*Culture and Customs
of Afghanistan*

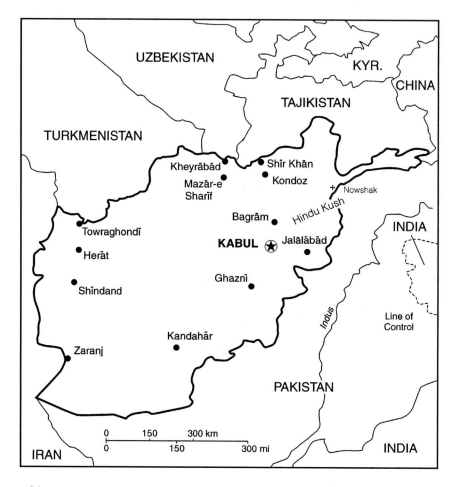

Afghanistan

Culture and Customs
of Afghanistan

∾∾

HAFIZULLAH EMADI

Culture and Customs of Asia
Hanchao Lu, Series Editor

GREENWOOD PRESS
Westport, Connecticut • London

958.1
EMA

Library of Congress Cataloging-in-Publication Data

Emadi, Hafizullah.
  Culture and customs of Afghanistan / Hafizullah Emadi.
      p. cm. — (Culture and customs of Asia, ISSN 1097-0738)
  Includes bibliographical references and index.
  ISBN 0-313-33089-1 (alk. paper)
  1. Afghanistan—Civilization. 2. Afghanistan—Social life and
customs. I. Title. II. Series.
  DS351.5.E53 2005
  958.1—dc22   2005003526

British Library Cataloguing in Publication Data is available.

Library of Congress Catalog Card Number: 2005003526
ISBN: 0-313-33089-1
ISSN: 1097-0738

First published in 2005

Greenwood Press, 88 Post Road West, Westport, CT 06881
An imprint of Greenwood Publishing Group, Inc.
www.greenwood.com

Printed in the United States of America

The paper used in this book complies with the
Permanent Paper Standard issued by the National
Information Standards Organization (Z39.48-1984).

10   9   8   7   6   5   4   3

Contents

Series Foreword   vii

Preface   xi

Acknowledgments   xiii

Chronology   xv

1   Land, People, and History   1

2   Religion and Religious Thought   53

3   Literature and the Arts   81

4   Architecture, Housing, and Settlements   111

5   Social Customs, Cuisine, and Traditional Dress   135

6   Family, Women, and Gender Issues   165

7   Lifestyles, Media, and Education   195

Glossary   221

Bibliography   227

Resource Guide   239

Index   241

Series Foreword

Geographically, Asia encompasses the vast area from Suez, the Bosporus, and the Ural Mountains eastward to the Bering Sea and from this line southward to the Indonesian archipelago, an expanse that covers about 30 percent of our earth. Conventionally, and especially insofar as culture and customs are concerned, Asia refers primarily to the region east of Iran and south of Russia. This area can be divided in turn into subregions commonly known as South, Southeast, and East Asia, which are the main focus of this series.

The United States has vast interests in this region. In the twentieth century the United States fought three major wars in Asia (namely the Pacific Wars of 1941–45, the Korean War of 1950–53, and the Vietnam War of 1965–75), and each had profound impact on life and politics in America. Today, America's major trading partners are in Asia, and in the foreseeable future the weight of Asia in American life will inevitably increase, for in Asia lie our great allies as well as our toughest competitors in virtually all arenas of global interest. Domestically, the role of Asian immigrants is more visible than at any other time in our history. In spite of these connections with Asia, however, our knowledge about this crucial region is far from adequate. For various reasons, Asia remains for most of us a relatively unfamiliar, if not stereotypical or even mysterious, "Oriental" land.

There are compelling reasons for Americans to obtain some level of concrete knowledge about Asia. It is one of the world's richest reservoirs of culture and over-evolving museum of human heritage. Rhoads Murphey, a prominent Asianist, once pointed out that in the part of Asia east of Afghanistan and south of Russia alone lies half the world, "half of its people and far more that half of its historical experience, for these are the oldest living civilized traditions." Prior to the modern era, with limited interaction and mutual influence between the East and the West, Asian civilizations developed largely independent from the West. In modern times, however, Asia and the West have come not only into close contact but also into frequent conflict: The result has been one of the most solemn and stirring dramas in world history. Today, integration and compromise are the trend in coping with cultural differences. The West—with some notable exceptions—has started to see Asian traditions not as something to fear but as something to be understood, appreciated, and even cherished. After all, Asian traditions are an indispensable part of the human legacy, a matter of global "common wealth" that few of us can afford to ignore.

As a result of Asia's enormous economic development since World War II, we can no longer neglect the study of this vibrant region. Japan's "economic miracle" of postwar development is no longer unique, but in various degrees has been matched by the booming economy of many other Asian countries and regions. The rise of the four "mini dragons" (South Korea, Taiwan, Hong Kong, and Singapore) suggests that there may be a common Asian pattern of development. At the same time, each economy in Asia has followed its own particular trajectory. Clearly, China is the next giant on the scene. Sweeping changes in China in the last two decades have already dramatically altered the world's economic map. Furthermore, growth has also been dramatic in much of Southeast Asia. Today, war-devastated Vietnam shows great enthusiasm for joining the "club" of nations engaged in the world economy. And in South Asia, India, the world's largest democracy, is rediscovering its role as a champion of market capitalism. The economic development of Asia presents a challenge to Americans but also provides them with unprecedented opportunities. It is largely against this background that more and more people in the United States, in particular among the younger generations, have started to pursue careers dealing with Asia.

This series is designed to meet the need for knowledge of Asia among students and the general public. Each book is written in an accessible and lively style by an expert (or experts) in the field of Asian studies. Each book focuses on culture and customs of a country or region. However, readers should be aware that culture is fluid, not always respecting national boundaries. While every nation seeks its own path to success and struggles to maintain its own identity, in the cultural domain mutual influence and integration among Asian nations are ubiquitous.

Each volume starts with an introduction to the land and the people of the nation or region and includes a brief history and an overview of the economy. This is followed by chapters dealing with a variety of topics that piece together a cultural panorama, such as thought, religion, ethics, literature and art, architecture and housing, cuisine, traditional dress, gender, courtship and marriage, festivals and leisure activities, music and dance, and social customs and lifestyle. In this series, we have chosen not to elaborate on elite life, ideology, or detailed questions of political structure and struggle, but instead to explore the world of common people, their sorrow and joy, their pattern of thinking, and their way of life. It is the culture and customs of the majority of the people (rather than just the rich and powerful elite) that we seek to understand. Without such understanding, it will be difficult for all of us to live peacefully and fruitfully with each other in this increasingly interdependent world.

As the world shrinks, modern technologies have made all nations on each continent "virtual" neighbors. The expression "global village" not only reveals the nature and the scope of the world in which we live but also, more importantly, highlights the serious need for mutual understanding of all people on our planet. If this series serves to help the reader obtain a better understanding of the "half of the world" that is Asia, the authors and I will be well rewarded.

Hanchao Lu
Georgia Institute of Technology

Preface

Afghanistan has been at the crossroads of many cultures and civilizations, occupying a unique place in the cultural geography of Central Asia and the Middle East. Invading tribes and armies passed through ancient Afghanistan and left their imprint on the culture, customs, and the way of life in the country.

Afghanistan has become the focus of international attention since the Soviet invasion and occupation, December 1979–February 1989, the brutal civil war that ensued shortly after the Soviet occupation army left the country, and subsequent intervention by the U.S.-led coalition force that toppled the rogue Taliban regime in late 2001 and installed a transitional government to lead the country.

A number of studies of Afghanistan since the 1980s deal exclusively with the religious and political aspects of development in the country, and the number of such works have substantially increased since the collapse of the Taliban rule. Their main theme revolves around issues such as *jihad*, the struggle to establish an Islamic state, geopolitics, politics of rehabilitation and reconstruction, and building civic institutions geared toward establishing a democratic system of governance. Little attention, to date, has been paid to topics such as culture and social mores of the country and its residents, and the reasons for such neglect of this aspect of Afghanistan derives from both a greater emphasis on the politics of national liberation during the Soviet occupation of the country and the concerted efforts to rebuild the war-torn nation in the post-Taliban era.

This reference is an attempt to remedy the lack of recent literature on the culture, customs, and cultural transformation of the country, a topic that has remained largely overlooked by the world scholarship since the outbreak of civil war in 1992. This book is an attempt to explore these topics and serve as a map to guide novice readers to gain a better understanding of the culture and customs of contemporary Afghanistan, a country that has experienced decades of wars and civil strife and yet shows the resilience to rebuild and integrate itself into the twenty-first century.

Acknowledgments

Writing on culture and customs, a subject that varies from one region to another, is an enormous task. The work could not have been completed without the generous support of friends and colleagues both in the private and public sectors who contributed ideas and provided relevant literature on the topic. Their discussions, views, and comments were stimulating in the writing of this book.

While I am indebted to those who shared thoughts and supported the project, I would like to express my deepest appreciation to Shafik Sachedina who has been a constant source of inspiration. He provided much-needed support during my fieldwork in Afghanistan in 2003–2004, which enabled me to access relevant literature at various libraries in Kabul. I am most indebted to Mohamed Alibhai for reviewing the first draft of Chapter 2, Religion and Religious Thought, and offering thoughtful suggestions on further improving it. My heartfelt thanks goes to Farooq Babrakzai for his critical remarks on various topics discussed throughout the text. His comments not only delivered me from some factual errors but also enriched this study. I am much obligated to Shah Muhammad Rais, head of Shah M. Book Company, who allowed me access to his rare collections on Afghanistan, for which I am grateful.

My gratitude and debt to Baz Mohammad Dehqanzadah cannot be properly expressed in just a few simple words. He accompanied and guided me during my fieldwork in Ishkashim, Yamagan, Darayam, and Jurm Districts of Badakhshan Province. In Kabul, individuals such as Azizullah Mehrzad, Sayed Amir Shah, Sayed Mohammad Ibrahim Bamiyani, and Sayed Qiyamuddin

Qiyam were instrumental in making my period of stay precious. I am grateful for their support and sharing their thoughts and views.

I am particularly grateful to Lori, always my best and most supportive critic. She was instrumental in the writing of this book and prepared the index. Without her support this project could not have been completed. Last but not least, I would like to express my gratitude to the Greenwood Publishing Group for bringing a side of Afghanistan that has not been studied recently to public attention.

Chronology

2000–1000 B.C.	Ancient Aryans residing in present-day Afghanistan moved toward the northern part of India.
1000 B.C.	Emergence of the Zoroastrian religion.
560–480 B.C.	Birth and death of Buddha.
549–545 B.C.	Persian conquest of ancient Afghanistan.
330–327 B.C.	Alexander's army invaded Afghanistan. Aikhanum, a Hellenic metropolis, was founded in the bank of the Amu River (Oxus River).
323 B.C.	Death of Alexander.
312 B.C.	The Indian Maurya dynasty had established their dominance over Afghanistan's Gandhara region.
250–128 B.C.	Establishment of the Greco-Bactrian kingdom in the city of Balkh.
570 A.D.	Birth of Prophet Muhammad, founder of Islam.
622	July 16, Prophet Muhammad left Mecca for Medina. This departure *(hijra)* marks the first day of the Muslim calendar.
632	Death of Muhammad.
652–664	Arab conquest of ancient Afghanistan, known as Aryana; the country was renamed Khurasan.

680	Muharram 10, date of the murder of religious leader *(Imam)* Hussein by Yazid in Karbala, Iraq; since then Shia Muslims of *Ithna Ashari,* or Twelver's, observe the anniversary of his death and mourn his murder.
765	Split in the Shia Muslim community after the death of Imam Jafar Sadiq.
873	Disappearance of Muhammad Mahdi, the 12th Imam of the Shias.
969	Establishment of the Fatimid caliphate (rulership of Islam) in Cairo, Egypt.
1092	A split occurred in the Isma'ili Muslim community into Mustalians and Nizaris after the death of Imam al-Mustansir.
962–1148	Ghaznawid era, the first Islamic empire in Afghanistan.
1186	Ghorid dynasty rose and replaced the Ghaznawid Empire.
1220	Mongol leader Genghis Khan invaded Afghanistan.
1370	Turkmen Mongol and military leader Timur-e-Lang, also known as Tamarlane, was crowned in the city of Balkh.
1405–1506	Timurid dynasty rules the cities of Herat and Balkh.
1504–1529	Zahir al-Din Muhammad Babur conquered Kabul and established his headquarters there.
1648	Persians captured the city of Qandahar.
1716	Abdali tribes rebelled in Herat.
1747	Ahmad Shah of the Sadozai Pushtun tribes was chosen king and ruled Afghanistan for 26 years.
1773	Timur Shah succeeded his father Ahmad Shah, transferred the capital from Qandahar to Kabul, and ruled the country for 20 years.

1798	Britain adopted a containment policy toward Afghanistan, fearing that it might invade India.
1809	British representative Mountstuart Elphinstone and Afghan King Shuja signed a defensive treaty that marked the beginning of a formal contract between Afghanistan and Britain.
1818	Armed conflict among the ruling elites for power paved the road for civil unrest, which lasted until 1835.
1839	First Anglo-Afghan War.
1841	December 23, assassination of British representative Macnaghten in Kabul.
1842	End of First Anglo-Afghan War.
1843	December, Dost Mohammad returned to Kabul, seized power, and ruled Afghanistan for 20 years.
1857	Anglo-Afghan Treaty signed in Peshawar. British agreed to provide a subsidy to Dost Mohammad.
1863	June 9, Dost Mohammad died and Shir Ali succeeded to the throne.
1878	Second Anglo-Afghan War.
1879	Amir Shir Ali died and his son Yaqoob ascended to the throne. Yaqoob abdicated the throne when the British invaded Kabul.
1880	British recognized Abd al-Rahman as King of Afghanistan.
1892	Hazara uprising against Abd al-Rahman suppressed.
1893	Abd al-Rahman signed the Durand Line Treaty with Britain, demarcating the southern boundaries between Afghanistan and British-controlled India. The line divides ethnic Pushtuns and Baluchis between Afghanistan and present-day Pakistan.

1896	Abd al-Rahman attacked and subjugated the region of Kafiristan, converted its residents to Islam, and named the region Nooristan.
1901	Abd al-Rahman died and his son Habibullah succeeded and ruled Afghanistan for 18 years.
1905	Afghanistan and Britain signed an agreement recognizing the validity of 1880 and 1893 agreements between the two countries.
1914	Afghanistan declared its neutrality during World War I.
1919	February 20, King Habibullah was assassinated. February 25, Amanullah proclaimed himself king of Afghanistan. April 13, Amanullah declared Afghanistan's independence paving the road for the Third Anglo-Afghan War on May 4. May 28, declaration of ceasefire. August 8, Afghanistan and Britain signed the Rawalpindi Peace Treaty and Britain recognized Afghanistan's independence.
1923	April 9, King Amanullah introduced a new constitution. October, criminal code introduced. November, statutes governing marriages introduced.
1924	March, the Khost Rebellion, a tribal revolt against Amanullah's modernization programs, was suppressed.
1927	April, a fortnightly private paper, *Anis,* begun its publication and later became a major national daily newspaper. December 10, Amanullah embarked on a grand tour of India, Egypt, and Europe.
1928	June 20, Amanullah returned to Afghanistan and initiated reforms encouraging people to wear Western dress. November, rebellion against state reforms begun by the Shinwari Pushtun tribes. December, an uprising begun by Habibullah Kalakani known as *bacha-e-saqaw* (water carrier's son).

1929	January 14, Amanullah abdicated the throne in favor of his brother Enayatullah and left for Qandahar and later to Rome, Italy. January 18, Kalakani captured Kabul and proclaimed himself king. October 14, General Mohammad Nadir and his brothers defeated Habibullah Kalakani, captured Kabul, and three days later Nadir declared himself king. November 3, Nadir tricked Kalakani to visit him in Kabul, arrested Kalakani, and executed him.
1930	Nadir endorsed the validity of 1921 and 1923 Britain-Afghanistan agreements.
1931	October 31, the new constitution of Afghanistan, *Usul-e-Asasi-ye Dawlat-e-Aliyya-e-Afghanistan*, the Fundamental Laws of the Government of Afghanistan, was approved.
1933	Construction of the Shibar Road linking Kabul to the northern cities completed. June 6, Nadir's brother Mohammad Aziz, ambassador to Germany was assassinated by an Amanullah supporter. November 8, Nadir was assassinated by Abdul Khaliq, a Hazara student at Nejat High School, and his son Mohammad Zahir succeeded him as king.
1934	February 16, general elections were held for the National Assembly. September 25, Afghanistan joined the League of Nations.
1940	January 12, the state declared that men aged 17 must serve in the army and imposed taxes to finance the purchasing of arms. Radio Afghanistan, with a 20-kw medium transmitter, was built in Kabul. August 17, Afghanistan declared its neutrality during World War II.
1941	Afghanistan expelled German and Italian nationals on the demands by the Soviet Union and Britain.
1943	May 16, Afghanistan established a consular office in New York.

1946	Kabul University, which was founded in 1933, became operational. May 9, Prime Minister Mohammad Hashim resigned and King Zahir's other uncle, Shah Mahmood, became Prime Minister. November 9, Afghanistan was admitted to the United Nations.
1948	Afghanistan began broadcasting news in support of Pushtunistan's independence.
1949	April 20, Louis G. Dryfus was appointed U.S. ambassador to Afghanistan. June 30, the 7th parliamentary session opened in Kabul, and it became known as the Liberal Assembly.
1950	January 13, Afghanistan recognized the Peoples' Republic of China. January 15, a proestablishment organization is founded: *Club-e-Milli* headed by Mohammad Daoud, the king's cousin.
1951	February 9, the United States provided technical aid to Afghanistan. March 19, the United States appointed George R. Merrell as its ambassador to Afghanistan.
1953	January 8, the United States provided a $1.5 million loan to Afghanistan for emergency purchasing of wheat and flour from the United States. September 6, Prime Minister Shah Mahmood resigned and the king appointed his cousin Mohammad Daoud prime minister.
1954	January 27, the Soviet Union loaned U.S. $3.5 million for construction of two grain mills and two silos.
1955	January 19, the People's Republic of China and Afghanistan established diplomatic ties at embassy level. March 29, Relations between Afghanistan and Pakistan deteriorated over the question of the rights to self-determination for the ethnic Pushtuns and Baluchis residing in Pakistan. March 30, progovernment forces marched on the Pakistan embassy in Kabul and the next day on the Pakistan

consulate in Qandahar. April 1, progovernment forces marched on Pakistan consulate in the city of Jalalabad. Pakistanis attacked the Afghanistan consulate in Peshawar. May 1, Pakistan asked Afghanistan to close its consulates in Pakistan and stated that it would close its consulates in Afghanistan. May 4, Afghanistan mobilized its forces across the border with Pakistan. May 13, Afghanistan and Pakistan accepted mediation by Saudi Arabia to resolve differences between them. December 18, Soviet leader Nikita Khrushchev visited Kabul and promised U.S. $100 million in economic aid to Afghanistan.

1956	June 27, the United States provided $14 million to develop Afghanistan's aviation industry. July 26, the Soviet Union embarked upon building the Nangarhar Irrigation Project.
1958	January 8, the Soviet Union began surveying oil deposits in the northern parts of Afghanistan. June 30, Prime Minister Mohammad Daoud visited the United States, and the United States agreed to asphalt the road between Kabul and Spin Boldak in Qandahar.
1959	May 28, the Soviet Union agreed to build the Qandahar-Herat Road. August, women of upper-class families appeared without their veils during the anniversary of Independence Day in Kabul.
1960	April 26, Amanullah died in Switzerland.
1961	September 3, flow of goods ceased between Afghanistan and Pakistan, and Pakistan closed its borders with Afghanistan. September 6, Afghanistan broke diplomatic ties with Pakistan.
1963	February 12, the United States agreed to ship all merchandise to Afghanistan via Iran due to the continued dispute between Afghanistan and Pakistan. March 10, Prime Minister Mohammad Daoud resigned and four days later the king appointed Mohammad Yusuf, minister of

mines and industries, as prime minister. May 29, Afghanistan and Pakistan improved ties leading to the opening of Afghanistan consulates in the cities of Peshawar and Quetta. October 12–17, Leonid Brezhnev, Soviet leader, visited Afghanistan.

1964   October 1, the *Loya Jirgah* approved the new constitution and the king endorsed it.

1965   January 1, the pro-Soviet *Hizb-e-Demokratik-e-Khalq-e-Afghanistan,* the People's Democratic Party of Afghanistan or PDPA, was founded with Noor Mohammad Taraki as general secretary of the party. July 24, the Soviet Union built a 97 km (60.27 mi.) pipeline to import natural gas from Shiberghan oil and gas fields. August 26–September 28, parliamentary elections were held. October 25, a major student demonstration known as *Seyum-e-Aqrab* broke out in Kabul. The government intervened and fired on the crowd, killing a number of people and wounding many others. The state closed down schools and banned public gathering and meetings. October 29, Prime Minister Yusuf resigned in the wake of student rallies and the king appointed Mohammad Hashim Maiwandwal prime minister. November 4, Maiwandwal visited Kabul University and participated at the condolence ceremony students held in memory of their fallen comrades.

1967   October 11, Maiwandwal resigned. November 1, the king appointed Noor Ahmad Etemadi prime minister.

1969   June 22, the government ordered the closure of all schools due to continuing student demonstrations.

1971   May 17, Etemadi resigned. June 8, the king appointed Abdul Zahir prime minister. August 22, a severe drought claimed the lives of thousands of people throughout the country.

1972   December 5, Abdul Zahir resigned and four days later the king appointed Mohammad Musa Shafiq prime minister.

1973	July 17, King Zahir's cousin, Mohammad Daoud, staged a coup while the king was on vacation in Rome and declared Afghanistan a republic.
1975	July 28, members of Islamic fundamentalists staged an uprising in Panjshir to overthrow Daoud, but state security forces suppressed them.
1977	Formation of *Jamiat-e-Enqilabi-e-Zanan-e-Afghanistan,* the Revolutionary Association of Women of Afghanistan (RAWA), headed by Meena. January 30, Daoud convened a *Milli Jirgah* to endorse the new constitution. February 14, the *Milli Jirgah* approved the constitution. February 24, Daoud promulgated the new constitution. November 16, Minister of Planning Ali Ahmad Khoram was assassinated in Kabul.
1978	April 17, Mir Akbar Khayber, a member of the PDPA was assassinated in Kabul. April 19, supporters of the PDPA participated at the funeral procession denouncing Khayber's murder. April 26, Daoud arrested key leaders of the PDPA. April 27, the PDPA staged a coup, seized power, and declared Afghanistan a democratic republic. The army formed a revolutionary council to govern the country. April 30, the Revolutionary Council elected Noor Mohammad Taraki president and prime minister. August 18, Minister of Defense Abdul Qadir was arrested on charges of organizing a coup, followed by the arrest of other key leaders of *Parcham* faction of the PDPA.
1979	January 28, armed uprising against the regime began in areas adjacent to the borders of Pakistan. February 14, U.S. Ambassador Adolph Dubs was kidnapped and killed by Kabul security forces during a rescue operation. February 22, U.S. President Jimmy Carter ordered reduction of U.S. aid to Afghanistan. March 16, government forces crushed a people's uprising in Herat, killing thousands of people. March 21, antistate rebellion began in Nooristan and Kunar. March 27, Hafizullah Amin, minister for foreign affairs, was

named prime minister. June 23, the Shia Hazaras in the Chindawul ghetto, Kabul rebelled and suffered major casualties when government forces suppressed them. August 5, army officers at the Bala Hisar Fort, loyal to *Sazman-e-Raha-e* and *Hizb-e-Islami,* rebelled and government forces crushed them. September 16, Hafizullah Amin removed Taraki from the leadership post and murdered him. October 10, Radio Kabul announced that Taraki died from an illness. Amin published a list of 12,000 prison inmates and condemned Taraki for murdering them. December 27, Soviet paramilitary troops stormed Amin's palace, killed him, and installed Babrak Karmal, head of the *Parcham* faction of the PDPA, as head of the state.

1980   January, President Carter requested provision of U.S. $300 million to Islamic militias to fight the Soviets. January 1, the Kabul regime claimed that it invited the Russian army to defend the country against external interferences. February 25, antistate demonstration continued and shops remained closed. February 26, security forces conducted a sweep and arrested hundreds of people. Anti-Soviet student protest demonstrations occurred in Kabul and continued for several days. April 27, paramilitary troops fired on demonstrators, killing three female students.

1981   August 12, Kabul regime rescinded the decree that restricted landownership by tribal and religious leaders.

1982   March 10, U.S. President Ronald Reagan declared March 21 as Afghanistan Day. June 16–25, the first U.N.-sponsored proxy talks between Afghanistan and Pakistan held in Geneva.

1984   July 26, the Appropriations Committee of the U.S. House of Representatives approved $50 million to help anti-Soviet Islamic militias.

1985   April 23, Karmal addressed members of the *Loya Jirgah* attempting to rally public support to fight

Islamic militias backed by Pakistan, Iran, and the United States. October 23, the Kabul regime ordered men up to age 40 to enlist for a three-year military service.

1986   May 4, Karmal was forced to resign as secretary general of the PDPA and Najibullah, former director of the intelligence department known as KHAD, was named secretary general of the party. Karmal was removed as president in November and was exiled to Moscow, and Najibullah became head of the state and the party.

1987   February 4, Meena, founder of RAWA was assassinated by an assassin loyal to *Hizb-e-Islami* in Quetta, Pakistan. November 29, Kabul regime convened a *Loya Jirgah* for approving the new constitution. November 30, the *Loya Jirgah* confirmed Najibullah as president.

1988   February 23, Pakistan-based Islamic militias announced the formation of Afghan Interim Government, AIG. April 14, Afghanistan and Pakistan signed the Geneva Accords concerning Soviet troop withdrawal from Afghanistan. The Soviet Union and the United States also signed the accord as the guarantors providing for the return of refugees and cessation of military support to their respective cliental parties. May 15, the Soviet Union began to withdraw its troops from Afghanistan.

1989   February 15, last contingent of Soviet troops left Afghanistan. June 16, nine Shia Muslim organizations united and formed *Hizb-e-Wahdat,* Party of Unity.

1990   June 27, Kabul regime renamed the ruling PDPA to *Hizb-e-Watan,* the Homeland Party.

1992   April 16, Najibullah sought refuge at the United Nations Office in Kabul. April 28, Kabul regime collapsed and Sebghatullah Mojaddadi, head of *Mahaz-e-Islami,* became head of the state and declared Afghanistan an Islamic state. June 28,

	Mojaddadi's short rule ends and Burhanuddin Rabbani head of *Jamiat-e-Islami* succeeded him. Armed confrontation among various Islamic militia groups intensified as each group tried to establish its domination over the country's politics. October 31, Rabbani's term ended and power was transferred to a council called *Shura-e-Ahel wa Aqd.* December 30, the council endorsed Rabbani as president of Afghanistan.
1993	March 11, leaders of the warring factions met in Mecca to resolve their differences and make peace. They signed an agreement that was countersigned by the Saudi leader, King Fahd, however, fighting continued among Islamic groups.
1994	November 5, Taliban militia captured Qandahar and established their bases of operations there.
1995	February 10, Taliban captured Maidan Shahr, Wardak and advanced eastward. March 13, Abdul Ali Mazari, head of *Hizb-e-Wahdat,* was captured and executed by Taliban militia. September 5 and 7, Taliban militia defeated Ismail Khan and captured Herat and Ghor.
1996	April 3, an estimated 1,000 clerics pledged allegiance to Mullah Mohammad Omar, recognizing him as *Amir al-Mominin,* commander of the believers. September 27, Taliban captured Kabul, entered the United Nations compound, dragged Najibullah and his brother Shahpoor Ahmadzai outside, and executed them. November 5, former Minister of Defense Shahnawaz Tanai declared his support to Taliban militia.
1997	May 25, Pakistan, United Arab Emirates, and Saudi Arabia extended diplomatic recognition to the Taliban regime.
1998	August 8, massacre of an estimated 2,000–5,000 ethnic Hazara Shia Muslims by Taliban militia in Mazar, Balkh. The Taliban murdered 11 Iranian diplomats in Mazar, which strained relations

between Tehran and Kabul. August 20, United States launched cruise missiles on Afghanistan to eliminate terrorist training camps run by Osama bin Laden.

2001   February 26, Taliban destroyed the Buddha statues in Bamiyan Province. September 11, al-Qaeda attacked the World Trade Center in New York and the Pentagon in Washington, D.C., using commercial airplanes as weapons of mass destruction. October 7, United States began its military assault on Taliban positions in Afghanistan. November 7, Taliban surrendered their main stronghold, Qandahar, and their leaders escaped to the countryside. November 27, the United States engineered the Bonn Conference, Germany, where representatives of Islamic groups agreed on a power-sharing scheme in the post-Taliban era. December 6, the Bonn Conference ended. December 22, the United States installed Hamid Karzai as head of an interim government.

2002   February 14, Abul Rahman, minister of aviation and tourism, was assassinated in Kabul. March 22, the Aga Khan, spiritual leader of the Isma'ili community, visited Kabul and participated in the opening of the school year. June 10–21, the *Loya Jirgah*, comprised of 1,500 (180 women) delegates, endorsed Karzai as head of the state. July 6, Vice President and former warlord Hajji Abdul Qadir of Nangarhar was assassinated in Kabul. Representatives of neighboring countries of China, Tajikistan, Uzbekistan, Turkmenistan, Iran, and Pakistan signed a nonaggression treaty in Kabul.

2003   May 1, U.S. Secretary of Defense Donald Rumsfeld visited Kabul and assured Kabul of continued U.S. support in the war against terrorism. May 9, explosion occurred near the U.S. embassy in Kabul when U.S. Deputy Secretary of State Richard Armitage was inside the building. November 3, the government unveiled the draft of the new

constitution. November 17, U.N. suspended
its operation in half of the southern parts of the
country due to assassination of one its employees and an attack on two others. Bomb exploded
near the U.N. office in Qandahar. December 14,
the constitutional *Loya Jirgah,* comprised of 502
delegates including 50 appointed delegates, was
officially inaugurated in Kabul.

2004   January 4, constitutional *Loya Jirgah* ended,
approving the draft of the new constitution, lay-
ing the ground for a strong presidential system
of government, and eliminating the post of the
prime ministry. March 17, U.S. Secretary of State
Colin Powell visited Afghanistan and promised
continued support to the U.S.-backed government of Hamid Karzai. March 29, the district of
Dai Kundi of Orazgan was elevated to the status
of a province in Afghanistan. April 12, district of
Panjshir was elevated to the status of a province
with Bazarak as its capital. May 23, first private
television station, Afghan Television Channel, was
established in Kabul. October 9, the first presidential election in Afghanistan. December 7, the
inauguration of Hamid Karzai as the first demo-
cratically elected president of Afghanistan.

1

Land, People, and History

Until recently, Afghanistan as a nation remained unknown. If the world thought of Afghanistan at all, it was in terms of the show dog—the Afghan hound. Afghanistan emerged from obscurity to international headlines in the 1980s when the Soviets occupied the country from December 1979 to February 1989. Reporters, writers, and scholars reflected on the heroic armed struggle waged by the people of Afghanistan to liberate their homeland. Since then, Afghanistan had been a major international media focus. Single-minded publicity of one event in the country's history lends a distorted view to the country and its people. However, just like any other country, Afghanistan has a diverse geography, people, and civilization.

THE LAND

Afghanistan's geographical coordinates are 33°N and 65°E. It is a land-locked country in Central and West Asia surrounded by Tajikistan, Uzbekistan, and Turkmenistan in the north, Iran to the west, and Pakistan to the south and southeast. In the east it shares a common border with Sinkiang, China. The country's landscape, dotted with high mountains and deep and narrow valleys, separates regions and people of different cultures and lifestyles. In the past, lack of modern transportation and communications, unfamiliar terrain, and pervasive illiteracy caused communities to be suspicious of anything beyond their immediate and familiar territory. Individuals would only leave their hometowns and travel to other regions in case of emergency. It usually took a few days to reach a destination in another part of the country.

View of present-day Kabul: a mix of modern buildings and traditional storefronts and homes, 2003.

Geography has contributed to perpetuation of the deeply rooted tribalism, localism, and regionalism.

Afghanistan is a land of variety and contrast. The Central Highland Ranges divide the country into three major geographic regions: the central, northern, and southern plains. The towering Hindu Kush Mountains (the words *Hindu Kush* translate as Hindu Killer) separate the northern plains from the southern regions, and its towering peaks alternate between deep gorges and barren slopes. The highest peaks of the Hindu Kush Range in the eastern parts are approximately 19,500 to 23,000 feet, and around the capital, Kabul, and in its adjacent areas it ranges from 14,750 to 19,500 feet in height. Areas in and around the Hindu Kush Mountains are prone to earthquakes. A powerful quake in 1955 demolished the city of Faizabad, the capital of Badakhshan, and another quake in the same region in 1998 reduced entire villages to rubble, killing 7,000 and affecting about 165,000 people.

The central region consists of high mountains with deep and narrow valleys.

The mountains extend from the Pamir Knot in the east and descend in altitude westward to Iran. Kuh-e-Baba lies in the central part of the country, and it is a continuation of the Hindu Kush Range, which begins in Bamiyan province and extends westward with its highest peak reaching about 15,000 feet. There are two mountains of lower altitudes on the western end of Kuh-e-Baba. Safid Kuh and Siyah Kuh lay north and south of Kuh-e-Baba, respectively.

The northern region covers a wide expanse of fertile foothills and agricultural lands that extend toward the Oxus River. The region is heavily populated, and its fertile agricultural land makes it the breadbasket of the country. The area is also endowed with natural gas resources. The average altitude in the region is estimated at 2,000 feet, except in the Oxus Valley, where it drops as low as 600 feet. The city of Balkh was a focal point of merchants, traders, and caravans that traveled the historic Silk Route through Afghanistan to China and Rome.

The southern region, with average altitude of 3,000 feet, consists of sandy deserts and semidesert plains, with the Rigistan Desert making up about one-fourth of the region. The high and arid plateau extends into Afghanistan's neighboring countries, Pakistan and Iran.

Two major mountains in the eastern part of Afghanistan include the Spin Ghar in the north and Siyah Kuh in the south. Spin Ghar, which extends east-west, lies between Nangarhar and Paktiya Provinces, and its northern and southern slopes are covered with dense forest. The Sulaiman Kuh range is also covered with forests and is divided into northern and southern parts. Its northern parts form a common boundary between Afghanistan and Pakistan, while its southwestern ridges separate Afghanistan from the basin of the Indus River.[1]

Most settlements in Afghanistan are concentrated around rivers and streams. Water level yields considerably in the spring and significantly lowers with a reduced amount of water in the summer. A few rivers have no water from April to June and November to December because many of their tributaries run dry prior to reaching their main rivers due to diversion of water for various types of irrigation systems. Rivers that originate from the glaciers and snow-covered mountains have less water in winter due to severe freezing, but usually have plenty of water in July and August when the snow and ice are melting. Major rivers include the Kabul, Oxus, Hari Rud, and Helmand Rivers.

The Kabul River originates from Onay (Gardana) Pass and runs through Kabul, and its course extends eastward through Tangi Gharu Gorge to Jalalabad, Nangarhar. The river provides water to the Naghlu, Mahipar, and Darunta hydroelectric plants, and its major tributaries are the rivers of Panjshir, Logar, Surkhab, Laghman, and Kunar. The river eventually merges with the Indus River in Pakistan and flows into the Indian Ocean.

The Oxus River originates from glaciers of the Pamir Knot and empties into the Aral Sea, situated between Turkmenistan and Qazaqistan. Its major tributaries are the Wakhan, Pamir, Panj, Kokcha, and Qunduz Rivers. The Hayratan Bridge, built in 1982, connects Balkh to the Termiz Port in the southern border of Uzbekistan, and the Shir Khan Port in Qunduz facilitates trade between Afghanistan and the former Soviet Central Asian states.

The Hari Rud River originates from an altitude of 9,000 feet from Lal and Sar Jangal regions on the western slope of the Kuh-e-Baba, runs westward to Herat, and then turns north to Iran. The Helmand River originates from the mountainous regions of Behsud, Panjab, and Dai Kundi and ends in the marshes and lakes of the Sistan depression. Its major tributaries are the Khash, Farah, and Arghandab Rivers. The Farah River is the longest of the three rivers that irrigate agricultural lands in Farah province.

There are a number of famous lakes throughout Afghanistan. Daryacha-e-Namakzar, Hamun-e-Pusak, and Hamun-e-Saberi are situated in the south-western region. Lake Band-e-Amir, comprising the five small lakes Haybat, Ghulaman, Zulfiqar, Qanbar, and Panir, is situated in the central region, Bamiyan. The lake is known for its exquisite coloring, milky-white running to dark green. Lake Sar-e-Qul is located in the Wakhan corridor, and Ab-e-Istada, which is a salt lake, originates from rivers in Ghazni.[2]

Climate, Vegetation, and Animals

Afghanistan's climate is as varied as its geographical landscape. The climate changes with the movement of air masses and precipitation that blows against high-altitude mountain ranges. Some high mountain ranges are covered with snow for most of the year. The weather is cold in winter and hot in summer. Dry, cold, and chilly weather prevail in the mountainous regions of the northeast. However, in the region adjacent to Pakistan, the Indian monsoon affects the climate that produces tropical air masses between July and September and brings increased humidity and rain into the central and southern regions. In winter, cold air masses from the north and northwest generate snow and extreme cold in the high mountainous regions and rain in the lower altitudes. In the western and southern regions, the wind blows sand dunes and dust with a tremendous force during the summer. It is known as the "wind of 120 days," and is very severe when combined with heat and drought.

The wide-ranging meteorological system in Afghanistan results in diverse plant life. At high altitudes there are arctic and alpine vegetation, while luxuriant plants grow in lower altitudes in the mountainous regions along the border with Pakistan. Date palms are found in the southwestern region adjacent to Farah. Vegetation is found in abundance across the rivers and creeks.

Mulberry and pistachio trees thrive in the northern plains. Pine, cedar, and fir trees grow on high mountains. Other trees include oak, walnut, ash, and juniper, and the most valuable trees are the deodar, a cedar that is primarily used for building houses and furniture.

There have been few in-depth surveys done in the past on Afghanistan's animal life, so knowledge of the fauna is at best fragmentary and certainly outdated. Entire species may have since vanished due to excessive hunting among those who can afford it, and later by the successive destructive wars. Many of the animal species did not originate there; however, some animals may have evolved into a unique version of its original species. Generally, geographic terrain and elevation divide the various animal species.

The higher, inhospitable mountain climates are home to the Marco Polo sheep (Ovis Poli) and the Siberian tiger, found in the Pamirs Region. The ibex, snow leopard, snow cock, piping hare, and brown bear are found in the Himalayas. Lower, in the steppes of Turkistan, are birds and susliks. Game birds found in the upland region include the kawk (chukar partridge), the sisi, a small partridge about the size of a quail, the bodena (lark), and sparrows. The deserts to the south and west contain gazelles, lesser plovers, and the jangals (wild pigs). In the southern part of the country mongoose, leopards, and cheetahs are found. The thick forests in Nooristan and Paktiya are home to large numbers of the short-tailed rhesus macaque (monkey). Black partridges inhabit sparsely wooded areas. Fish, particularly trout, are found in most streams. The *Mahi-Khaldar*, a German brown trout, is common in northern streams. Varieties of carp, also known as barbels, are found in streams around the Hindu Kush Mountains. The laka, similar to a catfish, inhabits the Amu River and northern streams. Freshwater crabs can be found all across the country.

Domesticated animals such as cattle, sheep, and goats are raised for their dairy products, and donkeys and horses are used for transportation. Camels of both the single and double-hump variety are native to the region, and nomadic tribes breed them for transportation. The country is also home to the well-known Persian cat, and to the elegant, longhaired dog known in the West as the Afghan hound. In its country of origin, the hound is known as tazi. The Western-inspired image of the kennel club show dog has silky hair and an imperious air that belies the hound's actual history as an intelligent and frighteningly effective hunter of both small and large game. The tazi has an ancient heritage in Afghanistan that goes back a few thousand years, when they first came to Afghanistan from the Middle East. Those with the thickest coats were bred and raised to guard flocks as well as to hunt game and predators large and small. The dogs' large, almond-shaped eyes are capable of sharp vision at long distances. They are known for their problem-solving capacity and ability to both hunt by sight and calculate the chase by anticipating the direction of fleeing prey. The tazi have long legs and powerful hips that are set higher and wider than average, and this unique hip structure makes for greater flexibility as they lope over rocky terrain. The tazi can stop on a dime or readily change direction without losing speed, and launch itself at prey with great force. They are popular as hunting dogs and can hunt and kill animals such as leopards and wolves without assistance.[3]

Mineral Resources

Afghanistan is relatively rich in mineral resources, but these resources are poorly developed. Available data suggest the existence of about 1,428 mineral reserves, such as lapis lazuli, chrome, gold, mica, nickel, silver, ruby, jade, quartz, zinc, manganese, asbestos, uranium, precious and semiprecious gemstones, copper, iron, and considerable iron-ore reserves.

Coal deposits are found in the Karkar and Ashpushta Regions in the northern part of the country. Coal is mined for domestic consumption, but production declined due to continuing civil war in the 1990s. Salt deposits are located in the region of Taliqan and in regions with lakebed salt reserves known as *Namaksar* in Andkhoy, Helmand, Herat, Chakhansoor, and Tashqurghan. Marble is found in Kabul, Nangarhar, and Helmand, and talc is mined at the Achin mine and Mama Khil mine in Nangarhar Province, while barite reserves are found in the regions of Sanglan, Herat, and in Faranjal, the Ghorband District of the Parwan Province. Mica has been mined in Nijrab, Kapisa.

Iron ore deposits are found at the Hajigak Pass and Khaish area in Bamiyan province as well as significant quantities of lime and quartz clay in the region. A Franco-German company conducted a feasibility study of the Hajigak deposit in 1972; however, the company and the government did not embark on its exploration. Iron ore also has been found in areas around Kabul, the central and eastern regions of the Hindu Kush Range, and valleys adjacent to the Oxus River as well as in areas around Qandahar.

Chromite deposits have been located in Logar province, nickel ore traced in Badakhshan, copper deposits are found in Darband, Kabul, and in Ainak region in Logar province. Gold is found in river sands in Kabul and Qandahar, and recently a small deposit was found and extracted in the Kayan Valley, Baghlan. Lead and zinc ores are found in the Kokcha River; sulfur is found in Takhar, Balkh, and Kabul; and Alabaster is mined in Galichah, southern regions bordering Pakistan. Badakhshan is known for its lapis lazuli, and, since the Soviet invasion, warlords mined lapis lazuli for export and used the revenue to finance their private armies.[4]

Administrative Divisions

In the eighteenth century Afghanistan was divided into four autonomous and semiautonomous regions of Herat, Qandahar, Turkistan, and Qataghan-Badakhshan with Kabul as the capital city. King Abd al-Rahman (1880–1901) subjugated autonomous regions to his rule and appointed his trusted men as governors to ensure that the regions remain under his control. During King Mohammad Nadir's rule (1929–1933) the country was divided into five major and four minor administrative areas. However, in 1964 the country was divided into 26 *Wilayat* (provinces), and by 2004 Afghanistan had 34 provinces. Each province is divided into several *Wuluswali* (districts) and *Alaqadari* (subdistricts), depending on the size of the population. Heads of the provinces are called *Wali* (governor). Heads of the *Wuluswali* and *Alaqadari* are called *Wuluswal* and *Alaqadar* respectively, and they are appointed by the central government. Villages in an *Alaqadari* are divided into several *qaryas*, and a *qarya* is headed by a chief known as *qaryadar, arbab, or malik*, and is elected by the people. Table 1.1 shows the administrative divisions in Afghanistan in 2004.

PEOPLE AND LANGUAGES

Afghanistan's geography and climate are full of contrast. Its inhabitants are also diverse in their ethnicity and languages. Each ethnic community has its own history, culture, and speaks its own language. Some 49 languages are spoken throughout the country. All ethnic groups have equally participated in the building of the country's political, social, and economic infrastructure, and they are equally responsible for its destruction in the 1990s. There is no precise data on the number of each ethnic and faith-based community, and members tend to exaggerate when asked about the number and size of their community. Although the Constitution recognized Persian (Farsi or Dari) and Pushtu as the two official languages, Persian is the dominant lingua franca. All languages use Arabic scripts, which are written from right to left and horizontally.

Pushtuns constitute the majority of the country's population as a single ethnic group, but they are a minority with regard to the total population of other ethnic communities. Pushtuns dominated the country's politics since the rise of Ahmad Shah Durani to power in 1747. Non-Pushtun ethnic communities refer to Pushtuns as *Afghans,* but Pushtuns refer to themselves as Pushtun or Pakhtun. Pushtuns reside primarily in the south and southeastern regions of the country, and the Durand Line separates them from the Pushtuns in Pakistan. A significant number of Pushtuns also reside in the northern

Table 1.1

Provinces and Their Capitals, 2004

Province	Provincial Capital	Area in square miles
Badakhshan	Faizabad	15,786
Badghis	Qalah-e-Naw	8,438
Baghlan	Baghlan	6,627
Balkh	Balkh	4,633
Bamiyan	Bamiyan	6,757
Dai Kundi	Khadir	—
Farah	Farah	21,666
Faryab	Maimana	8,226
Ghazni	Ghanzi	9,026
Ghor	Chigh-cheran	13,808
Herat	Herat	16,107
Helmand	Lashkargah	23,058
Jawzjan	Shiberghan	10,126
Kabul	Kabul	1,822
Kapisa	Mahmoodraqi	722
Khost	Khost	1,603
Kunar	Asadabad	3,742
Laghman	Mihterlam	2,790
Logar	Pul-e-Alam	1,702
Nangarhar	Jalalabad	7,195
Nimrooz	Zaranj	20,980
Nooristan	Nooristan	1,404
Orazgan	Tirinkot	11,169
Paktika	Sharan	3,860
Paktiya	Gardiz	7,336
Panjshir	Bazarak	273
Parwan	Charikar	2,282
Qandahar	Qandahar	19,062
Qunduz	Qunduz	2,867
Samangan	Aibak	6,425
Sar-e-Pool	Sar-e-Pool	6,177
Takhar	Taliqan	6,770
Wardak	Maidan-Shahr	3,745
Zabul	Qalat	6,590

parts of the country. Pushtuns are divided into numerous tribal groups such as Durani, Ghilzai, Afridi, Sadozai, Yusufzai, Waziri, Mohammadzai, Qanda-hari, and so forth. Each tribe speaks its own dialect of the Pushtu language, a variant of the Indo-European language family. Pushtuns are mainly Sun-nis of the Hanafi School of Islam, but a significant number are Shias. Most

Pushtuns believe they are descendants of the original Aryan people as well as Greek, Persian, Turkic, and Arabs, and some even trace their origin to the children of Israel.

The Tajiks trace their ancestry to the Greco-Bactrian dynasties that flourished in the oases around the Oxus River, and they are akin to Indo-European peoples and speak various dialects of the Persian language. Most Tajiks are Sunnis, while a significant number are Shia-Isma'ilis, residing primarily in Badakhshan, Parwan, and Kabul. Tajik intellectuals held junior political positions in the state bureaucracy prior to the Soviet invasion of the country, and they held leading positions after the collapse of the Soviet-backed government in April 1992. The Tajiks in the remote northern parts of the country such as Pamir, Darwaz, Shughnan, and other regions speak their own languages, which are called by their respective regional names. For example, Wakhi refers to the Wakhi tribes in the Pamir Knot and Shughni to the people resident of Shughnan.

The Hazaras are one of the native communities of Afghanistan, residing mainly in the central region known as Hazarajat. Their Mongolian-like features led some scholars to argue that Hazaras are direct descendents of the Mongols from when Genghis Khan's army invaded Afghanistan in the early thirteenth century. The Hazaras led a semiautonomous life until King Abd al-Rahman (1880–1901) subjugated them to his rule, suppressed the Hazaras, enslaved the men and women, and coerced them to follow the Sunni faith of Islam. This situation forced many Hazaras to leave the country and settle in Pakistan, Iran, and Russia. To forestall unity among the Hazaras, Abd al-Rahman divided Hazarajat and annexed it to the three provinces of Kabul, Qandahar, and Bamiyan. In 1964, Hazarajat was further partitioned into several administrative centers, such as Parwan, Bamiyan, Wardak, Ghazni, and Ghor. A significant number of Hazaras also reside in towns and villages in Samangan, Balkh, Takhar, Qunduz, and Baghlan as well as in Kabul. They speak Hazaragi, a dialect of the Persian language. Most Hazaras are Shias, while a significant number are Isma'ilis. Major Hazara tribal communities are Dai Kundi, Dai Zangi, Behsud, Yakawlang, and Jaghori.

The Uzbeks are divided between Afghanistan and Uzbekistan, and they constitute the largest Turkic-speaking community in Afghanistan. They speak their own language, Uzbeki, and also understand the Persian and Pushtu languages. Uzbeks are Sunnis, and most of them are sedentary farmers. A small number are engaged in business and crafts. The Uzbeks were allowed to publish newspapers and journals in their own language after the pro-Soviet People's Democratic Party of Afghanistan, the PDPA, seized power in 1978.

Turkmen are divided between Afghanistan and Turkmenistan. In Afghanistan they are divided into several tribal groups such as Chawdurha, Ersari,

Alili, Qara, Saloor, Sarooq-ha, Teka, Gugalan, and Yamut. Their mother tongue is the Turkic dialect; however, most understand and speak either the Persian or Pushtu languages. Turkmen are Sunnis and have maintained their literature, culture, and traditions. Turkmen are known for breeding qaraqul sheep and weaving carpets and rugs.

The Tatars reside primarily in northern parts of Bamiyan and in a few areas in Samangan. A small number of the Tatars also live in Bukhara and Uzbekistan. They are Sunnis and claim to be descendents of the Mongols.

The Aimaq are regarded to be of Turko-Mongolian descent and their economy is largely based on agriculture and cattle breeding. They led a semi-independent life until they were subjugated by Abd al-Rahman in the late nineteenth century. They are divided into the Jamshidi, Firooz Kohi, and Taimani groups; they are Sunnis and speak Persian with some Turkic words.

The Qirghiz are Sunnis and reside primarily in the Wakhan corridor of Badakhshan. They are nomadic people, migrating across the mountain borders of Afghanistan and Sinkiang, China. They live in yurts and speak a dialect of the Turkic language. Soon after the Soviet invasion, Rahman Qul, chief of the community, and most of the Qirghiz left Afghanistan, settled in Pakistan, and were subsequently repatriated to Anatolia, Turkey.

Qizilbash are Shias and speak Persian. They are primarily settled in urban areas such as Kabul, Balkh, Herat, Ghazni, Qunduz, and other regions. They trace their origin to the Turkish armies sent to occupy Kabul and other urban areas in the eighteenth century. Since then, successive rulers in Afghanistan recruited a significant number of Qizilbash as soldiers, and Qizilbash intellectuals nonetheless played an important role in the country as government officials, medical doctors, teachers, and so forth.

Nooristanis make up another branch of the Indo-European family. Some scholars argue that Nooristanis are descendents of ancient Aryan tribes who resided in the region around 3,000 years ago. In the nineteenth century, the Nooristanis were referred to as *Kafir* (infidels), and their place of residence was called *Kafiristan* (the place of infidels). King Abd al-Rahman converted them to Islam in 1896 and renamed *Kafiristan* to Nooristan, the land of light. The Nooristanis retained much of their cultural heritage; they speak the *Kafiri* dialect and follow the Sunni school of Islam.

Sayyeds are adherents to both Sunni and Shia schools of Islam. They make up a small segment of the country's population and trace their genealogy to Ali, the first Shia Imam and cousin of the Prophet Muhammad. Most Sayyeds are businessmen or traders, and some are in charge of religious affairs of the Shia communities.

A significant number of Arabs who speak a Tajiki dialect of Persian have settled in Balkh, Shiberghan, Taliqan, Takhar, and Badakhshan. They adhere to the Sunni school of Islam. They are mainly peasant farmers and business-men, and some are seasonal migrants moving with their herds.

There is a small group of people known as the Mongols, and they are Sun-nis. They originally lived in Ghor and later settled in central and northern regions as well as in the villages of Kundur and Kariz-e-Mullah in Herat. It is argued that these people are descendents of the Mongolian army of Genghis Khan. In the central and northern regions they speak Persian, while those residing in the southern region speak Pushtu, and their mother tongue is referred to as Mogholi.

The Pashayis reside in Kapisa, Laghman, and Kunar. Although they speak Pushtu, each tribal group has its own dialect. They are a distinct ethnic group that differs from the Pushtuns in their complexion and way of life. Most people are Sunnis, while a small number are Shia-Isma'ilis. A significant number of the Pashayi Isma'ilis left their hometown during the civil war and sought refuge in Peshawar, Pakistan. FOCUS Humanitarian Assistance, an affiliate of the Aga Khan Development Network (AKDN), repatriated them to Canada in 1996.

Baluchis are Sunnis, and they are divided among Afghanistan, Iran, and Pakistan and speak their own language, Baluchi. They are mostly nomads, and some live in small villages and towns. Baluchi intellectuals agitated for an independent homeland, but their struggle waned as the community failed to unite and rally under a common political platform.

Brahois are Sunnis and speak their own language, Dravidian. They are alternatively called Barahoiki, Brahoi, and Kur Galli. They are mainly peasant farmers, and some nomads, residing mainly in Baluchistan and in Chakhan-soor regions.

Farsiwan are a small group of people who reside in southern and western towns and villages in Herat. They are sometimes erroneously referred to as Tajiks. They are Shias and speak Persian.

Kohistanis, Gujar, Kati, Gawar-Bati, and many other ethnic groups are Sunnis, and each has its own unique cultural traditions. They speak their own mother tongues, however, all understand and converse in the Persian and Pushtu languages.

Two ethno-religious communities that stand out from the general popula-tion of Afghanistan are the Hindus and Sikhs. They migrated to Afghanistan from the Indian subcontinent as early as the eighteenth century. A significant number of Hindus and Sikhs settled in Afghanistan when King Amanullah (1919–1929) provided sanctuary to the Indian nationalists who fought for India's independence from the British rule, and a small number of others migrated to Afghanistan after partition of India in 1947. Hindus and Sikhs reside mainly in Kabul, Parwan, Nangarhar, Qandahar, and Balkh, and most are moneylenders and traders. During the constitutional period in 1964–1973 and afterward, a number of Hindus played a prominent role in the country's national politics. Incidents of harassment by fanatic Islamic militias collectively known as *Mujahidin* when they seized power in April 1992 forced a large number of Hindus and Sikhs to leave Afghanistan for India and Pakistan. Those who remained in Afghanistan bravely guarded their lifestyle and traditions. Charang Singh and Anar Kalay represented the Hindu communities of Khost and Awtar Singh represented the Sikh communities of Kabul during the constitutional *Loya Jirgah* convened in Kabul in December 2003.

The most uniform ethno-religious group in Afghanistan was the small Jewish community. It is thought that the Jews migrated to Afghanistan from Mashhad, Iran and settled in Herat, Balkh, and Kabul. Many of these Jews left the country for Israel and the United States as early as 1948. They were mainly moneylenders and traders. In 2000, Rabbai Ishaq Levin was the only Jew who remained in Kabul as caretaker of the only synagogue there.

An invisible community within the predominant Muslim society of Afghanistan is a small group of Christians who were converted to the faith by Christian missionaries when they worked in Afghanistan in the early 1960s. Members of the group identify themselves as Muslims in order to avoid harassment and persecution.[5]

Economy

Agriculture and animal husbandry are the main source of people's income. Major concentration of the population is around oases of cultivated land and villages located near creeks, streams, and bodies of water. The two decades of war in the 1980s and 1990s destroyed much of the country's economic infrastructures and forced one-third of the population to flee the country and seek refuge in the neighboring countries of Pakistan and Iran. The gross domestic product reduced dramatically due to migration of labor and capital as well as a succession of severe droughts that affected most regions of the country. Armed conflicts not only disrupted commerce, transport, trade, and imports and exports but also severely impacted the day-to-day lives of the people who suffer from lack of basic shelter, food, and medical care. The war also has prevented development and modernization of the country's industrial sectors.

Industry

Small-scale industrial development that began in the nineteenth century thrived in the post–World War II period. The government was at the forefront of industrialization and community development, monopolizing key industrial sectors. However, a small number of private firms were allowed to venture into industrial sectors. Major industries included three cotton spinning and weaving plants at Jab al-Seraj, Pul-e-Khumri, and Gulbahar, and a number of privately owned textile factories in Kabul and elsewhere produced cotton textiles for domestic consumption. Other industrial plants included the sugar refinery of Baghlan, the cement producing plants of Jab al-Seraj, the soap and ceramic plants of Qunduz, the woolen manufacturing plants in Qandahar, and the leather-tanning factory in Kabul. Several tanneries for fleshing, drying, and baling of *Qaraqul* skins are located in several regions in the northern parts of the country. The Jangalak factory in Kabul manufactured toys, truck bodies, hardware, steel doors and windows, cast iron stoves, iron beds, and so forth. In Kabul there were stocking and sock knitting plants, a shoe manufacturing plant, as well as an asphalt plant geared to supply local demand. Silos in Kabul, Qandahar, Herat, and Pul-e-Khumri produced flour and bread, and other industries in Qunduz, Mazar, Herat, and Helmand processed vegetable oils for domestic consumption. Industrial products account for 20 percent of the country's gross domestic product (GDP), of which 10 percent derives mainly from handicrafts and 1 percent from mining.

Energy is vital to the country's industrialization, and major sources of energy are fuel wood, coal, and electricity. Whenever possible, people grow varieties of poplar and willow trees for cooking and heating fuel. People also use dried cow dung and shrubs for cooking and heating purposes. Afghanistan once had plenty of timber for export, but today most of the timber resources have disappeared. Lack of power caused people to increasingly cut down large numbers of trees for heating the home and cooking food, and timber lords also exploited the lack of regulations to export timber. Overconsumption of timber and growing demands abroad resulted in a devastating deforestation of the land. Major rural industries include curing tobacco, processing brown sugar and milk, lime manufacturing, pottery, blacksmithing, and handicrafts. Development of hydroelectric plants also intensified in the post–World War II period. Since then, hydropower plants had been built in Kabul, Helmand, Qandahar, Mazar, Nimrooz, Zabul, Orazgan, and several other regions.

In 1950 oil was discovered at Angot, Jawzjan, and several years later the first oil refinery was built, processing 1,100,000 barrels of crude oil, 728,000 barrels of kerosene, 371,000 barrels of diesel, and 91,000 barrels of gasoline per year. In 1980 a pipeline was extended to Kabul to provide the needed oil for the city, but the civil war destroyed much of the oil wells and other power-generating plants. Natural gas reserves in Shiberghan are estimated to be 67 billion cubic meters, of which 48.5 billion cubic meters are sweet gas for export and manufacturing of fertilizers. A pipeline was built to carry gas to a thermal power plant and for the manufacturing of fertilizer at the fertilizer plant in Balkh. As early as 1967, gas was exported to Russia and a small amount of gas has been provided for domestic consumption and thermal plants.[6]

In late 1998 the UNOCAL Corporation, along with several other giant oil companies, planned to build a pipeline for exporting gas from the Dawlatabad Gas Fields of Turkmenistan to Pakistan and India, passing through territories in Afghanistan. The projected cost of the pipeline was U.S. $1.9 billion, and it is argued that the construction of the pipeline provided the United States $800 million per year.

Transportation and Communications

Afghanistan's gradual integration into the modern world began in the early twentieth century when the state built roads and established communication networks. Since the 1950s there were considerable increases in the number of vehicles such as trucks, lorries, buses, and small cars. However, mules and other animals still constitute a major part of the country's traditional system of transportation. The country has no railroads within its borders, but it is accessible by railroad networks in Pakistan, Iran, and the former Soviet Union. Balkh is close to a railroad station in Termiz near the Oxus River, and Herat is close to the railroad terminus in Kushk, and the railroad station in Mashhad of Iran is also in short distance from Herat. In the south, Pakistani railroad networks are accessible in Quetta, and Peshawar from Qandahar and Nangarhar respectively.

There are several major roads that link Kabul to major provinces and to neighboring countries. The Kabul-Nangarhar Road links Kabul with Islamabad, capital of Pakistan, via the Torkham Border in the east. The Kabul-Qandahar Road links Kabul to Quetta, Pakistan via Qandahar in the south, and the Qandahar-Herat Road links Kabul to Mashhad, Iran via Islam-Qala Port, Herat in the west. The Kabul-Mazar Road, passing through the Salang Pass, links Kabul to the ports of the Oxus River bordering Uzbekistan via Balkh in the north.

Modern transportation also included the aviation industry. In the 1960s, Afghanistan had 9 airports, and by 2002 there were 25 airports throughout the country. The Ariana Airlines, founded in 1955, serve destinations in London, Delhi, Tehran, Karachi, Beirut, and Tashkent. International airlines, mainly from Pakistan, India, Iran, and the Soviet Union, fly to Afghanistan. There are two international airports: Kabul International Airport was completed in 1960, and Qandahar International Airport was completed in 1964, with modern hangers and terminals. Both airports sustained severe damages during the two decades of civil war. Modern communications systems link Kabul to major cities inside and outside the country. In 1983 Kabul had approximately 31,200 telephone lines in use, but the war caused severe damage and reduced the use of telephones to 21,000 in 1998. By 1997 Kabul managed to establish satellite communications links with Nangarhar, Herat, Qandahar, and Balkh.

Commerce

The traditional barter system in which merchants and traders, particularly the nomads, exchanged animal products for grain and other items began to decline with the process of modern banking as early as the 1930s. Initially banking facilities were limited, and only a small number of people within the government used the services of the existing bank. People did not have confidence or trust in the government and the banking institutions preferred to engage in financial transactions that were based on traditional types of investment, such as land, property, cattle, and commodities, that they had personal control over and that were relatively immune from being stolen or destroyed.

Political stability in the 1950s helped convince citizens that it was more secure to trust the banks and use their services as far as savings accounts were concerned. This increased trust led to the growth of the banking system. There were five major banks with headquarters in Kabul: Da Afghanistan Bank, the National Bank of Afghanistan (Bank-e-Milli), the Agriculture and Cottage Industry Bank (Bank-e-Zeraati), Construction and Mortgage Bank, and Bank-e-Tejarati Pashtanay.

In conducting domestic business, people tended to turn to moneylenders for loans because they charged a minimal amount of interest. People preferred this type of traditional financial transaction because they did not have to go through bureaucratic banking procedures. They were unwilling or unable to wait for a procedure for approval ratings that was beyond their comprehension, whereas moneylenders were readily available with easy terms and conditions of loans and a simple procedure of contract, signed or agreed verbally between them. Financial transactions between the moneylender and borrower were primarily based on mutual trust, personal acquaintance, referral by a mutual friend or tribal chief, credit reputation, social and political connections, and the assurance of property, land, and a house as collateral.

In neighboring countries and the Middle East in general, regarding the transaction and exchange of money at the international level, most businessmen, traders, and merchants preferred the system of *Hawala,* a credit transaction through a known intermediary that is financially advantageous to both parties. In the *Hawala* system, a person who is about to venture on a personal or business trip abroad does not have to purchase foreign currency from an established bank that charges a considerable amount of fees for its service and pays a lower rate of exchange to the client. The person chooses to deal directly with money dealers who have agents or friends in a foreign country who could provide him with the required amount of money. The client would obtain the required amount of money he paid at home from his agent's client abroad immediately upon presentation of a simple note or a token that demonstrates that he is the right person whom his partner sent for collecting the required amount of money. The *Hawala* system continues to function, even at the present time, as expatriates still use the system when they send money to members of their family, either in Afghanistan or other neighboring countries. After the fall of the Taliban in late 2001, the U.S.-backed government worked to fully operationalize and modernize existing banks and permitted several foreign banks to open branches in Afghanistan.

Trade

Afghanistan's major import items include machinery, petroleum products, vehicles, tea, sugar, textiles, and miscellaneous manufactured products, such as medicinal and pharmaceutical products, rubber tubes, electronic machinery, metallic and nonmetallic manufactured items, and used clothing that comes mainly from the West. In 2001 Afghanistan's imports were valued at U.S. $1.3 billion, and its major import sources in 1999 included Pakistan, 19 percent; Japan, 16 percent; Kenya, 9 percent; South Korea, 7 percent; India, 6 percent; and Turkmenistan, 6 percent. The country's external debts were estimated at U.S. $5.5 billion in 1996. Afghanistan's principal export items consist of agricultural products, such as fresh and dried fruits, carpets, rugs, cotton, and Qaraqul fleece and hides. Its chief export markets in 1999 included: Pakistan, 32 percent; India, 8 percent; Russia, 5 percent; Germany, 5 percent; Belgium, 7 percent; and United Arab Emirates, 4 percent. A small number of items are also exported to the United States.[7] A significant amount of items are smuggled into Afghanistan mainly through the southern and western regions where nomadic tribes and refugees often cross borders to Pakistan and Iran.

Agriculture

Main agricultural products include wheat, corn, barley, rye, rice, fruits, and cotton. Cotton is cultivated in various regions such as Herat, Parwan, Alinagar, Kunar, Qandahar, Helmand, Farah, Badakhshan, Faryab, and Balkh. Afghanistan is known for its fruits such as grapes, apricots, peaches, palm, almond, berries, pomegranates, dates, melons, and watermelons. More than 50 types of grape vines are cultivated in Qandahar, Kabul, Balkh, and Faryab. Farmers dry the grapes in large quantities in order to make raisins. Fruit trees such as orange, lemon, and dates are cultivated mainly in Nangarhar. The olive plant is grown in the eastern and southeastern regions.

Afghanistan acquired notoriety in the 1990s for cultivation of opium poppies to the extent that the country became the world's major producer of opium, now a major source of cash economy as warlords derive the income from opium to support and maintain their private armies. The sap collected from poppies is refined in a few local laboratories and exported abroad, particularly to the West, by local drug lords controlling the narcotics traffic routes. According to the United Nations, in 1991 Afghanistan produced 2,637 tons of opium. In 2001, the Taliban banned cultivation of poppies in areas that they controlled to convince the international community to provide financial aid to enable the Taliban to maintain their hold on power. However, they did not publicize that they hoarded the existing stockpiles. Poppy cultivation continues to thrive to the present day.

Farmers cultivated opium for medical purposes and as painkillers in most regions where there is no medical facility available to provide medical treat-

Irrigated and rain-fed agriculture in rural Afghanistan.

ment to patients suffering from various illnesses. They also use opium for domestic purposes, such as extracting oil out of dried poppy seeds, manufacturing soap from the ashes of burned poppies, using the stalks for cooking food, as well as making *kunjara* (animal fodder) by mixing dried stalks with grass and hay.

A pervasive cultural trait in Afghanistan is the deep attachment the people have for their land and fiercely guarding it against intrusion and invasion. Owning land depends heavily on family size, status in the tribe, and development of alliances between family patriarchs. Generally, people live in the area of their birthplace, and because families live in close proximity to one another, landholdings can be combined or labor, equipment, or pack animals can be shared through arrangements such as the betrothal of sons and daughters to that of neighbors. A widow who inherits land will usually be married to her husband's next oldest brother to keep the land in the family. Land ownership is divided into four major types: private ownership, or *mulk-e-shakhsi*, is typical for families that have the means to purchase their shares and maintain their holdings without dependency on outside assistance. Sections of government-owned land may also be sold into private ownership or awarded as privately owned parcels to retired government employees or retired military as pensions. Joint ownership between blood relatives, called *mulk-e-khalisa*, is one way for relations to band together to increase the total size of their holdings and combine parcels and a family workforce large enough to set up and sustain farming activities.

Land ownership by religious organizations is called *mulk-e-waqfa*, and clerics in charge of these institutions control any revenue generated by the land. Alliances or sharing arrangements between single families or tribes and religious organizations provide status or influence for the former and a labor pool for the latter. Public ownership, called *mulk-e-ama*, involves a situation where land is shared and controlled collectively by families in a tribal clan, and the size of individual family shares is largely determined by the size of the family and the status of their patriarch. Tribal chiefs usually have the largest families and the highest status, and hence the largest land shares. In certain parts of the country, tribal chiefs have exclusive rights over tribal lands and flocks, and individuals within the community, blood relatives to their chief, work as tenant farmers and shepherds. This changes the relationship from one of kinship to one of occupation.

In addition to land, income generation has four other traditional sources: water, seeds, capital, and labor. Water ownership follows a pattern similar to that of land ownership, landowners have exclusive rights to water use and sell it to peasant farmers. In the few areas where the practice is different, peasant farmers determine the rights to water based on the size of their landholdings.

Kinship and tribal relations drive access to the traditional irrigation systems and water management practice. For example, rights to water from the public reservoir for irrigation purposes is only granted to married people, the idea being that single people are still dependents of their family and their parents already have a claim to a share of water use.[8]

Seeds, capital, and labor are commodities that can be used to gain use of land if outright ownership is beyond the reach of a family. A family providing seeds, equipment, or other investment to work a parcel of land shares a percentage of the proceeds from their activities with the owner. A landowner with several large parcels of land and not enough family members to work on them, or insufficient equipment or pack animals, enters into agreements with smaller clans or single families to work on lots and pay rent or a share of harvested crops for use of the land and water system.

Poor peasants work as tenant farmers on the lands of rich and absentee landlords under the terms of heavily disadvantageous land leases of a year or more. These contracts come in several varieties, all of them designed to favor the interests of the landowner. If a leaseholder owns his own agricultural equipment, seed, and/or plow animals, he must turn over one-half to two-thirds of his annual output to the landowner, the final amount depending on the location of the land. If any amount (but not all) of the equipment, animals, or seed is provided by the landowner, the leaseholder turns over four-fifths of his annual output. If all the equipment, animals, and seed are supplied to the leaseholder he becomes effectively a laborer hired to work the land. The leaseholder and his family are also expected to perform various services for the landlord, which may include repairing roads, cleaning ditches, and performing assorted household duties.

Afghanistan has a low average annual rainfall (estimated at about 11 inches annually) and depends on melting snow in their high mountains for a large part of its water supply. When the snow melts, the water is carried to lower altitudes by rivers and underground veins. Various complex irrigation systems and containment methods have been developed to take the best advantage of this critical resource and to carry water to every part of the field. Common water sources include the *kariz,* also known as *qanat* in other countries, which is a system of underground water channels, and *joi,* which are networks of springs and wells. Distribution of these water sources is regulated according to intended use, time of year, and status of the owner of the water source and of the user.

The most labor- and capital-intensive areas of the water supply system are the *kariz,* largely employed in the western part of the country. At its most basic, a *kariz* consists of channels dug into alluvial fans at the base of mountains that lead water from an underground aquifer to outlying areas where water would not otherwise naturally flow. A *kariz* system can run a length ranging from less than a mile to several miles. A series of wells are sunk at regular intervals into the alluvial fan, a reference to the fan-shape of the silt and gravel deposits left by rivers flowing from mountains as they lose velocity upon reaching the valley floor. The wells get progressively less deep until ground level is reached, resulting in a series of wells ending at the same predetermined depth, which is then connected with a channel that cross-sects with each other. Digging of the underground channel begins at the point of the mouth and the shallowest wells, and will continue at a slight slope until the deepest well, the head well, is reached. Once it is reached, water will begin flowing through the channel to the mouth. Surveying the land to find the precise spot on the alluvial fan for sinking wells requires a great deal of skill, and digging the channel underground is extremely dangerous and is part of the reason that this is the most expensive and complex of water supply systems. It also requires continuous maintenance, often by itinerant or resident specialists who have experience in building *kariz*. For individuals and communities who cannot afford the initial outlay and maintenance costs involved in building a *kariz,* other systems may be employed such as dams, or *jois* that are constructed above ground and serve to divert water to nearby areas via existing or manmade streams.

In most parts of the country, farmers till the land using primitive instruments such as wooden plows, harrows, and sickles. The main parts of a plow consist of a beam and a sole, and the plow shape is either flat or board triangle. The sole slips into an iron blade for plowing the soil. The plow beam is attached to a yoke that sits on the animal's shoulder between the neck and hump. A double yoke is used for a pair of bulls and held in position by two pairs of pegs tied around the neck by a rope. The yoke is adjusted for donkeys, mules, horses, and camels. A farmer will scatter seeds across field and then plow the land so the seeds are worked into the soil. Animals of the household are called for action. A dog occasionally herds the bulls to keep them going, and chickens follow behind looking for worms that rise to the surface as the soil is broken and lifted. Modern agricultural equipment such as tractors and thrashing machines are used by a handful of wealthy farmers and rich landowners.

Poor peasants often help each other by sharing equipment and pack animals, which include oxen, donkeys, and other animals. Farmers often work in pairs and groups and share in the work of plowing their lands, preparing seedbeds, and harvesting and threshing crops. In some areas, a shared oxen system, called *purghu,* is common. Two farmers, each the owner of one ox, will use both oxen together for common plowing of their lands or other activities requiring animal power, and can then accomplish their work more quickly and efficiently. This system is based on necessity rather than profit because a farmer could not effectively plow his land with only one ox.[9]

Animal husbandry is the second most common occupation. Cattle provide dairy products such as milk, butter, yogurt, whey, cheese, and meat. Farmers breed domestic animals such as cows, donkeys, oxen, and horses as a means of transportation, for plowing the land, and for the production of wool. Qaraqul sheep are found and bred mostly in several provinces in the north. Milk is consumed in most parts of the country, and families either take turns to drive the animals of the village out to pasture or hire shepherds to look after the animals and pay them with commodities at the end of the grazing season. The grazing period starts from early spring and continues to late fall, depending on weather conditions in different parts of the country.

Social Stratification

Ethnicity, tribalism, and regionalism created rifts in Afghanistan's polity. A dominant ethnic group would use its power to suppress the efforts of other ethnic and tribal communities to establish their own social bases, and marginalize their role in decision-making processes, so as to deprive them of the opportunity to express their views concerning the future of the country's politics. Tribal and regional conflict on the one hand and the widening gap between rich and poor on the other hand stalled the modernization process and paved the road to a bloody civil war in the 1990s that destroyed much of the country's political, social, and economic infrastructures. Afghanistan is a multitiered society, and at the top of its social ladder is the elite.

Elite

The ruling elite that governs the country comes mainly from landowning and wealthy business families. Their members can be found in top positions in the state apparatuses, serving as army generals, security officials, civil service officers, judges, governors, and legislators in the public and taking leading posts in the private sectors. The elite have access to formal higher education and professional training in Afghanistan, and a significant number study abroad. Relationships that develop between the urban-based elite and the rural elite (i.e., tribal chiefs known as *Mir, Malik, Khan,* and *Arbab*) are based on mutual benefit and cooperation. These arrangements are not equal, as the urban political elite have the backing of the state and its army and will exercise greater authority. The elite of the rural communities are less sophisticated in their worldview because they typically lack the educational background and access to other societies. The rural elite do have one advantage that makes it important to develop good relations with them—they have a longstanding grassroots understanding of politics of their respective communities and can exercise a marked influence over immense numbers of people. They can use this influence to rally people for or against any reforms or initiatives the government seeks to impose.

Landowners

Total agricultural land in 1978 was estimated at 62.61 million hectares, with another 54.7 million hectares of land for use as pastureland and meadows. Prior to the April 1978 coup, an estimated 5 percent of feudal landowners possessed 45 percent of the country's most cultivable lands, and 12 percent of the landowning families possessed 20 percent of the agricultural lands.[10] Landowners commonly influence rural politics in two ways: through their own economic positions and through their connections with conservative clerics, *mullahs,* who make up a large part of the "rural elite." Their influence can be used to obstruct the efforts of local government officials and to conduct activities such as tax collection, census taking, and recruitment in the army. Thus, in most cases, great efforts are made by the government to secure the cooperation of the largest landowners, most of whom are also tribal chiefs.

Peasantry

The peasantry is the largest social segment of the country's population. Prior to the April 1978 coup it was suggested that 83 percent of peasant farmers owned 35 percent of the land or about 2.025 to 4.05 hectares per farmer.[11] They tend to be the least educated social stratum and are isolated or have limited contact with groups outside their immediate community. Their primary political influence is in their numbers, and the ability of the clerics and tribal chiefs to rally them in support of their political agenda largely depends on the creation, nurturing, and sustenance of multiple linkages. One such powerful linkage includes an appeal to ethnicity, tribal pride, and religious beliefs.

Nomads

One segment of population consisted of nomads whose number was estimated to be 2.5 million in 1978–1979. The largest nomadic group is the Ghilzai Pushtuns, with a small number of Qirghiz, Turkmen, Baluchi, and Aimaq tribes. The nomads are classified into three groups: nomads, seminomads, and local seminomads. The first group is found mainly in the southern regions, engaged in the purchase and sale of camels and other goods. They conduct trade with various villages and also serve as an effective communication system for the settled populations, transporting news and gossip from village to village along with goods. Some nomads also served as moneylenders, and were a particularly important economic element in the lives of people in the more isolated communities. The annual migrations of various tribal groups were an integral part of rural life in Afghanistan. Many nomads became wealthy by trading their camels in for modern transportation (i.e., trucks and buses) and since the April 1978 coup and the resulting war, most had left Afghanistan and settled in Pakistan. While the nomads were traders more than stockbreeders, seminomadic herdsmen traveled from one region to another with flocks of animals (sheep, goats, yaks, camels, or horses), seeking pastureland and water. Some of them also engaged in trade with the communities they traveled among. Conflicts between the nomads and the sedentary farmers regarding use of water and land for grazing flared occasionally. Their movements are normally on the fringes of cultivated lands, and when they stop to let their flocks graze it is typically in areas where use is already agreed upon with the farmers, some of these arrangements are several centuries old.[12]

Before the Soviet invasion of Afghanistan in 1979, smuggling was frequently carried out by nomads or seminomads as they crossed borders on their seasonal migrations; except for the Russia-Afghanistan border and parts of the Afghanistan-China border, most borders are easy to cross without challenge. Items commonly smuggled were consumer goods to be used for bartering, although drugs (opium and hashish) and animal skins and Qaraqul fleece were also transported across borders. After the establishment of an Islamic order in April 1992 and the ensuing civil war that lasted until the Taliban was overthrown in 2001, non-Pushtuns did not allow these Pushtun nomads to freely move around in their communities and graze their flocks on their pastures and lands. As a result, many of them have ended up languishing in refugee camps, having lost most of their possessions and their livestock, unable to travel freely in a country now rife with warlord fiefdoms and violent territoriality. The Pushtuns that remain have become members of another class, the dispossessed, or have left the country altogether.

Religious Leaders

Clerical institutions play an important role in the country's social and political affairs. Traditional religious leaders are found in communities of all sizes and most wield significant influence over their constituency. They are known by the title *pir*, and each *pir* has a community of followers to whom they provide advice and guidance concerning issues vital to the religious life of the community. *Pirs* typically come from wealthy families who own large tracts of land and also possess property and land in urban areas. Most *pirs* are of Sayyed background and claim direct descent from the family of the Prophet Muhammad and his son-in-law, Ali; however, some of these claims are impossible to substantiate with certainty. Some *pirs* also claim descent from well-known *sufi* (Islamic mystics) families and other spiritual figures. *Pirs* are revered as liaisons between the people and God, and through their acts and guidance are the means for a family or community to become economically prosperous, to have a better life after death, and to be forgiven for past sins.

Clerics *(mullahs)* are another significant social group, and they are in charge of religious centers *(masjids)*, mosques, and religious schools *(madrasas)*. The most influential *mullahs* are in charge of large, magnificent mosques, while lesser *mullahs* are responsible for smaller-scale mosques and also teach children in *madrasas* for learning the art of Quranic recitation as well as gaining basic reading and writing skills. *Mullahs* in charge of village mosques are supported by the community, which provides money, a house to live in, and a small share from their crops for the religious services they perform and the guidance they give. An overwhelming majority of the population is illiterate, and they depend on *mullahs* for translating and writing letters and for interpretation of religious scriptures, which provides them with many opportunities for influence by presenting their interpretations of scripture and communications. *Mullahs* constitute a powerful group, and the level of their power and authority in their communities was often viewed as a threat to the central government.[13]

Intelligentsia

Afghanistan's intellectual stratum hails from diverse social, political, and economic backgrounds, and generally held junior-level positions within and outside the state apparatus, subordinate to the ruling elites. Educated and politically aware, espousing political ideologies such as liberalism, nationalism, and the doctrine of free market economy, they played a critical role in the country's social, economic, and political development. A significant number of the intelligentsia also advocated alternative development strategies based on socialism or on Islamic teachings. Intellectuals inclined to socialist ideology fell into one of two major groups: pro-Soviet reformists and revolutionaries. The pro-Soviet faction was represented by the People's Democratic Party of Afghanistan (PDPA) and supported a Soviet model of building a socialist society in Afghanistan. They seized power in a coup in April 1978 dubbed as the April Revolution and ruled the country until 1992, when they were forced to transfer power to a coalition of Islamic Parties. The revolutionaries supported a radical transformation of the country's social, political, and economic institutions and believed in the use of armed struggle and mass mobilization to achieve this objective. They vehemently opposed the Soviet-backed government and participated in the war of national liberation against the Soviet occupation.

Entrepreneurs

This class consisted of financial and commercial businessmen, money-lenders, industrialists, traders, and merchants. They established and ran corporations or owned and operated small shops or restaurants, and employed workers on a full- or part-time basis. These entrepreneurial groups, even if they operated in the private sector, were largely subordinated to the state, which monopolized key industrial and commercial sectors of the economy. Thus, their efforts to influence the direction of economic and political development in the country were subject to governmental interference and even outright obstruction. Despite this, they continued to attempt reforms and lent capital support to groups that engaged in fights for liberal and democratic rights. Most members of this group adopted conservative politics, and some of them associated with the Islamic parties, viewing their political ideology as compatible with their own—supportive of a free market economic system and its culture.

Workers

Workers constitute an important social group in Afghanistan who are employed mainly in state-owned industries, while a significant number work in private manufacturing and industries. Economic development in Afghanistan was uneven and this widened the gap between rural and urban living conditions, causing many rural poor to migrate to urban centers in search of employment. The vast majority of workers and laborers are in Kabul because most industrial and manufacturing industries were built in Kabul with a limited number set up in a few other provinces. Since the 1960s the working class has been active in the political arena. They organized protest demonstrations demanding higher wages, better working conditions, health benefits, and so forth. The PDPA that vocally supported the cause of the working class before they seized power now suppressed them. The ruling party imprisoned those who did not support state-repressive policies and executed a number of others who joined the revolutionary groups and fought to liberate Afghanistan when Soviet imperialism invaded the country in December 1979.

The Dispossessed

The lowest rungs of the social ladder are occupied by dispossessed groups of people in socially undesirable occupations such as tanners, gravediggers, and waste collectors. They are beneath the notice of the leadership and are invisible, as people, to society, regardless of the extent to which their services such as waste management or animal butchery may be utilized and needed. They often live a bare, subsistent existence in large urban areas, and their situation was further worsened over the decades of civil war that destroyed the economic infrastructure and civic institutions. The near total loss of their means to make a living exacerbated their hand-to-mouth lifestyle, while simultaneously doubling and tripling their numbers. This group of people remains the most vulnerable to exploitation and abuse by elements of society, such as the wealthy and the warlords, because they have no access to support services or assistance of any kind.[14]

HISTORY, POLITY, AND POLITICAL MOVEMENTS

Afghanistan has been a crossroads to various invading armies whose domination of the country transformed its countenance and civilization and used the region as a steppingstone to invade the Indian-subcontinent. It is argued that about 1000 B.C., the Indo-European speaking Aryan people had settled in the region that was known as Aryana, and the landscape was mentioned in the Rig Veda, the Sanskrit source of Hinduism, by people who moved to India. A reference to the region is also found in the Avesta, the teachings of a religious leader, Zarathustra who lived around 500 B.C. According to the Avesta, the first king of Aryans was named Yama, with his headquarters in Bactria or present day Balkh. Major Aryan dynasties ruled ancient Afghanistan including Paradate, Kawa, and Aspa. Yama belonged to the first dynasty, and his reign was marked by periodic wars between him and the Caledonian ruler Zahak. Kawa or Kayqubad was the founder of the Kawa dynasty who fought Afrasiyab, king of the Turanis. Lahra Aspa was the founder of the Aspa dynasty whose name referred to as the master of swift horses. He was duly succeeded by his two sons, Wesht Aspa and Gusht Aspa whose reigns paved the road for the emergence of the Zoroastrian faith. Zoroaster was related to the Aspa dynasty and began propagating his ideas concerning the doctrine of monotheism while he was in the court of the Wesht Aspa.

The Persian ruler Cyrus conquered ancient Afghanistan between 549–545 B.C., annexed the region to Persia, and laid the foundation of the Achaemenid rule. The Achaemenid rule collapsed almost two centuries later as a result of internecine war by feudal lords who led periodic rebellions against the Persian rulers. It was during this time that the region was subjugated by the invading armies of Alexander, son of Philip II of Macedonia, around 330 to 327 B.C. After Alexander's death around 323 B.C., his empire was split into three territories, and General Seleucus maintained his rule over the eastern parts, including Afghanistan. Around 250 B.C., a local Greek ruler declared the plains south of the Oxus River independent and eventually extended his rule to Kabul and Punjab, India. During this period, the eastern part of the country was ruled by Indian dynasties, while the western part was under the rule of Hellenic kings and later by Persian kingdoms.

Around 135 B.C., the Kushan tribes drove the Greeks out and laid the foundation of the Kushan rule, and their powerful King Kanishka extended his empire, which stretched from northern India to territories of China. The great historical caravan route known as the Silk Route connected Rome to China and India via Afghanistan, and exposed the country to the influences of several cultures and traditions. The Kushan rule crumbled around 250 A.D. with the emergence of conflicting principalities in different parts of the country that lasted until the first half of the seventh century. During this period, Afghanistan was under the domination of the Tokois of the Mongolian tribes with their center in Qunduz, the Sassanians with their headquarters in the western part of the country, and the Hephthalites, known as the White Huns, establishing their capital in Kapisa.[15]

In 652 A.D., the Muslim Arab invading armies launched a major offensive on Herat and regions in the central part of Afghanistan. The Arabs encountered severe resistance in Bamiyan, Ghazni, Kabul, and a few other regions, and eventually they established their dominance in Afghanistan. With Arab domination, the country's name was changed to Khurasan, the land of the rising Sun. Direct Arab domination of the country ended when Abu Muslim Khurasani exploited rivalries between the Ummayyad and Abbasid caliphs and sided with the latter against the former. After defeating the Arabs loyal to the Ummayyad, he declared himself king and ruled the country for several years until he was assassinated on his return from Mecca. His death paved the road to periodic armed conflicts between Afghanistan and the Arab ruler until the Tahirid rulers of Herat adopted a conciliatory approach toward the caliphs. After consolidating his power base, he declared his independence. The Tahirid (820–870) ruled the country until the Safarid dynasty led by Yaqub Lais Safari overthrew them and laid the foundation for the Safarid rule (870–890). It was during his rule that Persian was introduced as an official language of the court, ending the pervasive influence of Arabic language. The Arab rulers worked to reestablish their domination over Afghanistan, and for this reason they supported the Samanid of Balkh in their seizure of power. The Samanid established an independent state in northern Khurasan (874–999), defeated Yaqub Lais Safari's successor Ahmad (Yaqub's brother), captured him, and sent him as a prisoner to the caliph of Baghdad, Iraq. The Samanid ruled the country for 125 years until the Ghaznawid defeated them.

The rise of the Ghaznawid dynasty in 962–1148, with its power center in Ghazni, asserted its rule over Transoxiana, Bukhara, and in the regions adjacent to the Ganges region and Gujrat of India. The Ghaznawid ruler Mahmood enriched himself when his marauding armies looted the wealthy Hindu temples, and his religious missionaries converted a significant number of Hindus to Islam. The Ghaznawid rule collapsed when the Saljuqid (1038–1157) established their domination over several regions in the northern areas until the Ghorid seized power (1150–1217). Ala al-Din Ghori set fire on the city of Ghazni, which lasted for a week, and he ordered the massacre of Ghazni's residents and sanctioned the destruction of other cities as he conquered them. The Ghorid were defeated by the Kharazm tribes that ruled the country until the armies of the Mongolian chief Genghis Khan conquered Afghanistan in 1220. People who suffered under the brutal rule of various kings always welcomed their downfall. Residents of the city of Balkh, including religious leaders, welcomed the Mongol invader Genghis Khan when he crossed into the region. Genghis's army showed no mercy to those who did not submit to them. When Genghis's grandson was killed in a battle in Bamiyan in 1221, he retaliated with a scorched-earth rampage upon residents of the city, killing men, women, and children. The site is known as *Shahr-e-Ghulghulah* or the City of Screams—the screams of dying citizens of the valley.

The Mongols could not destroy the Islamic way of life and Genghis's great grandson eventually converted to Islam. Genghis's descendants ruled the country for a century and a half and allowed local rulers who pledged allegiance to him to remain in power. Timur, known as Tamerlane, a descendent of Genghis Khan through his mother, rebelled against the Chaghatai government and declared himself king. Tamerlane (1336–1405) established his capital in Samarqand and his empire extended from India to Turkey. Tamerlane was known for his brutal display of towers built from the skulls of defeated foes. His successor Shah Rukh (1407–1447) transferred the capital to Herat and was succeeded by his son Ulugh Beg. In 1500–1747, Afghanistan remained a cause of disagreement between two feuding rival powers, the Safawid in the west and the Moghul dynasty in India. Tamerlane descendent Zahir al-Din Muhammad Babur (Babur means tiger) conquered Afghanistan and established his rule in Kabul in 1504 and sent an expedition to India in 1526. He established his capital in Agra and laid the foundation of the Moghul rule that dominated India for almost 200 years. Babur was known for his love of poetry and gardening, and his famous garden is called the Garden of Felicity. When Babur died in 1529, he requested that he be buried in Kabul and was succeeded by his son Homayun. The Moghul domination of Kabul ended after the death of Awrangzib in 1706, when Safawid rulers of Iran conquered Afghanistan.[16]

Rise of Pushtun Aristocracy and Tribal Conflict

The fragmented Pushtun tribes were referred to as Afghans around the fourteenth century, but the usage of the word Afghans gradually expanded to include all Pushtun residents of the country by the eighteenth century when the Pushtuns emerged as a cohesive political group. The Indians referred to the Pushtuns as Pathans, a derivative of the word Patna, when a small number of them had settled in the Patna Region of India in the fourteenth century. By the nineteenth century the use of the word Afghans extended to include all ethnic communities that resided in the country. The toponym Afghanistan is comprised of two words, *Afghan* (Pushtun) and *Stan* (Land) meaning "land of the Afghans," and was incorrectly applied to include all the country's ethnic communities.

In 1709, Mirwais, chief of the Hotak Ghilzai tribe, mobilized his men to put an end to the domination of Afghanistan by the Shia Safawids. After a pilgrimage to Mecca he secured a religious edict *(fatwa)* proclaiming war on the Safawid governor, Gurgin. After Mirwais's death, his son Mahmood fought and overthrew the Safawids. Mahmood's rule ended when his cousin Ashraf murdered him in 1725. Ashraf's cruelty cost him his life when Nadir Quli of Khurasan, Iran seized Herat in 1732 and conquered Qandahar, Ghazni, Kabul, and India. In 1739 he defeated the Moghuls at Karnal, a few miles north of Delhi and seized valuable treasures including the Koh-e-Noor diamond, and transferred the Peacock Throne to Iran. Nadir showed no mercy to those who tried to oust him, including his son, whom he blinded for trying to seize power. In 1747 he was killed and his security guard, Ahmad Shah Abdali, established his rule in Qandahar.[17]

Ahmad Shah changed his last name, Abdali, which was associated to his tribe Abdal, to the neutral name of Durani in order to unite the tribal communities. He made Qandahar his base, and the tribal chiefs pledged allegiance to him and awarded him the title of *Dur-e-Duran,* pearl of pearls. Ahmad Shah mobilized his tribes and subjugated much of Afghanistan by 1750. He extended his rule to the northeastern parts of Iran, and marched into Baluchistan and India where his marauding tribal armies plundered the areas they conquered. The rise of Ahmad Shah heralded the beginning of the Pushtun domination of the country's politics. In 1773 Ahmad Shah died, and his son Timur moved the capital from Qandahar to Kabul in 1776 and ruled until his death in 1793. After his death, armed conflict intensified among his 23 sons, each trying to seize power. In 1801 Mahmood fought his brother Zaman, captured and blinded him and kept him in jail. In 1803 his brother Shuja overthrew him and ruled until 1810, but Mahmood maneuvered his way back to power, toppled Shuja, and ruled until 1819. He delegated most of the responsibilities to his trusted aide, Fatih, and his brothers. However, Mahmood soon viewed Fatih's growing popularity as a threat to his rule and blinded him on accusations of plotting to overthrow him. Fatih's brothers formed an alliance with Shuja to fight Mahmood. Mahmood tried in vain to reconcile with his brothers and then murdered Fatih. This murderous act and the continuing rivalry among the brothers contributed to the decline of the Durani rule.[18]

Colonial Intervention

Dost Mohammad, son of Payenda, a powerful Mohammadzai tribal chief, fought the Duranis to avenge his brother Fatih's death, defeated them, and seized power in 1826. During this period, Afghanistan became an arena of conflict among rival communities. The Uzbeks and other tribal communities declared their independence. The period in which Dost Mohammad ruled coincided with the growing rivalry between Russian and British colonial powers. The British intended to contain the Russian drive toward the Indian Ocean and supported Dost Mohammad. Dost Mohammad launched a war to capture Peshawar, former capital of Afghanistan, from Ranjit Singh, the Sikh ruler of Punjab, but he was defeated. The British refusal to recognize Peshawar as part of Afghanistan caused Dost Mohammad to turn to Russia for help. This move caused the British to invade Afghanistan in 1839, resulting in the first Anglo-Afghan war (1839–1842). The British seized Qandahar and Kabul, drove Dost Mohammad to the north, and installed former King Shuja to the throne. Shuja immediately arrested Dost Mohammad and exiled him to India. Shuja relied on the British for protection, however, the people in Kabul regarded Shuja as an illegitimate ruler, revolted against him, and attacked his forces, killing the British envoy William Macnaghten and his army. Only one British subject, William Brydon, survived the onslaught and reached Jalalabad battered and slumped across his feeble horse. In reprisal, the British burned the bazaar in Kabul and Qalah-e-Chawk in Ghazni and installed Dost Mohammad to the throne in hopes that he could defend their interests. Dost Mohammad maintained friendly ties with the British until his death in 1863.

Dost Mohammad's successor Shir Ali improved ties with the Russians, which resulted in another British invasion of the country, paving the road for the second Anglo-Afghan war (1878–1879). The British installed Shir Ali's son Yaqub Khan to the throne (1879–1880), who concluded the Gandumak Treaty with the British in May 1879, which transformed Afghanistan into a British protectorate. When Russian forces occupied Panjdeh, a district less than 100 miles north of Herat, the British mobilized its forces to defend the city and repulse the Russians. During negotiations, the Russians agreed to halt their advance southward, paving the road for the Anglo-Russian Treaty of 1895 that resulted in the demarcation of the boundary between Russia and Afghanistan. The Russians recognized the Wakhan corridor as part of Afghanistan, and the British agreed with the treaty because the corridor served as a buffer zone between Russia and British-India. This development also led to demarcation of Russian-Afghanistan boundaries along the Oxus River. The British also delineated the eastern and southern boundaries of Afghanistan when the Durand Line, drawn in 1893 by Mortimer Durand, split the Pushtun and Baluch tribes between Afghanistan and Pakistan.[19]

Shir Ali's nephew Abd al-Rahman, who ruled in 1880–1901, remained loyal to the British and received military equipment that enabled him consolidate his rule. With British assistance, Abd al-Rahman launched a war on Hazarajat and other regions and subjugated the tribal chiefs to his rule.[20] Abd al-Rahman neglected development of the country except for the manufacturing and industrial sectors that served his interests and those of the ruling circles and aristocratic families. Abd al-Rahman's successor, Habibullah (1901–1919), followed his father's domestic and foreign policies and remained subservient to the British. He embarked upon small-scale modernization programs, evidenced in the establishment of a number of state-owned manufacturing industries, such as European medicine, automobiles, telephones, telegraphs, and so forth.

The October socialist revolution in Russia in 1917 influenced developments in Afghanistan and ignited anticolonial sentiment in the Indian subcontinent. Liberal and radical intellectuals agitated for independence from the British. This development is believed to have led to the mysterious murder of Habibullah in 1919 in Jalalabad, Nangarhar, while on vacation. His brother Nasrullah succeeded him but was soon ousted by Habibullah's son Amanullah. Amanullah declared Afghanistan's independence from the British, which led to the third Anglo-Afghan war in May 1919. The British lost this war and on August 8, 1919, were forced to sign the Treaty of Rawalpindi that recognized Afghanistan's independence.[21]

Postindependence Development

Amanullah intended to modernize the country's social and political institutions. To achieve this he promulgated a new constitution in 1923 that accorded equal rights to ethnic communities. The Constitution abrogated slavery, which led to the freedom of thousands of Shia Hazaras working as slaves and bonded servants in the houses of the upper and middle classes. The

Constitution permitted the Shias to freely practice their faith and respected the rights and equality of the non-Muslim minority communities of Hindus and Sikhs before the law. Amanullah also embarked upon building roads, establishing modern communications networks to boost the country's economy, and industrialization. Amanullah sought to expand Afghanistan's ties with the international community. The Soviet Union was the first to recognize Afghanistan's independence and pledged to provide support for its modernization programs. Amanullah supported anticolonial and Pan-Islamic struggles and allowed Indian nationalists and revolutionaries to establish an office in Kabul, and assigned Raja Mahendra Pratap of the Ghadr Party as a member of Afghanistan's delegation to China. The British viewed Amanullah's Pan-Islamic ideas, his support of the anticolonial movements in the Indian-subcontinent, and his closer ties with the Soviet Union as a threat to their domination and worked to instigate anti-Amanullah unrest.

British efforts as well as fear and anger at the sudden changes imposed from above gave rise to rumbles of dissent among the citizenry. A major civil rebellion broke out in Khost in March 1924 against Amanullah's reforms, but it was immediately suppressed. To defuse the situation and to prevent similar uprisings in the future, Amanullah temporarily rescinded some of the reform measures. Between December 1927 and June 1928 Amanullah, his wife, Soraya, and members of their entourage visited several European countries and were warmly greeted by their hosts. Technological, economic, and social developments in these countries impressed Amanullah to the extent that he became determined to modernize the country on the basis of a European model of development.

During a *Loya Jirgah* (Grand Assembly of Tribal Elders) held in Kabul in August 1928, Amanullah presented his policies concerning modernization of educational, social, political, and economic infrastructures and argued passionately in favor of women's equality. His wife, Soraya, who accompanied him to the *Loya Jirgah* discarded her veil and was supported in this action when a hundred other women, mainly wives of government officials, also discarded their veils.[22] This measure and other radical programs that Amanullah initiated ignited public unrest in most parts of the country. Amanullah was 27 years old when he became king and 37 years old when rising opposition to his leadership forced him to abdicate the throne. He lacked the experience and political maturity necessary to effectively deal with sensitive and complicated social, religious, and tribal politics, and his infatuation with Western civilization and his unrealistically radical approach to modernize the country led to disaster. Aided and abetted by the British, anti-Amanullah forces launched a concerted campaign to discredit him and call for his overthrow.

Tajik Domination of Politics

To garner public support for their agenda, anti-Amanullah forces circulated and distributed photographs of Amanullah's wife, Soraya, wearing low-cut gowns among the conservative tribal communities. They claimed that Amanullah and Soraya violated Islamic values and called for a holy war, *jihad*, to overthrow him and restore Islamic rule. Sadiq Mojaddadi, brother of an influential religious leader, Fazl Omar Mojaddadi, collected signatures of 400 clerics who issued a religious decree *(fatwa)* condemning Amanullah for violating Islamic values and pronouncing him unfit to rule, paving the road for a major rebellion by the Shinwari tribes in November 1928. The rebellion forced Amanullah to rescind some of his reforms in order to placate opponents. For example, he recalled girls who were studying in Constantinople, closed some of the schools for girls, and released prisoners, including the Mojaddadi family, but the rebellions continued.

On January 14, 1929, Habibullah of Kohdaman launched a frontal attack on Kabul and forced Amanullah to retreat to Qandahar where he organized a tribal army, fought, was defeated, and left the country for Italy in March 1929. Habibullah had been born and raised in Kalakan and was recruited in Amanullah's army, the *Qita-e-Namuna* (model battalion). Habibullah's opponents called him *bacha-e-saqaw*, water carrier's son, because of a job his father had. During the Khost rebellion in 1924, Habibullah deserted the army and went to Peshawar, British-controlled Pakistan, where he ran a teahouse until he returned to Kalakan after some years. Habibullah became popular as he amassed substantial wealth and was warmly received by people in his hometown.

Habibullah seized power for nine months and was awarded the title of *Khadim-e-din-e-Rasulallah,* the Servant of the faith of the Prophet, by conservative clerics and religious leaders. He appointed trusted men from his hometown to key posts and launched an offensive to subdue tribal chiefs and individuals still loyal to Amanullah. Within five months his forces gained control of Badakhshan, Balkh, Maimana, Herat, Qandahar, and Kabul. However, in Hazarajat and a few other regions people did not submit to his rule and fought to restore Amanullah to power. General Mohammad Nadir, a great-grandson of one of Dost Mohammad's brothers and Afghanistan's ambassador to France in 1924–1926, returned home along with his brothers. Backed by the British, Nadir was determined to overthrow Habibullah and seize power. To rally the people and gain their support for his crusade against Habibullah, Nadir declared that he had no intention of seizing power. He stated that he sought to restore the deposed king to the throne in Kabul.

Nadir rallied the Pushtun tribes of Paktiya who helped him seize power and engaged in a concerted campaign that depicted Habibullah as a Tajik bandit who seized power form the Pushtuns. Two times Nadir moved toward Kabul but retreated, and in October 1929 he and his brothers defeated Habibullah and seized Kabul. The tribal army that helped Nadir defeat Habibullah looted public and private properties in Kabul, regarding them war booty, and they proclaimed Nadir the new king.[23]

Rise of the Mohammadzai Dynasty

Nadir was born in 1883 to a family exiled to British India by King Abd al-Rahman. He and his family returned to Afghanistan after Abd al-Rahman's successor Habibullah issued a general amnesty to political prisoners. Nadir became a general in Habibullah's army and commander-in-chief in 1913 and became a powerful player when Amanullah succeeded his father in 1919. As a conservative politician, Nadir opposed Amanullah's radical policies of nation building, and for this reason he was sent to diplomatic exile in France.

Nadir sent an envoy to convince Habibullah of Kalakan to return to Kabul for a meeting to discuss the structure of the political system. Habibullah did not trust Nadir and asked for assurances that Nadir would not harm him if he visited Kabul. Nadir promised that he would not do anything to harm him and as a demonstration of keeping his promise he wrote a note in the margins of the Quran, signed it, affixed his seal and sent the Quran to Habibullah. Habibullah was naïve and inexperienced in politics, trusted Nadir, and along with his close aides returned to Kabul to meet Nadir. Soon after their arrival they were arrested and summarily executed. Religious leaders who supported Habibullah's rise to power and called him *Ghazi* (a warrior) and *Khadim-e-din-e-Rasulallah,* now called him a bandit.

Nadir consolidated his rule by relying on his brothers and immediate family members and by strengthening ties with conservative religious leaders. He awarded honorary titles such as colonels and majors to some of the tribal chiefs to gain their support. He exempted the Pushtun tribes who helped him seize power from paying taxes and recruitment in the army and appointed Pushtun rulers as governors and administrators in non-Pushtun communities. Nadir appointed his immediate family members and cronies to key positions in the state bureaucracy and brutalized those who did not agree with him.

Nadir encountered opposition to his leadership by people throughout the country. In May 1930 the Shinwari tribes led a rebellion in favor of Amanullah but Nadir quelled the uprising by bribing a number of the tribal chiefs. He also crushed an uprising to his rule by the Ghilzai tribes residing in the southwestern region of Kabul. When the people of Kohistan rebelled against Nadir in July 1930, he dispatched the Pushtun tribal armies who killed Purdil, the leader of the rebellion and plundered property while brutally murdering innocent men and women. To this day, people in Kohistan vividly remember the massacre. To legitimize his leadership in September 1930, Nadir convened a *Loya Jirgah*, which was dominated by handpicked delegates who endorsed his leadership. Nadir abrogated Amanullah's progressive reforms, embarked upon a regressive policy of nation building, and arrested and executed a number of nationalist and patriotic forces who remained loyal to Amanullah. In 1931 Nadir consolidated his power base as his army defeated rival opponents in the southern, western, and northern regions. To maintain peace and stability, Nadir embarked upon building roads to facilitate the quick dispatching of armies to deal with tribal insurgency as well as improve the communications and transportation system. The road that links Kabul to the northern regions via the Shibar Pass was completed just prior to Nadir's assassination in 1933, and retained its strategic importance as a north-south route until the opening of the Salang Tunnel in 1964. In October 1931, Nadir promulgated a new constitution that restricted civil liberties and individual freedom. He embarked upon a limited scale of modernization of state institutions and encouraged the growth of private sectors that mainly engaged in import and export but did not support industrialization of the country, effectively hindering independent development in Afghanistan.

Nadir's pro-British policy and regressive domestic programs dismayed progressive, radical, and liberal intellectuals who tried to liberate the country from his rule. In June 1933, Sayed Kamal assassinated Nadir's brother, Mohammad Aziz, who was the country's ambassador to Germany. Abdul Khaliq, a Hazara student at Nijat High School, assassinated Nadir on November 8, 1933, during a student award distribution ceremony. Khaliq was arrested along with his family and friends, and the state used this opportunity to arrest potential opponents on allegations of having a role in the assassination of Nadir. Security officers tortured Khaliq by cutting his tongue and gouging his eyes and soldiers killed him with bayonets while his family and friends were forced to watch.[24] This act was meant to teach a lesson to others who may contemplate committing a similar action against members of the ruling family.

Mohammad Zahir succeeded his father but was very young at that time, and his two uncles Mohammad Hashim and Shah Mahmood effectively ruled the country for several years. Prime Minister Hashim effectively suppressed opposition members and countercultural and political movements. His coercive methods of governance caused disenchantment among intellectuals and members of the middle classes who engaged in a movement to establish a democratic system of governance. Members of the king's family were not happy with the growing public dismay and forced Hashim to resign and appointed King Zahir's other uncle, Shah Mahmood, as prime minister in 1946. Shah Mahmood tried to project a more benign image of the monarchy and initiated a number of reforms including amnesty to political prisoners, free parliamentary elections, freedom of association, and freedom of the press.

It was during this time that several political groups agitating policies from liberalism to nationalist and progressive approaches were formed. *Wishzalma-yan*, the Awakened Youths, comprised mainly of Pushtun intellectuals who were in favor of cosmetic reforms and avoided confrontations with the ruling elite. *Hizb-e-Watan*, Homeland Party, was critical of government policy and advocated progressive policies of development. To counter the growing influence of the antiestablishments, the ruling elite headed by Mohammad Daoud, cousin of King Zahir, founded a semisecret political group, *Itihad-iya-e-Azadi-e-Pushtunistan*, Union for Freedom of Pushtunistan. When the organization failed to win recruits, Daoud founded a new organization, *Club-e-Milli*, National Club, on January 15, 1950 and used this organization to secure needed support for assuming power in 1953.

During Shah Mahmood's tenure, radical and patriotic individuals contested the seventh parliamentary elections in 1949, and a number of them were elected on the basis of free and secret balloting. The liberal parliament passed a law concerning freedom of the press and association, which led to the formation of several independent papers. *Angar* was edited by Faiz Mohammad Angar, *Nida-e-Khalq* by Dr. Abd al-Rahman Mahmoodi, *Watan* by Mir Ghulam Mohammad Ghubar, and *Wulus* by Gul Pacha Ulfat.[25] The government also allowed the formation of a union by students of Kabul University in 1950. As antiestablishment and liberal struggle escalated, the government cracked down on the liberal intellectuals, forcing many to flee to Pakistan where they continued their antigovernment activity and published newsletters and smuggled them to Afghanistan. The ruling elite perceived the growing radicalization of the country's politics, and Shah Mahmood's inability to harness it, as a potential threat to the status quo, and decided to take action. Shah Mahmood was forced to resign and the king appointed his cousin, Mohammad Daoud, prime minister.

The decade of Daoud's tenure, 1953–1963, was a period of state-sponsored modernization. Daoud asked the United States for military aid to offset growing U.S. military aid to Pakistan. The refusal of the United States to provide arms to Afghanistan compelled Daoud to strengthen ties with the Soviet Union and its bloc countries. The Soviet Union had long aspired to dominate Afghanistan and use it as a launching pad to influence events in the Indian subcontinent. To this end, in January 1954 the Soviet Union provided U.S.

$3.5 million in economic aid to build two grain silos and bakeries in Kabul and Pul-e-Khumri, as well as financial aid to modernize the country's armed forces. It also granted scholarships for students and government personnel to study in institutions of higher education in the Soviet Union.

In March 1955, relations between Afghanistan and Pakistan deteriorated over the validity of the Durand border lines, which led to the closure of the borders for five months. During this time, Daoud requested the United States to facilitate the transport of imported goods through the Chabahar Port in Iran. The United States refused on the grounds that it was not economically feasible, compelling Daoud to seek Soviet assistance, which led to improved Kabul-Moscow relations and furthered Afghanistan's dependency on the Soviet Union. Soviet economic, military, and technical aid increased in subsequent years, which transformed Afghanistan into a client state. As relations improved between the two countries, the Soviet leader Nikita Khrushchev visited Kabul in December 1955 and promised U.S. $100 million in economic aid to Afghanistan subject to repayment in several installments with a 2 percent interest rate. The Soviet leadership also declared that it supported Afghanistan policy regarding the rights of the Pushtuns residing in Pakistan for self-determination. Conclusion of a bilateral agreement between Kabul and Moscow paved the road for greater Soviet involvement in economic development, such as improving irrigation dams and building hydroelectric plants, automotive repair plants, modern roads, schools, and hospitals.

Despite increased Soviet technical, economic, and military aid to Afghanistan, the United States also provided aid in an effort to influence political developments in the country. Afghanistan became an arena for superpower rivalry, evidenced in the formation of client political parties who advocated a free market economy and its ideology as well as a Soviet model of socialism. U.S. development projects included building the road that linked Kabul to Pakistan and building a modern airport in Qandahar at a cost of an estimated U.S. $15 million, of which $5 million was a loan and the remainder grants. The United States also provided aid for the building of a dormitory at the campus of the Kabul University and scholarships for students and civil service personnel to study in the United States.

During his tenure, Daoud consolidated his rule and gained loyalty within the army and security departments, projecting an image of a strong man whose popularity overshadowed that of the king. Opposition to Daoud's autocratic rule gradually grew stronger within and outside the state apparatus, which eventually forced him to resign in 1963. The king appointed Minister of Mines and Industries Mohammad Yusuf, who was not a member of the king's family as caretaker prime minister to form a new government.

Constitutional Decade

During the constitutional period (1964–1973) the king tried to make his presence felt by the people and traveled throughout the country, meeting tribal chiefs and common people because at that time most people in remote areas still believed that Amanullah was in charge of the country. The king appointed a committee to draft a new constitution, and a *Loya Jirgah* that was convened in September 1964 in Kabul approved the Constitution. The Constitution recognized freedom of speech, freedom of assembly, and freedom of association, and it barred involvement of the king's immediate family members into high government posts; however, they used their position and ties with bureaucratic officials to influence the direction of political development in the country.

During this period, several political organizations emerged that advocated policies such as liberalism, nationalism, Islamic fundamentalism, and socialism. Prominent among them were the Afghan *Millat,* the Afghan Social Democratic Party, who advocated ultranationalist approaches and supported the cause of the Pushtuns in Pakistan. *Sazman-e-Jawanan-e-Musalman,* Islamic Youths Organization known as *Ikhwan al-Muslimin* or Islamic Brotherhood fought for restoration of Islamic values. *Itihad-e-Milli,* National Unity, a pro-establishment group that became known as *Hizb-e-Zarnigar* and was headed by Khalilullah Khalili, special advisor to the king, and later by other technocrats. The pro-Soviet *Hizb-e-Demokratik-e-Khalq-e-Afghanistan,* the People's Democratic Party of Afghanistan, PDPA was founded in 1965, split into *Khalq* (masses) and *Parcham* (banner) factions. Both factions advocated peaceful transition to socialism. *Sazman-e-Jawanan-e-Mutaraqi,* the Progressive Youth Organization or PYO that split into several factions in the mid-1970s (Akhgar, Paikar, Khurasan, *Sazman-e-Azadi Bakhsh-e-Mardum-e-Afghanistan,* People's Liberation Organization or SAMA, *Sazman-e-Azadi-e-Afghanistan,* Afghanistan Liberation Organization or ALO, and others) advocated revolutionary armed struggle as the only means to bring fundamental political and economic changes. *Setam-e-Milli,* an ultra nationalist party, supported the rights of the oppressed ethnic communities and equality among the country's constituent national communities. Freedom of the press allowed political groups and individuals to have newspapers of their own. A new election law that was approved in May 1965 paved the road to general elections in August-September that year. There were 216 representatives elected to the *Shura-e-Milli,* House of Representatives that included three members of the PDPA such as Anahita Ratibzad, Babrak Karmal, and Hafizullah Amin, as well a significant number of candidates from *Hizb-e-Wahdat-e-Milli* and conservative, liberal, and patriotic individuals.

With growing student and labor movements, Prime Minister Yusuf resigned in October 1965 and the king appointed Mohammad Hashim Maiwandwal, former ambassador to the United States and later minister of information and culture, as prime minister. Maiwandwal promised to improve the economy and initiate reforms in the state bureaucracy to serve the public in a more efficient manner. Maiwandwal's ascension to power dismayed the Russians, who expressed concern over the direction of developments. It is reported that a Russian official chided his American counterpart in a cocktail party saying that, "Well, you Americans should be happy, at last your man got in."[26] Maiwandwal formed the Progressive Democratic Party in 1966 with a publication of *Masawat* (Equality), that supported liberal capitalist ideology, politics, and economic development. When Maiwandwal was accused of being a CIA agent in an article published in the *Rampart* magazine in the United States, he resigned in October 1967 and his treatment at the Andrew Air Force Hospital outside Washington, D.C., reinforced such allegations. Noor Ahmad Etemadi, a distant relative of King Zahir who succeeded Maiwandwal, failed to reform the bureaucracy or improve the economy and resigned in May 1971, and was succeeded by Abdul Zahir. Like his predecessors, Zahir also failed to improve the economy and curb growing unemployment during his tenure (1971–1972). This factor on the one hand and the severe drought that claimed the lives of thousands of people (50,000 to 100,000 in Hazarajat alone) on the other hand led to his resignation. Mohammad Musa Shafiq who succeeded him could not deliver an immediate panacea to growing economic difficulties that gripped the country, forcing many skilled and semiskilled laborers to leave the country for Iran and other oil-producing countries in the Middle East in search of employment. He was labeled a traitor when he signed a treaty with Iran that regulated the flow of the Helmand River to Iran.

Republican Order, 1973–1978

The corruption, nepotism, and favoritism that permeated every level of the governmental structure generated public dismay and necessitated a major reform in the social and political arena in order to fuse the state and civil society. Several individuals, such as former Prime Ministers Daoud, Maiwandwal, and the king's son-in-law, General Abdul Wali, were rumored to be planning to topple the monarchy. Daoud was trying to recruit loyalists to support him, including Babrak Karmal, head of the Parcham faction of the PDPA. It is alleged that when Daoud discussed the issue with Karmal he advised Daoud that working with the king, his cousin, is the only way to serve the country and liberate the people.[27] The constitutional period had been characterized as follows:

Favoritism and nepotism, corollaries of a tribal system superimposed on a government and long rampant in Afghanistan, remain widespread. Some collateral members of the royal family have never completely accepted the democracy-e-naw [new democracy] and look on its structure as simply a personal inconvenience. They ask official favors of cabinet ministers and other high ranking officials, and, if rebuffed, they usually manage to have their requests approved somewhere in the middle-range bureaucratic levels, in return for reciprocities, present or anticipated. Many tribal leaders go to the royal family with petitions, which are then transmitted to acquiescent middle-range bureaucrats in the ministries concerned.... Of course, such motives and actions exist in varying degree in all states, democratic and non-democratic alike.[28]

On July 17, 1973, King Zahir was in Rome, Italy, when his cousin Mohammad Daoud staged a coup, seized power, and declared Afghanistan a republic. The king abdicated the throne and remained in Rome with his family. People reacted calmly, regarding Daoud's takeover simply as a "changing of the guard" without any significant alteration in the system of governance. To legitimize the takeover of power, Daoud condemned the monarchy for miseries people endured and declared that he would do his best to improve the economy, raise the standards of living, and fight nepotism, corruption, and divisive politics that fractured the nation.

Soon after consolidation of his rule, Daoud permitted members of the former king's family to leave the country and join their families in the West and provided a monthly maintenance salary to the former king. Daoud came to power with the help of pro-Soviet army officers and appointed four of these individuals as members of his cabinet. The revolutionaries did not support Daoud because they were skeptical about the sincerity of his intentions in initiating fundamental changes that would benefit the public. However, Daoud depicted the regime as revolutionary and progressive and himself as an iconoclastic leader who delivered the people from their miseries sustained under the kingdom. For this reason, he dropped the title of *sardar,* prince, attached to his name (he was addressed Sardar Daoud by his cronies and *sardar-e-diwanah,* lunatic prince by his opponents). The public did not trust him because they saw Daoud and former King Zahir as a fox and a jackal in the same family, and they vividly remembered Daoud's autocratic style of leadership during his tenure as prime minister in 1953–1963. Still, pro-Soviet intellectuals called Daoud "Red Prince," Father of the Nation, and leader of the revolution.

Daoud abrogated the 1964 Constitution and promised to promulgate a new constitution and carry out land reforms. He stressed development of heavy industries and encouraged private investment. In the political arena, he stated that his government would work to resolve the nationality question on principles of equality and friendship. Among the reforms were: stabilization of the prices of basic staples, reduction of working hours to a maximum of 45 hours per week at state-owned institutions, and raising the minimum wage from 450 Afs. to 900 Afs.

Daoud declared other political parties illegal and cracked down on those he suspected of working against him. In September 1973, former Prime Minister Maiwandwal was arrested on allegations of planning a coup and was executed. Daoud's support for the right to self-determination of the Pushtuns and Baluchis residing in Pakistan compelled Zulfiqar Ali Bhutto to destabilize his regime by supporting Daoud's opponents. Bhutto capitalized on the grievances of the Hazaras in Afghanistan and launched a program in the Hazaragi dialect of the Persian language from Quetta, urging Hazaras to rise against Daoud.

There was a shift in Daoud's foreign policy orientation after he consolidated his power base. He improved ties with Iran and Pakistan and distanced himself from the Soviet Union. In October 1974, the Shah of Iran promised to provide him with U.S. $2 billion in economic aid, which would reduce Afghanistan's dependence on the Soviet Union for economic and technical aid. In the process, Daoud dismissed pro-Soviet forces from his government. On January 30, 1977, Daoud convened a *Milli Jirgah* that endorsed his leadership and approved the new constitution, which adopted a single party system. Daoud's own political party, *Hizb-e-Enqilab-e-Milli* (National Revolution Party) was the only political group recognized as a legal political organization.

Daoud's closer ties with pro-U.S. countries in the region alarmed the Soviet Union. To maintain its imperial influence on Afghanistan, the Soviet leadership decided to help the client party, the PDPA, to seize power. To this end, the Kremlin leadership resolved differences between the *Khalq* and *Parcham* factions of the PDPA as early as March 1977, which led to the issuance of a unity statement by the party in July of that year. When Daoud visited Moscow on April 13, 1977, he discussed bilateral issues with Moscow and during a meeting Soviet leader Leonid Brezhnev, expressed his concerns about growing Western experts in Afghanistan. He told Daoud to expel all imperialist advisors and experts from Afghanistan. This action provoked Daoud to the point of rage that he told Brezhnev:

> We do not allow anyone to dictate to us on how to run our country and who to employ. As to how and where we employ foreign experts it is the sole responsibility of the state of Afghanistan, if Afghanistan deems that it will remain poor but retain the right to decide its own affairs.[29]

Tension between Daoud and pro-Soviet forces grew to the extent that in November 1977, the minister of planning, Ali Ahmad Khuram, was assassinated and on April 17, 1978, a leading member of *Parcham,* Mir Akbar Khaybar was also assassinated in Kabul. Pro-Soviets condemned Khaybar's murder during his funeral procession on April 19, and this factor alarmed Daoud to monitor their activities. On April 26, Daoud arrested key leaders of the party and ordered the standing army to be on full alert. Despite Daoud's anticipation of troubles and his readiness to confront his adversaries, army officers loyal to the PDPA carried out a preplanned coup on April 27, 1978, stormed the presidential palace, killed Daoud and his associates, and declared Afghanistan a "democratic" republic.[30]

The April 1978 Coup

There was some cheering in the streets of Kabul as jet fighters scoured the sky and tanks patrolled the city. People were caught by surprise when Radio Afghanistan made a public announcement that Daoud's government was overthrown and a revolutionary government had been established. Noor Mohammad Taraki, General Secretary of the *Khalq* faction of the PDPA, was installed as president, prime minister, and chairman of the Revolutionary Council. Babrak Karmal, head of the *Parcham* faction of the PDPA, became vice-chair and deputy prime minister. The leadership described the coup as a revolution and a model to be followed by other counties, a shortcut that transferred power to the working and laboring people. Members of the ruling party praised Taraki with the objective to promote him as a leader capable of leading the country into a new era.

The regime abolished the Constitution and issued an 11-point charter of rules to govern the country under the ruling party's guidance and declared general amnesty to prisoners, which led to the release of an estimated 5,000 prisoners. It dismissed senior and junior bureaucrats associated with the former regime and appointed party members to key government posts even though they lacked necessary knowledge, expertise, and experience in the political arena. To consolidate its domination of the country's armed forces and security apparatuses, the ruling party opened political training courses to imbue soldiers, cadets, and officers with the party's politics. The party revamped the educational curriculum in schools and passed a resolution that readmitted 25,000 eighth-grade school graduates to high schools. The measure was intended to enlist support of students for the regime.

The pro-Soviet regime embarked upon a repressive policy of building a society based on the Soviet model of socialism and issued decrees from the top without seeking active participation of the public in the process as well, making efforts to make the material conditions conducive to changes. Prominent decrees that dealt with economic reforms included decree numbers 6 and 8. Decree number 6 exempted peasants who possessed 4.5 hectares of land from paying debts and mortgages to the landlords, and Decree number 8 limited the amount of landholding to 6 hectares of better land, with the rest being confiscated by the state.

The regime established the National Agency for the Campaign Against Illiteracy and used it as an instrument of ideological propagation to imbue citizens of the country with the ideology of the ruling party. Party members forced people to attend literacy classes, and those who resisted were severely punished and some were even executed, as the ruling party viewed them as antirevolution. Coercive policies of modernization led to mass arrests of people of various backgrounds, including tribal chiefs, landlords, farmers, artisans, students, civil servants, and clerics. The regime executed an estimated 12,000 prisoners held in Kabul's notorious central prison, *Pul-e-Charkhi*, between April 1978 to September 1979. The regime believed that building a communist society demanded that those who resist the reform must be eliminated. A member of the Khalq faction of the ruling party, Sayed Abdullah, a notorious guard in charge of the *Pul-e-Charkhi* prison, is quoted as saying: "A million Afghans are all that should remain alive—a million communists and the rest, we do not need. We'll get rid of all of them."[31]

Differences between *Khalq* and *Parcham* over the course of development intensified, which led to the dismissal of top *Parcham* figures from key posts in the party, state government, and their appointments as ambassadors to several Afghanistan embassies abroad. Karmal was appointed ambassador to Czechoslovakia, Anahita Ratibzad to Yugoslavia, Noor Ahmad Noor to the United State, Abdul Wakil to England, and Karmal's half brother, Baryalai, as ambassador to Pakistan. Karmal and Ratibzad left their posts and went to Moscow, where they stayed until the Soviet Union invaded the country in December 1979. This development further intensified differences and divided the ruling party, which weakened their strength to effectively deal with the growing opposition within and outside the party.

Popular armed insurgencies were on the rise. A major insurrection occurred on August 5, 1979, at the Bala-Hisar military garrison in Kabul, which was carried out mainly by supporters of *Gruh-e-Enqilabi*, the Revolutionary Group (RG). The state crushed the insurrection and arrested and executed individuals associated with the RG and several other radical and revolutionary organizations. Major revolutionary organizations active in the urban areas included SAMA, Akhgar, ALO, RAWA, SAWO, Khurasan, Paykar, and several others. Members of the groups were arrested, tortured, and executed by the regime.[32]

The Soviet Union was not happy with events in Afghanistan and the grow-ing insurgency that threatened the Kabul regime and tried to reconcile dif-ferences between *Parcham* and *Khalq*. During Taraki's visit to Moscow and his meeting with Kremlin leaders, a decision was made to remove Hafizul-lah Amin, deputy prime minister and minister for foreign affairs, who was regarded as the main culprit for all the troubles. Amin's aide, who was Taraki's bodyguard and had accompanied Taraki to Moscow, informed Amin of the plot against him. When Taraki returned to Kabul he summoned Amin to his office for a meeting. Amin asked for assurances that he would be safe and was informed that the Soviet ambassador would be present at the meeting to mediate between them. Amin went to the presidential palace to see Taraki and on his way to Taraki's office shots were fired on him, killing his body-guards, but Amin escaped unharmed.

Amin alerted his supporters in the Ministry of Defense and ordered the arrest of Taraki and his men. Amin executed Taraki, and a few days later the state announced Taraki's death. On September 16, 1979, Amin convened a meeting of the central committee of the party to elect him president and prime minister. Amin blamed Taraki and his associates for the murder of innocent people and declared that his government would honor legality, security, and justice as the main theme of his policy. To consolidate his rule, Amin dismissed individuals loyal to Taraki and appointed his closest supporters and family members to top government posts. His brother, Abdullah Amin, was in charge of several northern provinces and his nephew, Asadullah Amin, was head of the state intelligence agency, known by its acronym, AGSA and later as KAM.

Despite declarations of legality, justice, and security, political repression intensified. *Parcham* members of the PDPA conspired against Amin and hin-dered his ability to deal with growing Islamic insurgents, collectively known as Mujahidin, backed by the United States, Pakistan, and Saudi Arabia. Amin tried to normalize relations with Pakistan and the West in hopes that these countries would not provide military and financial support to his adversaries, the Islamic fundamentalist parties operating from bases inside Pakistan and Iran. The Soviet Union was not happy with Amin's weakness and shifting policies and his rapprochement with Pakistan and the West and decided to replace him. The Kremlin leadership convinced Amin that they supported him and made him agree to the deployment of a contingent of the Red Army to defend Kabul and his government against growing attacks by the Mujahi-din. Amin did not receive assurances from Pakistan and the United States and so agreed to the deployment of the Soviet forces. He believed that the Soviet troops would maintain security of the city of Kabul and his forces would be spared from Kabul and could easily beat the insurgents outside Kabul and other provinces.

Soviet Occupation, 1979–1989

Soviets forces already stationed in Kabul stormed Amin's residence, killed him and his supporters in the army, and installed Babrak Karmal as head of the state on December 27, 1979. The puppet government promulgated a new charter, the Fundamental Principles of the Democratic Republic of Afghanistan on April 20–21, 1980, that contained 68 articles. The ruling party remained the most powerful institution that issued guidelines concerning development policies. The regime called upon patriotic, nationalist, and progressive forces to join the front in the struggle to defend the regime against the Islamic parties. Karmal declared general amnesty and issued decrees that revised earlier state policies concerning economic reforms in order to win support among the peasantry. A decree was issued in August 1981 that allotted religious institutions their lands and property and permitted clerics and other religious figures to retain the income, *waqf* or *zakat* they received from the public. The regime sent a large number of youths, students, and party sympathizers to the Soviet Union and its bloc countries for political indoctrination. It sponsored the publication of *Darafsh-e-Jawanan* (Youth Banner) in 1980 as a means of mobilizing the youths in defense of the regime. To gain support of ethnic minority communities, the state supported and financed publication of papers in their languages, which former regimes did not allow.

While Islamic parties established their headquarters in Pakistan and Iran, revolutionary groups and organizations such as SAMA, Akhgar, ALO, SAWO, RAWA, and others had their bases of operation inside the country. These militant organizations intensified their underground activities against the puppet regime. However, they remained divided, each with its own analysis of the situation and strategies for action. Although the Soviet-backed government targeted revolutionary organizations, SAMA suffered a major setback when the regime arrested its celebrated leader, Abdul Majid Kalakani, in February 1980. Kalakani visited Kabul to attend a condolence party and offer his sympathy to the deceased family. Informants tipped off security officers about Kalakani's visit to a house in the Microrayon housing complex, which led to his arrest and his execution in June that year. Kalakani was respected by a wide spectrum of the people, who called him Majid Agha, and the Western media portrayed him as Afghanistan's Robin Hood.

Continued Soviet occupation and their involvement in the country's politics eroded Karmal's base of support and tarnished his image. People called him Shah Shuja in reference to the king who was installed to the throne by the British in the early nineteenth century, while Karmal was propelled to power by the Russian bayonets and tanks. People referred to Karmal, whose name literally means friend of labor, by the nickname *Karghal,* meaning a traitor to the laborers. When Karmal failed to stabilize the situation and win public support, Moscow decided to dismiss him from his post and install a new leader. On May 4, 1986, Karmal was replaced as secretary general of the party by Najibullah, and by November of that year he was relieved from his remaining posts and exiled to Moscow.

Najibullah, director of the state intelligence department, *Khidamat-e-Ittilaat-e-Dawlat* or KHAD, became secretary general of the party and president of the country. Najibullah was known as *Najib-e-Gaw,* the bull, and relied on the Soviet Union for military and economic support. He nonetheless sought to depict himself as independent of the Russians and appointed non-party members to key government posts, permitted the formation of independent civic institutions, and revoked some earlier reforms with the intention of expanding his power base. However, he encountered severe opposition to his leadership by members of the *Khalq* faction of the PDPA, as well as those who remained loyal to Karmal and survived several coup attempts by officers loyal to the *Khalq* who tried to oust him. Growing opposition inside and outside to the Soviet occupation of Afghanistan on the one hand and inability of the Soviet occupation army to crush the U.S.-backed *Mujahidin* on the other hand, compelled the Kremlin leadership to withdraw its troops from Afghanistan. Moscow supported Najibullah, believing that he would be able to maintain control of the state after the Soviet Union withdrew its troops. The Kabul regime endorsed the Geneva Accord signed between Afghanistan and Pakistan concerning Soviet troop withdrawal and repatriation of refugees. During the years of its occupation, the Russians failed to maintain its imperial domination and suffered an estimated 15,000 deaths. The Kremlin leadership began troop withdrawal, and the last Soviet regiment left Afghanistan in February 1989.

To win public support for his policies, Najibullah changed the name of the ruling party to *Hizb-e-Watan* (Homeland Party) in 1990. With the continuation of armed conflict, Najibullah had no option but to support the United Nations' efforts to find a peaceful solution to the conflict. With the United Nations mediation, Najibullah agreed to transfer powers to a coalition of Islamic parties and leave Afghanistan for India. On April 16, 1992, Najibullah tried to board a plane to New Delhi, India, but his opponents prevented him from leaving the country. He was forced to seek refuge in the United Nations compound in Kabul. On April 28, 1992, the Kabul regime collapsed when the U.S.-backed Islamic parties seized Kabul. Najibullah remained at the United Nations compound until 1996, when the Taliban seized Kabul, killed him, mutilated his body, and displayed it and that of his brother, Shahpoor Ahmadzai, in a public square in Kabul.

One of the destroyed buildings in Kabul that bears the scars of brutal armed conflicts among Islamic militia groups in the 1990s, each fighting to establish its dominance.

Islamic Fundamentalism

Sebghatullah Mojadaddi, head of *Jabha-e-Milli-e-Nijat-e-Islami-e Afghanistan*, the National Islamic Front of Afghanistan was sworn in as head of the state. He declared a general amnesty and called upon the people to cooperate with the government in its efforts to rebuild the country. His short rule ended in June 1992, and Burhanuddin Rabbani, a Tajik from Badakhshan and head of *Jamiat-e-Islami-e-Afghanistan,* Islamic Society of Afghanistan became president. When Rabbani's term ended in October 1992, he maneuvered his way to a second term. Opponents accused him of vote rigging and five out of nine parties contested the reliability of the election results. This factor on the one hand, and Rabbani's unwillingness to share power with opponents and form a broad-based government on the other hand, paved the road for continued armed conflict among Islamic parties.

To eliminate their opponents, Rabbani, his defense minister Ahmad Shah Masoud, a Tajik, and their ally Abdul Rasul Sayyaf launched a blitzkrieg attack on the Shia Hazaras in west of Kabul in March 1995, massacring men, women, and children and destroying their residences. To counter their offensive, the Hazaras turned to Gulbuddin Hikmatyar, head of *Hizb-e-Islami-e-Afghanistan* (Islamic Party of Afghanistan) for support. Warring factions that fought for control of Kabul and other provinces had no regard for the lives of the people. Their hostility toward captured men and women of rival groups ranged from gouging their eyes and cutting their noses and ears to humiliating them to immolation. Armed clashes among Islamic parties continued until a more regressive and oppressive Islamic group, the Taliban, emerged and eventually drove Rabbani and Masoud and other warring factions out of Kabul and seized power in 1996.[33]

The Taliban

The word Taliban means "student of religious studies," and this group emerged as a force when they seized Qandahar in 1994. The Taliban declared their goal to rid the country of factional fighting, restore true Islamic rules, and unite and rebuild the country. Their reclusive spiritual leader Mullah Mohammad Omar remained at his headquarters in Qandahar and was rarely seen by the public except for a close circle of advisors and his trusted man Mullah Rabbani, who was in charge of state affairs in Kabul. Taliban militia captured more territories in eastern and western parts of the country and received aid from two major U.S. allies, Pakistan and Saudi Arabia. Pakistan's notorious Inter-Service Intelligence agency known as ISI was the main agency responsible for creating and molding the Taliban. Pakistan's main objective was to use the Taliban to maintain its political influence on Kabul, while Saudi Arabia intended to use the Taliban to propagate their brand of Islam, Wahabism. The United States supported the Taliban in order to use them as a force to contain growing Iranian influence in Afghanistan and Central Asia, leading to a visit in Afghanistan in April 1998 by Bill Richardson, U.S. ambassador to the United Nations. The United States believed that the Taliban, who are Pushtun in ethnicity and Sunni in their religious beliefs, were the best ally to fight Iran. The U.S. leadership did not trust the Tajik-dominated government of Rabbani or the Hazara leadership to be a reliable ally in the U.S. policy of containing Iran because both had close ties with the ruling clerics in Tehran.

The Taliban seized Kabul in 1996 and began a war of conquest toward the north and Hazarajat. In the fight against the Taliban, Rabbani and heads of other religious parties who opposed the Taliban forged an alliance known as the Northern Alliance. Taliban militias exploited internal differences within the Northern Alliance group. In the process, they utilized personal and political differences between the warlords of the Hazara community, Karim Khalili and Mohammad Akbari, and co-opted the latter and drove Khalili from Bamiyan. The Taliban also exploited differences between the Uzbek warlords (Abdul Rashid Dostam and his aide Abdul Malik), fought Dostam, defeated him, and established their domination in several northern regions. The Taliban defeated Hajji Qadir in Nangarhar and other warlords in the Pushtun-belt regions as well as Ismail Khan, governor of Herat, and Mansoor Naderi, chief of the Isma'ilis of Bamiyan and Baghlan. The Taliban and their ally al-Qaeda organization operating in Afghanistan engineered the murder of Ahmad Shah Masoud on September 9, 2001, when two assassins armed with bombs posed as journalists to get close to him. Although a significant number of Arabs were given citizenship and were allowed legal residence in Afghanistan soon after the establishment of an Islamic regime in Kabul in 1992, the Taliban welcomed more Wahabi Arab militants who declared their readiness to join the Taliban in the fight against the Northern Alliance. The Taliban maintained friendly ties with Osama bin Laden, a wealthy Saudi businessman and head of al-Qaeda (the Base) organization, and welcomed him to Afghanistan when he was expelled from Sudan, Africa, and provided him and his networks facilities for military training.

U.S. Intervention in Afghanistan

The United States that once supported Islamic fundamentalists as a bulwark against communism and revolutionary movements no longer needed them when the Soviet Union and its bloc disintegrated in the early 1990s. Since then, the United States decided to dismantle the terrorist network worldwide, including Afghanistan. The United States accused bin Laden and his men of the bombing of U.S. embassies in Africa and the attack on a U.S. warship in the port of Yemen and demanded that Taliban hand him over to U.S. authorities for trial. The Taliban's refusal to expel bin Laden and dismantle his organization caused the Clinton administration to launch cruise missiles to destroy military training camps used by bin Laden in the eastern region of Afghanistan.

When al-Qaeda attacked the World Trade Center building in New York City and the Pentagon in Washington, D.C., on September 11, 2001, using commercial airplanes as weapons of mass destruction, it forced the United States to act to overthrow the Taliban. The September 11 attacks on the United States by supporters of al-Qaeda were a turning point in the process of Afghanistan's political development. The United States condemned the Taliban for sheltering Osama bin Laden and his terrorist networks and decided to eliminate the Taliban and al-Qaeda bases throughout Afghanistan. On October 7, the United States began its military offensives on Afghanistan, code-named Operation Enduring Freedom, and relentlessly bombed Taliban positions, which forced them to surrender their last and principal center, Qandahar, on November 7. Taliban and al-Qaeda leaders fled to the countryside and remain at large. In late November, the United States also engineered the Bonn Conference in Germany, where representatives of several Islamic parties agreed on a power-sharing mechanism in a post-Taliban period and joined the United States in the war against the Taliban and al-Qaeda. The United States installed ethnic Pushtun, Hamid Karzai, as head of the state in Kabul. The U.S.-led coalition, with their base in Bagram, maintains security in Kabul and continues the war on what the United States calls terrorist networks. To most of the dispossessed and suffering Afghans, September 11 heralded a new era that liberated them from a tyrannical rule unprecedented in the country's history. People who had endured years of oppression and brutality at the hands of various Islamic fundamentalist groups and the Taliban welcomed the new era, believing it would bring significant changes in the years to come.

Karzai made concerted efforts to build his image as a national leader with a popular mandate to rule the country. To this end, he convened a *Loya Jirgah* in June 2002 and maneuvered his way through the process, and delegates cast votes of confidence and elected him head of the state. Another *Loya Jirgah* was convened on December 14, 2003–January 4, 2004 and endorsed the draft of a new constitution. The 502 delegates, comprised mostly of warlords and their men as well as 50 people appointed by Karzai, deliberated the Constitution and eventually approved it, which gave the president greater power to govern and rebuild the country. Karzai won a popular mandate when people cast their votes during the presidential election on October 9, 2004.

The Karzai government remains weak and relies on the International Force to maintain peace and stability in Afghanistan. The small-scale economic and educational progress Afghanistan had achieved has been completely destroyed during the two decades of war. The country remains dependent on foreign aid and technology, and the poor and dispossessed will continue to endure years of suffering with no immediate remedy to help them rebuild their lives.

NOTES

1. See also, Hamidullah Amin and Gordon B. Schilz, *A Geography of Afghanistan* (Omaha, Nebraska: Center for Afghanistan Studies, 1976), pp. 30–35.
2. For details, see Harvey H. Smith, Donald W. Bernier, Frederica M. Bunge, Frances Chadwick Rintz, Rinn-Sup Shinn, and Suzanne Teleki, *Area Handbook for Afghanistan*, 4th ed. (Washington, D.C.: U.S. Government Printing Office, 1973);

United States, Central Intelligence Agency, CIA, *The World Factbook* (Washington, D.C.: CIA, 2002).

3. See also, Jerry D. Hassinger, "A Survey of the Mammals of Afghanistan: Resulting from the 1965 Street Expedition (Excluding Bats)," *Fieldiana: Zoology* 60 (6 April 1973); Amin and Schilz, *A Geography of Afghanistan.*

4. See also, United Nations. Economic and Social Commission for Asia and the Pacific, *Atlas of Mineral Resources of the ESCAP Region. Vol. 11, Geology and Mineral Resources of Afghanistan* (New York: United Nations, 1995).

5. See also, Barbara F. Grimes (ed.), *Ethnologue: Languages of the World* (Dallas: Summer Institute of Linguistics, 1992); Faiz Mohammad Katib, *Nijad Namah-e-Afghan* [Ethnography of the Afghans] (Peshawar, Pakistan: Al-Azhar Ketabkhanah, 2000); Hafizullah Emadi, "The Hazaras and Their Role in the Process of Political Transformation in Afghanistan." *Central Asian Survey* 16, no. 3 (1997): 363–387; Hassan Poladi, *The Hazaras* (Stockton, CA: Mughal, 1989); Mohammad Ehsan Pajohish, *Nazari ba tarikh-e Qizilbash-ha dar Afghanistan* [A glance at the history of the Qizilbash in Afghanistan] (Peshawar, Pakistan: Ketabkhanah-e-Shams, 1379/2000).

6. Amin and Schilz, *A Geography of Afghanistan*, p. 108.

7. For details see, CIA, *The World Factbook.*

8. See also, Smith et al., *Area Handbook for Afghanistan.*

9. Sayed Bahaouddin Majrooh and Sayed Mohammad Yusuf Elmi, *The Sovietization of Afghanistan* (Peshawar, Pakistan: Afghan Information Center, 1986), pp.163–164.

10. Raja Anwar, *The Tragedy of Afghanistan: A First Hand Account*, tr. Khalid Hasan (London: Verso, 1988), p. 130; Salih Mohammad Ziray, *Manasibat-e-fiyudali dar kishwar wa Islahat-e-demokratik-e-Arzi* [Feudal relations and democratic land reform in Afghanistan] (Kabul: Ministry of Information and Culture, Government Press, 1357/1978).

11. Anwar, *The Tragedy of Afghanistan*, p. 130

12. Anwar, *The Tragedy of Afghanistan*, p. 129.

13. Yu V. Gankovsky, M. R. Annova, V. G. Korgun, V. A. Masson, and G. A. Muradov, *A History of Afghanistan*, tr. Vitaly Baskakov (Moscow, Russia: Progress Publishers, 1985), p. 280.

14. For details see, Hafizullah Emadi, *State, Revolution, and Superpowers in Afghanistan* (New York: Praeger Publishers, 1990); Mir Ghulam Mohammad Ghubar, *Afghanistan dar Masir-e-Tarikh* [Afghanistan in the path of history] (Tehran: Entisharat-e Jamhoori, 1374/1995).

15. See also, Ghubar, *Afghanistan dar Masir-e-Tarikh*; Gankovsky et al., *A History of Afghanistan.*

16. Gankovsky et al., *A History of Afghanistan.*

17. Mir Mohammad Siddiq Farhang. *Afghanistan dar panj Qarn-e-Akhir* [Afghanistan in the last five centuries], vols. 1–3 (Peshawar, Pakistan: Author, 1373/1994).

18. For details see, Ghubar, *Afghanistan dar Masir-e-Tarikh.*

19. See also, Gankovsky et al., *A History of Afghanistan.*

20. For details see, Poladi, *The Hazaras.*

21. Ghubar, *Afghanistan dar Masir-e-Tarikh*, p. 774.

22. Mohammad Alam Fayzzad, *Jirgaha-e-Bozurg-e-Milli Afghanistan, Loya Jirgahs, wa Jirgaha-e-Namnihad wa Tahti Tasalut-e-Kamunistha wa Rus-ha* [Grand National Assemblies of Afghanistan, Loya Jirgahs, and so-called Jirgahs Held Under Communists and Russians] (Islamabad, Pakistan: Author, 1368/1989), p. 123.

23. Emadi, *State, Revolution, and Superpowers in Afghanistan*, p. 5.

24. For details see, Ghubar, *Afghanistan dar Masir-e-Tarikh*, vol. 2.

25. Gankovsky et al., *A History of Afghanistan*, pp. 238–246.

26. Louis Dupree, *Afghanistan* (Karachi, Pakistan: Oxford University Press, 2002), p. 593.

27. Mohammad Hasan Sharq, *Karbas Push-ha-e-Berahnapa: Khatirati Mohammad Hasan Sharq az 1310–1370* [Shabby clothed and bare-feet people: Memoirs of Mohammad Hasan Sharq from 1931–1991] (Peshawar, Pakistan: Saba Ketabkhanah, n.d.), p. 107.

28. Dupree, *Afghanistan*, pp. 657–658.

29. Sharq, *Karbas Push-ha-e-Berahnapa: Khatirati Mohammad Hassan Sharq, 1310–1370*, pp. 153–154.

30. See also, Farhang, *Afghanistan dar panj Qarn-e-Akhir*.

31. Edward Girardet, *Afghanistan: The Soviet War* (New York: St. Martin's Press, 1985), p. 107.

32. Hafizullah Emadi, "Radical Political Movements in Afghanistan and their Politics of Peoples' Empowerment and Liberation," *Central Asian Survey* 20, no. 4 (2001): 439–440.

33. For details see, Hafizullah Emadi, "Radical Islam, Jihad, and Civil War in Afghanistan," *Internationales Asienforum* 30, nos. 1–2 (1999): 5–26.

2

Religion and Religious Thought

Religion has played a major role in various eras of Afghanistan's history, from ancient worship of natural forces to the concept of a supreme deity as expressed in Zoroastrianism. Buddhism also influenced social and artistic development in the country before Islam ascended and spread throughout the country. Islam is practiced in a variety of ways, and in Afghanistan people struggle to live peacefully with one another. Their practice of and belief in their view of Islam plays a fundamental role in providing daily moral, ethical, and social guidance.

ANCIENT RELIGIOUS BELIEFS

The Indo-Aryans were scattered over a wide area, including ancient Afghanistan. They believed in the divine power of nature, and worshipped nature as gods: sky as the god Varuna; storm as the god Indra; fire as the god Agni; and a mountain plant, which they believed to be the elixir of life, as the god Soma. A second major ancient religion in Afghanistan, Zoroastrianism, emerged around 1000 B.C. and made a significant contribution to the development of human thought. Zoroastrians believe in the existence of a supreme deity, Ahura Mazda (the wise deity), heaven and hell, balance and accountability in life. Zoroaster (Zarathustra), the founder of the faith, cherished honesty, integrity, and good deeds as cardinal virtues of life. He provided moral guidance that prohibited wrongdoings such as robbery, rapaciousness, and plundering. The Zoroastrian belief system was based on the three principles: benevolent thought, benevolent speech, and benevolent deeds.[1]

Simple agricultural activity constituted the lifeblood of the early Zoro-astrian civilization. Animal husbandry was important for the production of food as well as a hallmark of wealth and welfare. For this reason, people adopted names that related to animals. Zoroaster's mother was named Dugh-dova meaning "milking cows," and his father was called Purushaspa, mean-ing "a person possessing spotted horses." One of Zoroaster's avid followers was named Frashaoshtra, meaning "a person who owns good camels," and another follower was named Jamaspa meaning "one who leads horses."

Zoroaster thought that the world is ruled by two cosmic forces, Light and Darkness, that are locked in a struggle for control. He believed that the power of Light would prevail over that of Darkness. According to him, only a pow-erful and mundane ruler commands the destruction of evil, restoration of peace, and bringing prosperity. The annual celebration of *Naw Rooz,* March 21, marks the first day of the year and heralds the beginning of *Bahar,* spring season. *Naw Rooz* is one of the most important components of the cultural heritage of the Zoroastrian religion, and was practiced in most regions of the country and territories in northern India, even after Alexander invaded that country.

Buddhism spread and found adherents in different parts of ancient Afghan-istan, particularly in the reign of Kanishka, ruled by one of the most powerful kings of the Kushanid dynasty. Although Kanishka accepted Buddhism, he advocated religious pluralism and tolerated the worshipping of other deities, and even inscribed the names of all deities on the coins he minted. He was said to be the founder of a large Buddhist council and a strong patron of monasteries, and he supported the works of Buddhist theologians and phi-losophers. During the Kushanid rule, Greco-Buddhism dominated arts and culture throughout the country to such an extent that between the third and fifth centuries B.C., Bamiyan became one of the major centers of Buddhism; two giant Buddha statues were carved out of the face of a cliff in Bamiyan. The Hephthalite and Sassanian rulers adhered to the practice of Hindu and Buddhist faith. Buddhism and other forms of religious practices continued until Islam conquered the country.[2]

THE SPREAD OF ISLAM INTO AFGHANISTAN

A significant development in Afghanistan's history is its Islamization after its conquest by Muslim armies. The founder of Islam, Muhammad, died in 632 A.D. after successfully forging the Arab tribes into a new community of believers in one supreme lord of creation, Allah, who was preeminently the lord of justice. Muhammad's mission and lifework was dominated by a con-cern to rid Arab tribal society of all forms of injustice. After his death, his successors, the caliphs, embarked on a series of military expeditions that would, within 30 years, bring Egypt, Byzantium, and Persia under Muslim rule.

In 652 A.D., an advancing Arab expedition army defeated fierce resistance by tribal chiefs and their subjects and established their rule in the western part of Afghanistan. However, Kabul, Ghor, and the mountainous regions did not convert to Islam until the ninth and eleventh centuries, whereas Nooristan (formerly known as Kafiristan) held out until the turn of the twentieth century. When the tribal chiefs began converting to Islam, their subjects also embraced it. Although Islamic teachings stressed the equality of believers and the abolishment of old social orders, Arab settlers in practice pursued policies that contradicted this basic Islamic philosophy of egalitarianism. Arab rulers regarded the conquered lands as public property *(bait al-mal)* and distributed them among Arab settlers and rulers as well as among the local chiefs who paid taxes for the land. These policies had the effect of strengthening feudalism in territories they conquered and incorporated into the expanding Islamic world.[3]

Local rulers paid tribute to the caliphs, and the people were subject to different types of taxes on income from their crops. Non-Muslims were subject

Mausoleum of Ali, son-in-law and cousin of Islam's Prophet Muhammad, in Balkh, is one of the magnificent examples of seventh-century Islamic architecture. Photograph courtesy of Najibullah Abbassi

to paying higher taxes, such as one-tenth of the crops plus per capita taxes and other fees. Many of these people eventually embraced Islam in order to avoid having to pay heavy taxes on the land and property they owned. Domination of Islamic rule paved the road for Arab cultural influence, the use of the Arabic language, and the elimination of Zoroastrian and Buddhist practices and traditions. However, a small community of Zoroastrians and Jews had survived and maintained their culture and traditions, but only in major cities. Despite the Arab conquest of Afghanistan and Arabic cultural influence, it was the Persian language used as a medium for the dissemination of Islamic teachings. Although people accepted Islam, they nevertheless grew to despise Arab political domination of their homeland. Under the leadership of Abu Muslim Khurasani, people fought and put an end to Arab domination. Islam is not a monolithic but a pluralistic community, where various interpretations and practices of Islamic faith and paths *(tariqah)* exist. However, of these many interpretive traditions, only two are dominant in the Islamic world: Sunni and Shia. In Afghanistan, 99 percent of the population are Muslim and adhere to various branches of the Islamic faith.

Sunnis

After Prophet Muhammad's death, the Muslims were divided into the Sunnis, the Shias, and Kharijites factions. Most Arabs argued that Muhammad did not leave precise instructions for the appointing of his successor. To them, consensus by the tribal council was the best method of choosing a leader. The group became known as Sunnis, those who adhere to the *Sunna,* or practices of the Prophet. Others believed that Muhammad had designated Ali, his cousin and son-in-law, to lead the Muslims; they are known as Shias or partisans of Ali. The Kharijites comprised a small segment of the Muslims. They argued that any qualified person, even an Ethiopian slave, could become a leader of the Muslim world.

Sunnis adhered to a strict observance of the *Sharia,* the religious law of Islam, based on four major sources: the Quran (the Islamic holy book), the *Sunna* (custom, tradition of Islam), *Ijma* (consensus of the community), and *qiyas* (reasoning by analogy). Sunnis maintain that Muhammad's deeds and sayings, which were recorded and collected and form the *hadith* (traditions of Prophet Muhammad), supplement the Quran and serve as the authority for Muslim beliefs and practices. Muslims recognize Jewish and Christian figures, chief among them Adam, Abraham, Moses, and Jesus, as prophets of Islam, but they believe that Muhammad is the greatest, the final, and the Seal of the prophets who preceded him. The Sunnis do not attribute any divine quality to Muhammad but respect him as one of the messengers of Allah. They maintain that Muhammad was a human and was chosen by God to deliver humankind from the worship of idols and to call on humanity to submit to the will of God, the sole creator of the universe and humans. According to them, God cannot be reincarnated as a human being, male or female. Sunnis believe that the soul is immortal and individuals are responsible for their deeds and will have to account for them on the Day of Judgment, when God will decide whether to send them to heaven or hell.

Sunnis follow the four major schools of law that are named after their founders: Hanafi, Maliki, Shafi'i, and Hanbali. The Hanifa School was founded in Iraq by a prominent jurist, Abu Hanafi (d. 767). It is based on the principle of deduction whereby a judge renders a decision based on his deduction and understanding of the intent of the Quran and *Sunna*. Hanafi jurisprudence recognizes consensus, analogy, and private opinion in administering laws and does not stress a literal interpretation of the Quran. The Maliki School founded by Malik Ibn Anas (d. 795) recognizes the authority of consensus but does not vocally support consensus, analogy, and private opinion in the adjudication of laws. The Shafi'i School founded by al-Shafi'i (d. 820) accepts a wider application of consensus than the Malikis and regards it as the highest legislative authority. The Hanbali School founded by Ahmad Ibn Hanbal does not accept consensus, private opinion, and analogy in the dispensation of legal matters. It maintains that the Quran and the traditions are two valid legal authorities in Islam.

In Afghanistan, most Sunnis follow the Hanafi School of jurisprudence, which is compatible with local traditions, customs, and cultures. However, the Shafi'i School also found some adherents throughout the country; and a number of people, mainly in the northern parts, adhere to the Hanbali School of jurisprudence.[4] Although there is no clergy in the Sunni branch of Islam, *mullahs* are powerful religious leaders who regard themselves as the sole custodians of Islamic faith.

Shias

The Shias pledged allegiance to Ali and his descendants through his wife, Fatima, daughter of Muhammad. Shias believe that righteousness can prevail only if Ali and his descendants rule the Islamic world. They were defeated by the Sunnis and deprived of their rights and equality. Over the centuries, they fought tyrant rulers who attempted to seize power. Ali's son, Hussein, and a number of his comrades-in-arms were murdered by Yazid, the Ummayad Caliph Muawiya's son, in October 680 A.D. in the desert of Karbala in Iraq. The month of *Muharram*, in which Hussein was killed, became a symbol of

unity for the Shias, who celebrate the occasion on an annual basis by organizing passion plays stressing self-sacrifice and atonement.

The Shias, like the Sunnis, recognize the five pillars of Islam, but they
developed their own school of jurisprudence. They elaborated a doctrinal
position regarding the divine leader, the *Imam,* and developed the concept
of *zahir* and *batin,* exoteric and esoteric meaning of the Quranic text. They
argued that the inner meaning of the Quran can be obtained only through
tawil, allegorical interpretation, and that only the *Imam* is endowed with
the divine ability to interpret the Quran and reveal its inner meaning to
the community of followers. The Shias split after the death of their leader,
Jafar Sadiq, in 765 A.D. because of a dispute over succession. Those who
followed his younger son, Musa al-Kazim, became known as *Ithna Ashari*
(Twelvers), and those who followed his other son, Ismail, are duly called
Isma'ilis. The last *Ithna Ashari* Imam, Muhammad Mahdi, disappeared
around 873. Ithna Asharis believe that he will eventually return to deliver
the earth of its miseries and anxiously await his return. Until such a day,
clerics in order of their rank such as *Mujtahid, Hujjat al-Islam,* and *Ayatollah* lead the community. The highest rank in the Shia clerical system is the
Grand Ayatollah.[5]

The Shia Hazaras did not have a leader in the rank of ayatollah until
recently and followed instructions from the ayatollahs and other lower-ranking
clerics residing in Iran and Iraq. At present, there are several individuals who
received religious education and attained the title of ayatollah and supervise
the religious affairs of the community in Hazarajat. The Sunni dominated
governments subjected the Shias to the Sunni legal system, deprived them of
their basic rights and equality before the law, and treated them as second-class
citizens.

Isma'ilis

Isma'ilis, like their Shia counterparts, the Twelvers, believe that the Imam
is the only qualified person who can reveal the inner meaning of the Quran.
But unlike the Twelver Shias, the Isma'ilis believe that the line of Imamat has
continued unbroken to the present, that the world cannot function even for a
day in the absence of the Imam. Under the leadership of the Imam al-Muizz,
the Isma'ilis conquered Egypt in 969 and laid the foundation of the new
city of Cairo as the capital of their Fatimid Caliphate. They made tremendous progress in the areas of sciences, architecture, education, commerce, and
trade. The Isma'ili Imams pursued policies that accommodated the interests
of diverse religious and faith-based communities such as the Sunnis, Jews,
Christians, and others.

A major dispute over the succession to the Imam al-Mustansir Billah occurred in 1092. Badr al-Jamal was chief of the army in al-Mustansir's court and wielded considerable power because his daughter was married to one of al-Mustansir's sons, Mustali. Jamal's son al-Afzal became chief of the army after the death of his father, and shortly before al-Mustansir's death he supported Mustali's rise to Imamat. In so doing, he divided the community into two factions, the Mustalians and the Nizaris. The Mustalians ruled over Egypt, Yemen, and western India until 1174 A.D., when they were defeated by the Ayubbids. By the thirteenth century, the Mustalians had disappeared from Egypt, but they survived in India, where they are known as Bohra Isma'ilis.[6]

Nizari Isma'ilis emerged in Persia when acclaimed Isma'ili leader Hasan Sabbah consolidated his power base in Alamut, in northern Iran, captured more territories, and fought the oppressive Saljuqid ruler and other enemies of the Nizaris. Writers and chroniclers who were not familiar with Isma'ili traditions had wrongly portrayed them as assassins. They had relied on Italian explorer Marco Polo's fanciful description of the Isma'ili community. He claimed that Sabbah had built pavilions with streams flowing with milk, water, wine, and honey, while beautiful young girls danced to entertain the guests. He alleged that Sabbah lured young men to the pavilion to make them believe that they were in paradise. When they found themselves back in the real world, then Sabbah's men would approach them and tell them if they wished to return they must murder enemies of the Isma'ilis. Such a characterization distorts reality. Isma'ilis adhered to *asas,* a Persian word meaning the foundation or principles of their faith, they are called *asasiyun* or followers of the *asas.*[7]

Sabbah was a theoretician, a strategist, a poet, and a philosopher who composed treatises that elaborated upon the Isma'ili doctrines and built a library that housed a large volume of literature on religion, philosophy, and history. Sabbah devoted the last years of his life at Alamut to writing prose and poetry on religious topics. Most of his writings have perished but a few fragments survived and were preserved by the Isma'ilis. His writings reflect his deep conviction to Islam and his devotion to Allah.

> There is a desert in which
> I have utterly lost my way;
> the path is dreadful and I am
> without help or companion.
> I am alone and confused,
> not knowing which way to go,
> and thinking like this makes
> my head turn with giddiness.
> O my Lord! What difference

does it make between
my good and bad if both are
as particles of dust to You?
And if I were to sit or
stand improperly, accept me
As I am. O Holy One, do not
reject me, whatever I am![8]

Isma'ili rule in Persia ended when the Mongol ruler Hulegu launched an
offensive, killed their leader, Khayrshah in 1257, dismantled their strong-
holds, and set fire to the library that housed a valuable collection of books.
The Mongol ruler forced many Isma'ilis to flee to Central Asia and the mountainous regions of Hazarajat and Pamir, in Badakhshan. They were forced to
maintain *taqiyya,* dissimulation in the practice of their faith, to avoid persecution by hostile forces arrayed against them. The Nizari Isma'ilis emerged from
obscurity when their leader, the Aga Khan I, rebelled unsuccessfully against
the Shah of Iran in 1838 and 1840. He and a number of his followers were
forced to leave for British India via Afghanistan.

The Aga Khan I remained in India and appointed local individuals as
religious leaders *(pirs)* to supervise religious and other issues related to the
community. The *pirs* later were called *Mukhi* and *Kamadia,* Gujrati words
meaning treasurer and assistant treasurer. Before his death in 1957, Imam
Sultan Mohammad Shah, Aga Khan III, designated his grandson, Karim,
to succeed him as Imam and Aga Khan IV.[9] Karim Aga Khan IV, a staunch
advocate of Third World development, is the present 49th Imam of the community. He was born on December 13, 1936 in Geneva, Switzerland, and
graduated from Harvard University in 1959. Since then, the Aga Khan IV has
worked tirelessly to improve the welfare of the Isma'ili communities.

In Afghanistan, the conservatives and fundamentalist Sunni and Shia clerics regarded the Isma'ilis as infidels, and their hostility toward them grew
bitter when the Isma'ilis supported the Soviet-backed government, beginning with the April 1978 coup. However, a significant number of Isma'ilis
participated in the war of national liberation during the Soviet occupation,
1979–1989. The Isma'ilis, like the Twelver Shias, were subjected to the Sunni
legal system, were deprived of their legal rights and equality, and were forced
to follow the religious practices of the Sunni community.

Sufis

Islamic mystics emerged around the eighth century and spread throughout the Muslim world. The word *Sufi* is derived from the word "*suf,*" which

means "wool" in Arabic because the pioneering mystics wore coarse woolen robes. The Sufis, who came mainly from the middle classes, emerged as a new group who despised tyrant rulers and rigid social and political environment. They adopted a passive and utopian approach in their opposition to societal injustices. Their basic philosophical orientation was based on the concepts of nonattachment to material things and the mortification and purification of one's soul as the only way for people to escape suffering. The Sufis rejected intellectual knowledge *(ilm)* and advocated a philosophy of personal experiences as a way to seek union with the Supreme Being, God. They congregated in convents, known as *Khanaqah,* for meditation and contemplation, and for performing *Zikr,* ecstatic recitation of various names of God.[10]

The Sufis held religious meetings, mostly accompanied by music and dances involving rhythmical breathing and movement around a spot symbolizing their continuous quest for the truth. The Sufis express their ideas by using symbols and metaphors that are difficult for others to decipher. Sanai Ghaznawi flourished in Ghazni between the eleventh and twelfth centuries. He authored a major mystical epic. Another notable Sufi is Abdullah Ansari, known by the title of *Pir-e-Herat.* He was born around 1005 and died around 1088 in Herat. In his works, he described the experience of personal union with the Supreme Being:

> From the unmanifest I came,
> And pitched my tent, in the Forest of Material existence.
> I passed through
> Mineral and vegetable kingdoms,
> Then my mental equipment
> Carried me into the animal kingdom;
> Having reached there I crossed beyond it;
> Then in the crystal clear shell of human heart
> I nursed the drop of self into a Pearl,
> And in association with good men
> Wandered around the Prayer House,
> And having experienced that, crossed beyond it;
> Then I took the road that leads to Him,
> And became a slave at His gate;
> Then the duality disappeared
> And I became absorbed in Him.[11]

Despite growing Islamic orthodoxy that led to persecution and execution of a number of Sufis, the tradition continued. Sufis are divided into various *tariqahs,* such as *Naqshbandiyya, Cheshtiyya, Qadiriyya,* and so forth. In

Afghanistan, some prominent religious leaders such as the Mojaddadi family belong to the *Naqshbandiyya,* while Sayed Ahmad Gilani belongs to the *Qadiriyya* branch of the Sufi order; both leaders have significant followers, mainly among the Pushtun tribes.

OTHER RELIGIONS

Non-Muslims account for about 1 percent of the population of Afghanistan. Among them are adherents of Hinduism, Sikhism, Judaism, and Christianity, as well as Bahais and Parsees. In 2000, the Hindu population was estimated to be 79,521; the number of Sikhs was approximately 4,545. Although the Hindus and Sikhs migrated to Afghanistan as early as the eighteenth century, a significant number settled in other regions of the country after the partition of India and Pakistan in 1947. They built temples for the practice of their faith and their respective house of worship is known as *Dharamsala* and *Gurudwara.* Rigid Islamization policies pursued by the Taliban regime stipulated that Hindus and Sikhs must wear a yellow badge on their clothing, ostensibly to except them from the purview of the religious police. However this also served to immediately identify non-Muslim citizens of Afghanistan. The Taliban also ordered women of the Hindu and Sikh communities to cover their faces like other women in Afghanistan, and the dwindling Hindu and Sikh population, one of the few non-Muslim communities left in the country, was severely affected by this policy.

The Jews are known by the name *Yahud* and they are regarded as *ahl al-Ketab,* "people of the book." The number of Jews in Afghanistan was extremely small and it is suggested that Jews settled in Afghanistan as early as the eleventh century. During King Mahmood's rule (998–1030), the prominent Jew Issac served as his agent supervising the king's lead mines. In addition to being subject to annual pool tax, Jews in the early 1950s were barred from services in the military, and for this were bound to pay a fee called *harbiya.* A community council comprised of heads of families was established wherever there was a significant Jewish community, and was charged with looking after the community's needs and coordinating the delivery of the various tax revenues to the government. The Jewish community spoke a Judeo-Persian dialect and composed religious literature and poetry in Judeo-Persian. Garji and Shaul from Herat were two renowned Jewish scholars and writers who published commentaries on the Bible and the Torah in Judeo-Persian.

Muslims also regard Christians as people of the book. In 2000, the number of local Christians was determined to be about 3,000. They were converted to Christianity by missionaries who came to Kabul under the guise of students studying at Kabul University and also by aid workers in the early 1960s. To propagate the faith, the missionaries built a church in Kabul on the road to Dar al-Aman, adjacent to the Russian Embassy. Since foreign nationals were not allowed to purchase property in Afghanistan, the missionaries bribed government officials to let them purchase a plot of land from Nasir Ahmad Shansab. Mohammad Kabir Nooristani, an official of the Kabul municipality, approved the sale of the land to the missionaries for building a church. Christian missionaries continued their work until the early 1970s, when Prime Minister Mohammad Musa Shafiq, an Islamic fundamentalist, ordered the destruction of the church. Before its destruction, a number of local engineers pleaded with Shafiq not to destroy the building as it was regarded as an architectural masterpiece. Shafiq ignored the plea and arrested the engineers who had tried to save the church. Shafiq also ordered the closure of the Ghulghulah Restaurant in Shahr-e-Naw, adjacent to the Hajji Yaqub mosque in Kabul, as he regarded it as a center that promoted anti-Islamic cultural values. He closed the Marastun Theater for similar reasons. Shafiq instructed officials of Radio Afghanistan to broadcast the call to prayer *(Azan)* five times daily. Soon afterward, a religious leader said public prayers via radio to bless the government for its success.[12]

Population figures of other minority religious groups such as Bahais and Parsees are negligible. In 2000, their numbers were claimed to be 23,075 and 340,806 respectively.

Superstitions

Superstitious beliefs persist among all segments of the people and it is strongest among the illiterate rural and urban population. It is a commonly held superstition that certain people possess the "evil eye," and with that comes the power to cause others misfortune. Grandmothers still tell children stories about *jins* (genies) and evil spirits, and ensure that the belief in the supernatural and good and bad luck as causative factors in daily life will persist through future generations.

The practice of witchcraft is not prevalent in Afghanistan, but some people continue to believe that it can have an effect in the defensive sense. For instance, two feuding families nursing a grudge may resort to their impression of acts of witchcraft to avert malicious intent by the other. Some people also believe in the power of spirits and visit the shrines of well-known saints seeking their blessing, protection, or an instance of good luck. It is also common for people to flock to fortune-tellers, who use rosary beads and passages from a book called the *Falnamah* to interpret their client's future.

ISLAMIC VALUES AND IDENTITY

Islam is the religion of people of diverse social and cultural backgrounds, and it plays an important role in shaping the social, cultural, ethical, and moral values of the Muslims. It constitutes the core of people's identity. Islam is a religion that supports pluralism and diversity as the creation of God and believes in harmony and peace. During the heyday of Islamic civilization, metropolitan centers such as Constantinople (Istanbul), Baghdad, Cairo, and other cities under Muslim rule showed great tolerance to the practice of other faiths, advocated a policy of peaceful coexistence, and had forward-looking institutions.

Authoritarian and despotic rulers and elites in the Muslim world used Islam to legitimize their rule and exercised coercion to eliminate countercultural movements and pluralism of the faith, viewing them as a threat to their rule. Clerics associated with them often presented Islam as a monolithic faith, deliberately ignoring the diversity of the faith, which compelled the adherents of different traditions and *tariqah* to oppose a monolithic approach to nation building.

The rise of colonial and imperial powers and their domination of the Muslim world have awakened a nostalgic feeling of a return to the golden era of Islam within a segment of the intelligentsia. To achieve their objective, they resort to a holy war *(jihad)* to transform the status quo. They maintain that *jihad* means the defense of one's homeland, honor, religion, and beliefs by Muslims of all backgrounds, and those who die on the battlefield in defense of Islam's values are memorialized and are called martyrs, *shahid.* The title warrior, *ghazi,* is awarded to those who have struck a fatal blow to an aggressor who violates Muslim law or invades their homeland. The concept of *jihad* has been interpreted differently by individuals and leaders to suit their understanding of Islam. However, a vast majority of progressive Muslim theologians and scholars maintain that *jihad* means an effort to promote the liberation and welfare of the community of believers, *ummah.* To them, Islam and modernity are two sides of a coin. These progressive Muslims believe that secularism safeguards Muslims from the danger of continued monolithic exploitation by despotic and authoritarian religious leaders and elites within the state apparatus and civil society; and these progressive Muslims seek at the same time to bring about the renaissance of the Muslim world.

RELIGION AND BRITISH COLONIALISM

Religion played a vital role in the liberation struggle against colonial powers trying to establish their domination of the country. Muslim theologians, clerics, and radical individuals mobilized their people for the war of national liberation; some lost their lives fighting puppet regimes that defended the interests of the colonial masters. Although a handful of clerics of upper-class backgrounds sided with tyrant rulers and alien powers, clerics and religious leaders from the lower classes supported the cause of the poor and fought local tyrants and imperial domination. For example, during a popular uprising against the British invasion in 1879, the cleric Ghulam Qadir Opyani of Charikar mobilized the public to fight the British. To finance his campaign against them, he minted coins from the gold and silver donated by men and woman who supported him. These lines were inscribed on the coins:

> *Mikunam diwanagi ta bar saram ghawgha shawad*
> I will act insanely until people notice me
> *Seka bar zar mizanam ta sahibash payda shawad.*[13]
> I mint coins until he [the next king] is discovered.

Religious leaders who participated in the war were motivated not by any selfish agenda of their own but by dedication to promote the unity of the Muslims and their liberation from colonial and imperial powers. Despotic rulers harassed, jailed, and even executed clerics and religious leaders who defended the interests of the poor and sent others into exile.

Sayed Jamal al-Din Afghani (1838–1896) was an eminent Islamic revivalist who opposed the growing colonial interference and domination of the Muslims. His radical ideas concerning modernity, social, economic, and political development and reform within the Islamic world served as a beacon to inspire people and guide the anticolonial forces to rise and fight for independence. Afghani believed that disunity among the Muslims was the main cause of their subjugation to alien powers. He lectured passionately on independence through unity and brotherhood among the Muslims, and stressed the need to resurrect Islamic art and philosophy.

RELIGION IN THE POSTINDEPENDENCE PERIOD

Prior to Afghanistan's independence in 1919, the educational institutions known as *madrasa* were under the control and supervision of the clerics and *ulamas,* who taught subjects related to Islamic philosophy, arts, and sciences. The curriculum gave priority to topics that dealt with ethical and moral codes of conduct compatible with the ethos of Islam. Religious subjects also constituted the bulk of the curriculum of existing public schools, and students who graduated from the India-based Deoband School of Theology were recruited, by the state, as teachers at a number of seminaries throughout the country.

There was no school for girls because conservative clerics and *ulamas* viewed education for women as a waste of time. There were a few exceptions among the upper and middle class families, including enlightened clerics and religious leaders who supported education for women, but only a few women received an education, which was no more than a rudimentary education delivered at home.

In the postindependence period, King Amanullah initiated reforms to modernize the country. Major reforms included a ban on the graduates of the Deoband School to teach in the *madrasas;* instead, religious teachers and clerics were required to obtain a certificate for teaching Islamic studies. The reforms restricted the authority of religious leaders and *mullahs* in political and cultural affairs and their interference in the running of the state affairs, which supported education for women and built schools for girls.

Conservative clerics viewed the social and political reforms, particularly educational programs for women and women's rights and equality, as anathema to Islamic values. They opposed the reforms and called for a *jihad* to overthrow the state and establish an Islamic order. They accused the state of decreeing that indigenous dress be replaced with European costumes, that men shave their beards, and that the Islamic holiday on Friday be abolished and replaced by Thursday as the day of rest. Opposition forces led by Habibullah, known as *bacha-e-saqaw,* launched a campaign against Amanullah that forced him to leave the country for Italy. The clerics pledged their allegiance to the government of Habibullah after he seized Kabul in January 1929. Habibullah abolished social, cultural, and political reforms initiated by Amanullah and reinstated the rights of religious leaders and clerics in the country's affairs.

Religion was used as an instrument of legitimacy when General Mohammad Nadir seized power in 1929. He promoted religion to shield himself and the ruling elite from those who denounced the monopoly of power by a handful of people. Although the ruling elite defended religion and projected themselves as pious and religious men, in practice they did not abide by Islamic values and ethics. The state under Nadir worked to appease the *ulama* (religious leaders), scholars, and clerics, and declared that his government was abiding by Islamic Sharia law and was implementing the Hanafi School of jurisprudence to deal with court cases involving criminal and legal issues. Furthermore, the state declared the wearing of head covering *(hijab)* by women, in accordance with Islamic law and the tradition of Prophet Muhammad. It also decreed that those who drink alcohol, which is prohibited in Islam, would receive punishment as prescribed by Sharia law. Progovernment clerics issued an edict *(fatwa)* declaring the people of Kohdaman as imposters to Islam and enemies of God and Muhammad who must be dealt with on a proactive basis because Habibullah was from that region and they were members of his tribal community.

To appease religious leaders and clerics, the state approved a proposal to establish *Jamiat al-Ulama-e-Islami,* Society of Islamic Scholars, in Kabul in December 1929. Members of the society included clerics and theologians who supported Nadir and wielded considerable influence, so much so that every Wednesday they had a meeting with the king to discuss religious matters. The society assumed a greater role as it became a parallel institution to the two chambers of the Parliament, the House of Representatives or *Shura* and the Senate; whenever a cleric died, it was mandatory for the state to send a letter of condolence to the family of the deceased. Influential clerics, such as Fazl Omar Mojaddadi, Fazl Ahmad, and Amir Ata Mohammad, occupied key cabinet positions; others, including Salahuddin Saljuqi, were appointed to Afghanistan's embassies abroad.

Religion continued to be a strong influence on government policies after Nadir was assassinated in 1933 and his son, King Mohammad Zahir, took over and ruled the country until 1973. In the post–World War II period, clerics advocated establishing an Islamic regime; among them was Ismail Balkhi, who studied in Iran and Iraq and advocated an Islamic regime upon his return home in the 1950s. He was imprisoned for 15 years and died in 1963 of a mysterious illness. Radical Islamic ideas gained dominance in the 1960s and led to the establishment of an Islamic organization, *Ikhwan al-Muslimin,* Islamic Brotherhood. The *Ikhwans* published a weekly paper, *Gahiz* (Morning), for propagating their views on society and development based on Islamic ideology. The spread of radical Islam culminated in the establishment of *Jamiat-e-Islami,* Islamic Society, in 1967 to counter the growing influence of liberal, democratic, progressive, and communist activities.[14]

One of the prominent figures in the propagation of radical religious ideas was Ghulam Mohammad Niazi, dean of the college of Islamic Studies at Kabul University. He was inspired by and supported the Islamic radicals, *Ikhwan al-Muslimin,* in the Middle East and was sentenced to life imprisonment in 1974, one year after the monarchy was overthrown and Afghanistan was declared a republic, he was executed soon after a pro-Soviet regime was established in April 1978. Islamic radicals opposed the growing cultural influences of the West, such as nightclubs, movies, and women's movements. They clashed with supporters of *Sazman-e-Jawanan-e-Mutaraqi* or Progressive Youth Organization, PYO, also known as *Shula-e-Jawid,* Eternal Flame, and murdered one of their spokespeople and activists, Saidal Sukhandan, on the campus of Kabul University in June, 1972. During the republican order headed by Mohammad Daoud, 1973–1978, Islamic radicals clashed with Daoud, regarding him as a Russian agent as he had a number of pro-Soviet party members in his cabinet. They declared *jihad* and attacked government installations in the Panjshir Valley but were defeated and their top leaders sought refuge in Pakistan.

RELIGION UNDER THE PRO-SOVIET REGIME, 1978–1979

After the pro-Soviet forces of the PDPA seized power in April 1978, they strove to transform Afghanistan into a socialist society based on the Soviet model of political system. They viewed religious institutions as a stumbling block in their endeavors to achieve their objectives and waged war on religious leaders, progressives, liberals, patriots, and revolutionary forces. The regime purged the Islamic symbols, *Mihrab* and *Minbar* (*Mihrab* is the principal prayer niche in a mosque where the Imam leads people in prayer and *Minbar* is a pulpit for sermons), from the emblem of the country's flag, and substituted them with a golden emblem and a five-centered star with the inscription, *De Afghanistan Demokratik Jamhuriat*, Democratic Republic of Afghanistan; and they changed the color of the flag to red to represent the April 1978 coup as a revolution. On the day the flag was hoisted, live pigeons were smeared with red ink and let loose, residents of Kabul were ordered to apply red paint to the exterior of their houses and apartments, and students were instructed to paint their chairs and desks red.

The war on religion also led to the removal of the *Kalima* (*bismillah al-rahman al-rahim,* "In the name of God the most merciful, the most compassionate") from official events. The *Kalima* was traditionally recited at the beginning of every official announcement, lecture, and official declaration. Young party members desecrated mosques, defiled religious sites, and transformed President Taraki's residence into a museum of the revolution, an act that the conservatives regarded as sacrilegious. In so doing, the regime further isolated itself from the people, who fought to defend their faith against the verbal and physical attacks by the regime.

The Kabul regime arrested and executed a number of religious leaders, influential tribal chiefs, clerics, and revolutionary and patriotic intellectuals. Many were thrown out of airplanes flying at night on orders of the regime, which had warned that those who conspired against them in darkness would be eliminated in darkness. Security agents would invade people's homes at night and beat and arrest those whom they suspected of conspiracy against the regime. Family members of the much-respected religious leader, Sebghatullah Mojaddadi, were imprisoned and nearly all the male members of the family were summarily executed. The regime arrested Sayed Muazam, son of the influential religious leader of Karrukh, and his family and many others in Herat on charges of opposing the regime's social and economic reforms.

These arrests on the one hand and radical socioeconomic reforms and political repression on the hand led to a public uprising on March 5, 1979. People carried green flags and marched toward the provincial center, and seized control of the city, holding onto it until March 16. During the armed insurrection, many army officers, including several Russian military advisors, were killed, but government forces finally crushed the uprising and regained control of the city. The regime used modern military arsenal against the insurgents and civilians. They bombed the city relentlessly, killing thousands of people. The pro-Soviet regime blamed Ayatollah Shariatmadari, an influential Iranian cleric, for his role in the uprising, claiming that Iran had sent agents to Herat to organize and lead the insurrection.[15]

On March 21, 1979, people in Nooristan and Dara-e-Paich of Kunar Province rebelled and laid siege to government forces, who retaliated by bombing villages in the area. When the army forced people of the Kerala village to participate in a progovernment rally, the people chanted antigovernment slogans and epithets. The army fired into the crowd, killing scores of men, women, and children. The Kabul regime naively believed that it could easily eliminate any religiously inspired opposition and rebellion to their rule. When conservative clerics, religious leaders, and people at large opposed the coercive methods of governance, the party's leadership labeled the clerics and religious leaders *Ikhwan al-Shayatin* (Satanic Brothers) and denounced them as foreign agents. The party appealed to the peasantry, farmers, and liberal and democratic forces to fight the *mullahs,* whom the Kabul regime described as "*Ikhwanis* made in London and Paris."

A major religious-oriented uprising occurred in the Chindawul ghetto of Kabul on June 23, 1979, by the Shia Hazaras. Residents of the district attacked a police station on Jada-e-Maiwand Street, seized its depots, and continued their march toward the main center of the city, hoping that others would join in the crusade against the regime. The Kabul regime brutally crushed the uprising, which claimed the lives of numerous people. The next day, state security forces arrested an estimated 2,000 Hazaras and executed most of them, throwing their bodies into a mass grave.[16]

Religion and nationalism served as a unifying force against social and political oppression. Progressive religious leaders and clerics, Sunni and Shia, called upon the Muslims to unite in the fight against the pro-Soviet regime. They called for the restoration of an Islamic order and encouraged their respective followers to heed the call for *jihad.* Opposition to the regime escalated in most rural areas, while in urban areas, antigovernment forces such as liberals, progressives, and revolutionaries intensified their struggle and distributed "night letters" *(shabnamah)* to encourage people to oppose and fight the Soviet-backed government. Such actions caused the Kabul regime to arrest those who they believed were key figures behind the growing anti-regime movement.

Political repression by the Kabul regime forced a number of renowned religious leaders, clerics, *ulamas,* and revolutionaries to leave Afghanistan and settle in Pakistan and Iran. From their bases in exile, they encouraged people to continue their struggle and appealed to civil servants, soldiers, and security personnel to desert the Kabul regime and join the resistance movement. Continued political repression forced moderate and liberal religious leaders to leave the country and settle in Pakistan and Iran, where they soon established organizations of their own to lead the struggle against Kabul. Leaders of the Islamic fundamentalist parties of *Jamiat-e-Islami* and *Hizb-e-Islami,* which established their headquarters in Pakistan before the April 1978 coup, received substantial financial support from the United States and its regional allies, Pakistan and Saudi Arabia. This support enabled them to establish leading roles in the fight against the Kabul regime in comparison to other Islamic groups.

Shia leaders forged closer ties with Iran, established offices in Tehran and other cities in Iran, and received financial and military support from Iran. By 1979, the Shia Hazaras liberated most of Hazarajat and established *Shura-e-Itifaq* (Solidarity Council) to lead the struggle and maintain law and order in Hazarajat. Sayed Ali Behishti, a reputable cleric in the region, headed the council.

In 1978–1979, armed struggle against the Kabul regime escalated in most rural areas. The clerics in charge encouraged people to refrain from cooperating with government agencies; and they appealed to civil service officers, teachers, and soldiers to abandon their posts and join them in the *jihad* to restore the Islamic order. Those who did not heed their call were murdered, and their mutilated bodies were left exposed to the public to intimidate other government officials into abandoning their posts. Such acts by Islamic fundamentalists backfired and forced many to support the government and to enlist in the state militia units.

RELIGION UNDER SOVIET OCCUPATION

Religion and nationalism played equally significant roles in the armed struggle against Soviet imperialism from the moment its forces invaded the country on December 27, 1979, and until colonial domination ended in February of 1989. The invasion enraged public opinion and caused revolutionary, patriotic, liberal, and religiously oriented groups and individuals to fight for the liberation of their homeland. The puppet regime headed by Babrak Karmal made concerted efforts to win the support of religious leaders and students, even freeing political prisoners. Karmal designated January 13, 1980, as a day of national mourning to honor the memory of those who had been executed by the regimes of Taraki and Amin in 1978–1979; indeed Karmal himself participated in one of these events in a city mosque in Kabul. Karmal proclaimed the Soviet invasion a new era, where people would no longer be subjected to witch-hunts by state security agencies. But these concessions by Karmal did not create public support for him; instead, they caused the people to continue their struggle against him.

A major uprising occurred in April of 1980. Anti-Soviet pamphlets were distributed during that night, asking the public to protest the Soviet occupation. The uprising originated in several districts of Kabul, such as Qalah-e-Shadah, Dasht-e-Barchi, and Afshar. People congregated at local mosques and used loudspeakers to call people to *jihad.* They left the mosques carrying green flags as well as pistols, hand grenades, and machine guns under their long coats. They attacked government installations, the Soviet embassy, the house of the former henchman, Amin, and several police stations, where they seized arms and equipment. As a sign of protest, people closed stores while students boycotted schools. For several days in a row, antigovernment epithets and the call of *Allah Akbar,* "God is Great," could be heard at night throughout the city. The regime used the standing army to crush the rebellion, killing an estimated 300 people and arresting over 5,000 others.[17] The regime warned businessmen that if they did not open their stores, they would be arrested and prosecuted. Despite this threat, anti-Soviet protests continued throughout Kabul and other cities.

To deal more effectively with growing anti-Soviet and antiregime activities, Karmal established *Jabha-e-Milli-e-Padar Watan* (National Fatherland Front) and invited tribal leaders, clerics, and others to join the front, declaring that the regime was ready to negotiate with the Islamic parties. The regime resorted to forcing people to join the army to fight the Islamic opposition parties. This policy led many young soldiers to desert the army and either return to their villages, if they had been liberated from the government's control, or go to Pakistan where they joined the anti-Soviet resistance movement. The increasing rate of desertion in the army forced the regime to undertake new measures. Security forces searched houses and roamed through the city's hotels and restaurants, public gathering areas, and mosques to find the deserters and other youth and force them to join the army. Such a coercive policy further isolated the social base of the regime's support.

Islamic militias continued their relentless war on the regime, but they also experienced desertion in their ranks. The major Sunni political parties, collectively known as *Gruh-e-Haftganah* ("the group of seven") with their headquarters in Pakistan, included the following:

- *Hizb-e-Islami* (Islamic Party), led by Gulbuddin Hikmatyar.
- *Hizb-e-Islami* (Islamic Party), a splinter group that broke from Hikmatyar's party, led by Mohammad Yunus Khalis.
- *Jamiat-e-Islami* (Islamic Society), led by Burhanuddin Rabbani.
- *Mahaz-e-Islami* (National Islamic Front), led by Sayed Ahmad Gilani.
- *Jabha-e-Milli-Nijat* (National Liberation Front), led by Sebghatullah Mojaddadi.
- *Harakat-e-Enqilabi-e-Islami* (Islamic Revolutionary Movement), led by Mohammad Nabi Mohammadi.
- *Ittehadi Islami-e-Mujahidin* (Islamic Unity of Mujahidin), led by Abdur Rabb Rasoul Sayaf.

The Shias came under the growing influence of Iranian clerics who tried to promote their own brand of Islamic revolution to counter the influence of Sunni Islam supported by Saudi Arabia, Pakistan, and other Sunni countries. The Iranian leadership dispatched representatives to Hazarajat to study the situation and identify and set up organizations that supported their political agenda. This policy damaged the unity among the Hazaras and paved the way for continuous clashes amongst themselves. The major Shia parties included the following:

- *Shura-e-Itifaq* (Council of the Union), led by Sayed Ali Behishti.
- *Harakat-e-Islami* (Islamic Movement), led by Mohammad Asif Mohsini.
- *Sazman-e-Mujahidin-e-Mustazafin* (Organization of Warriors of the Dispossessed).
- *Sazman-e-Nasr* (Victory Organization), led by a council of four people.
- *Sepah-e-Pasdaran* (Revolutionary Guard Corps), led by Mohammad Akbari.
- *Hizbullah* (Party of God), led by Shaikh Wusoqi.

In 1989, these and other small Shia parties united and formed *Hizb-e-Wahdat* (Unity Party), with Abdul Ali Mazari elected as its head. The Shias continued to receive financial aid and some military equipment from the clerical institutions in Iran; some of their members even received basic military training at military camps in Iran. The Shias in Afghanistan supported Iran during its eight years of war with Iraq, and even sent some of their men to fight at the war front.[18]

The Isma'ili community did not have an established political party to defend its interests, and it had no representation outside the country to liaise between the Shia and Sunni political parties. The Isma'ilis were not mobilized on the basis of Islamic ideology, as the other political parties had done when they were formed in the 1960s. Most Isma'ili intellectuals supported secular political movements and rallied in support of the pro-Soviet PDPA and the militant revolutionary organizations that had split from *Shula-e-Jawid* in the 1970s. A number of these Isma'ili intellectuals as well as tribal leaders also participated in the war of national liberation.

Commander Noor Mohammad and Khodayar Faiyaz led the partisan war in the Shibar District, while Manuchehr led a similar group in Baghlan. When the Soviet-backed regime co-opted the Isma'ili chief Mansoor Naderi and helped him to build a strong progovernment militia that was later promoted to a mechanized army division, the 80th Army Division, the independent Isma'ili partisan movements in the two regions lost their power and domination of the regions. The Tajik Isma'ilis in Badakhshan supported the Kabul regime because they saw their Isma'ili counterparts on the other side of the Oxus River, in Khorog, Tajikistan, and in Sinkiang, China, enjoying better standards of living. They believed that their lot would not improve under the Islamic fundamentalists, so they continued to support the Kabul regime.

RELIGION, CIVIL WAR, AND THE TALIBAN

Armed conflict during the Soviet occupation period forced a large number of people to leave the country for Iran and Pakistan. Migration inside and outside the country provided opportunities for refugee children to attend different schools and experience a different lifestyle, which to some extent changed their perspective so that they no longer maintained the strong attachment to the traditional way of life their own families had experienced at home.

During the war of national liberation, religion and nationalism significantly transformed people's social and political perspectives in such a manner that the culture of tribal warfare gradually lost its significance as a motivating factor in the fight against alien domination. The culture of *jihad* to promote Islamic culture and identity was given more prominence as regional commanders of the Shia and Sunni parties as well as traditional religious leaders tried to mobilize the people in the war against the Soviets and the Kabul regime. Aggrandizement of the *jihad* culture led to the revision and rewriting of the school curriculum to imbue the younger generation with Islamic identity. For example, a mathematics teacher in a classroom would teach students that one plus one is equal to two Kalashnikovs (Russian-made assault rifles), or two plus two is equal to four dead enemies of Islam.

The establishment of *madrasas* and universities by Islamic fundamentalist parties in Pakistan further contributed to the promotion of the culture of *jihad,* a culture that did not attach much importance to natural science subjects as well as topics related to improving the welfare of the Muslims. The provision of religious education for a number of refugee students at religious schools in Iran instilled younger people with radical Shia politics. During and after the war of national liberation, the Sunnis and Shias remained apart, unable to find a common ground to unite and rebuild the war-torn country after the Soviet-backed government collapsed in 1992.

Differences between the Shia and Sunni leaders intensified when Sebghatullah Mojaddadi's short rule ended and Burhanuddin Rabbani of *Jamiat-e-Islami* became head of the state in late June, 1992. Shia demands concerning recognition of the Shia jurisprudence, as well as their proposals for the political, social, and economic development of the Hazara region, were rejected by fundamentalists within the government. This factor on the one hand and opposition by a number of Pushtuns who were not happy with dominance of the Tajiks on the other hand paved the road for armed conflict among the Islamic parties that eventually transformed the war into a war of ethnic cleansing. Leaders of each ethnic group appealed to their own ethnic community for support, a policy that led to the destruction of Kabul and the killing of thousands of people.

Competition between the Shia clerical institutions of Iran and the Sunni leadership of Pakistan and Saudi Arabia to establish their domination in Afghanistan added fuel to religious bigotry and the war of ethnic cleansing. Although the Shia political groups united in 1989, they remained divided. *Hizb-e-Wahdat* adopted a nationalist approach that stressed the unity of the Hazaras to defend their vested interests, irrespective of their religious beliefs. *Harakat-e-Islami,* headed by Asif Mohsini, adopted policies that gave prominence and priority to religion in political and social development and vehemently denied the role of tribal, ethnic, and regional issues in societal development.

The continuation of armed conflict among various Islamic parties for domination of the country's politics led to the destruction of economic, social, and political institutions throughout the country and caused people to despise their leaders. People condemned the policies and practices of the Islamic parties; they questioned their belief and sincerity in Islam when the parties did not honor a peace treaty they signed in Mecca, Saudi Arabia (Mecca is regarded as the holiest city of Islam). They had no means to fight these parties and anxiously awaited the arrival of a day when the warlords would be overthrown. It was during this period that the Taliban emerged as a power and eventually established their domination over most parts of the country between 1996–2001. Although Taliban means 'students of religious studies,' the typical Talib lacked formal education or even a rudimentary knowledge about the history of Islam and of Afghanistan, and were strangers to the modern sciences, arts, philosophy, and politics of the twenty-first century. The views of some of their top leaders were heavily influenced by the teachings of Mawlawi Fazl al-Rahman, head of *Jamiat-al-Ulama-e-Islami* (Association of Islamic Scholars) in Pakistan.

The Taliban spiritual leader, Mullah Mohammad Omar, who lost one eye during the battle with the Soviet army, was called by the title of *Amir al-Mominin,* commander of the faithful. As a one-eyed man, Omar tried to promote his cult of personality as a spiritual man who dispenses justice to all and sees all the faithful through one eye, without any discrimination. Omar justified his leadership on the basis of a dream he had in which Prophet Muhammad appeared to him and ordained him with the task of delivering the community of the faithful from the miseries and sufferings they have endured for years. Although all Islamic parties fought to implement their version of Islamic law and imposed severe penalty on those who violated their injunctions, the Taliban's policies for building an Islamic society did not differ much in their principles from those of their rivals. They adhered to a strict and literal interpretation of the Quran and instituted harsh measures for implementing the Islamic Sharia law, as they understood it. The Taliban policy of building a highly regimented Islamic society led to the creation of the Ministry for the Supervision of Vice and the Promotion of Virtue ("Vice and Virtue"), with the task to ensure strict observance of Islamic law.

The Taliban regarded the Hazaras as infidels and declared *jihad* on them. When Taliban militias launched an offensive on Mazar, in Balkh Province on August 8, 1998, they massacred an estimated 2,000–5,000 civilians, mostly Hazaras. They justified their war on the Hazaras on the grounds that they were avenging the deaths of a large number of their men who had been killed by the Hazaras during an earlier offensive in Mazar, Balkh. When Taliban militias captured Bamiyan in 1998, they burned people's houses and executed a large number of their captives on the simple charge that they were Shias and Hazaras.

ISLAM AND DEVELOPMENT: THE AGA KHAN DEVELOPMENT NETWORK

The concept of development was alien to Afghanistan's religious leaders, theologians, scholars, and clerics. They focused exclusively on religious aspects of their followers' lives by supporting the building of mosques, *takyakhanas* (shrines to Imam Hussein), and *madrasas* and asking their followers to donate funds to maintain such institutions. Religious leaders often spoke of life after death and reward and punishment on the Day of Judgment and called upon the people to abide by Islamic codes of conduct. They did not concern themselves with improving the quality of life, both in urban and rural ghettos, or with promoting the concepts of a clean environment, sanitation, repairing public roads and utilities, and engaging in income-generating projects for improving the standard of living of Muslims.

Religious leaders and clerics did not become advocates and champions of a safe and clean environment. They did not actively participate in debates concerning the devising of strategies of nation-building and the sponsoring of development projects such as building and repairing roads and building hospitals and schools, considering such activities to be beyond the scope of their social obligation, thereby limiting themselves to delivering sermons at mosques and religious schools. They did not position themselves at the fore-front of community development to elevate themselves as role models to be followed.

A religious leader who is at the forefront of development is the Isma'ili spiritual leader, the Aga Khan. The Isma'ili community has decades of experience in community development, a process begun by Sultan Mohammad Shah, Aga Khan III and 48th Imam of the Isma'ilis, who embarked upon projects that promoted social welfare, education, and economic development for the Isma'ili community worldwide.

Karim Aga Khan IV continues building on the tradition of his grandfather. He is not only concerned with the spiritual and material development of the Isma'ili community, but he also involved himself in the development process of countries both in the developed and developing world. The Aga Khan Development Network (AKDN) is a network of several institutions, each with its own specific mandate, providing funds and services in the areas of education, culture, architecture, rural development, social welfare programs, and so forth.

AKDN did not engage in works in development projects in Afghanistan until 1996. The political situation was not conducive for the Aga Khan to visit Afghanistan and meet his followers and devise strategies for the development of the community. Lack of direct access to the Imam created opportunities for local Isma'ili religious leaders to remain independent of the Imam's headquarters. Many of them took advantage of this situation and built their own cult of personality, to the extent that they were viewed as the supreme religious leaders of the Isma'ili community.

Armed conflicts in Afghanistan wreaked havoc on the lives of the poor and resulted in the destruction of the local economy and displacement of a large number of people inside the country, forcing thousands to seek refuge in neighboring countries. The Aga Khan directed his institutions to provide emergency humanitarian aid to affected communities, regardless of their ethnic background, religious beliefs, and political association. In the process, he also intended to help Isma'ilis who had not received aid from the international aid agencies. On July 30, 1996, a delegation visited Badakhshan. The objective was to meet members of the community and develop appropriate strategies to provide aid and to participate in the long-term development of remote and neglected communities in the region.[19]

FOCUS Humanitarian Assistance, an affiliate of the AKDN, engaged in small-scale emergency relief programs in Badakhshan as early as March 1997 and expanded its operation to other regions, establishing offices in Kabul, Pul-e-Khumri of Baghlan, and Mazar in Balkh. FOCUS also provided aid for community projects to enable people to improve their shattered lives and donated funds for schools and hospitals.[20]

After the Taliban regime was overthrown and Hamid Karzai was installed as head of the transitional government, the Aga Khan pledged to support his government to rebuild the country and contributed U.S. $75 million to Afghanistan in January 2002. The Aga Khan visited Kabul in March 2002 and was warmly received by the government; he declared that his institutions would expand their development programs in Afghanistan.

Major development projects by AKDN include contribution of funds for the restoration of historic sites, such as the Timur Shah mausoleum; renovation of the historic mosque, *Masjid-e-Guzar-e-Uzbek-ha* in Shoor Bazaar and the Babur Garden; renovation of schools such as Tajwar Sultana; and provision of funds to improve health and agriculture. The Aga Khan Fund for Economic Development (AKFED), an affiliate of the AKDN, is engaged in promoting the tourism industry and in repairing and expanding the Kabul Hotel, with an estimated cost of U.S. $27.8 million, and converting it to Serena Hotel. AKFED's subsidiary organization, Serena Tourism Promotion Services, manages the day-to-day operation of the hotel. AKDN also undertook projects to repair roads, as evidenced in the building of five bridges that link Badakhshan Proper to Khorog in Tajikistan. The bridges, which cost U.S. $2 million to build, eliminate Badakhshan's geographical isolation and link it to the markets of Central Asian states. AKFED also provided U.S. $55 million to establish a telecommunication system, GSM network, which began providing services to Kabul, Herat, Qandahar, Balkh, Nangarhar, and Qunduz by the end of 2003.[21]

Parallel to his decision to commit resources for the rebuilding of Afghanistan, the Aga Khan also decided to modernize his community there. To this end, he abolished the old hereditary system of leadership of *pirs* and *khalifas* and established modern institutional structures, such as the National Council for Afghanistan (NCA) and Educational and Religious Tariqah Board, and he appointed qualified men and women from the younger generations to positions of leadership. The NCA is the leading institution of the Isma'ili community, with 38 male and 8 female members. The leaders of all institutions are appointed for a three-year term that is renewable only once for a second term. By establishing modern institutions and by appointing a new generation of leaders for the Isma'ili community, the Aga Khan aims to help the community integrate itself into the twenty-first century.[22]

NOTES

1. Mir Ghulam Mohammad Ghubar, *Afghanistan dar Masir-e-Tarikh* [Afghanistan in the path of history] (Tehran, Iran: Entisharat-e Jamhoori, 1374/1995), pp. 36–38.

2. Ghubar, *Afghanistan dar Masir-e-Tarikh*, p. 55.

3. Ghubar, *Afghanistan dar Masir-e-Tarikh*, pp. 83–85.

4. Ghubar, *Afghanistan dar Masir-e-Tarikh*, pp. 154–156.

5. Hafizullah Emadi, "The Hazaras and Their Role in the Process of Political Transformation in Afghanistan," *Central Asian Survey* 16, no. 3 (1997): 363–387.

6. Farhad Daftary, *The Isma'ilis: Their History and Doctrines* (Cambridge, MA: Cambridge University Press, 1990).

7. Emadi, "The Hazaras and Their Role in the Process of Political Transformation in Afghanistan," p. 365.

8. Hasan-i-Sabbah, "Particle of Dust," in *Shimmering Light: An Anthology of Isma'ili Poetry*, tr. Faquir M. Hunzai (London, England: I.B. Tauris, 1996), p. 77.

9. Daftary, *The Isma'ilis: Their History and Doctrines*.

10. Ghubar, *Afghanistan dar Masir-e-Tarikh*, pp. 166–175.

11. J. Singh, *The Persian Mystics, the Invocation of Sheikh Abdullah Ansari of Herat*, A.D. *1005–1090* in *Afghanistan*, ed. Louis Dupree (Karachi, Pakistan: Oxford University Press, 2002), p. 79.

12. Sabahuddin Kushkaki, *Daha-e-Qanun-e-Asasi: Ghaflat Zadagi-e-Afghanha wa Fursat Talabi-e-Rus-ha* [The decade of the constitution: Afghans ignorance and Russian opportunism] (Peshawar, Pakistan: Shura-e-Saqafati Jihad-e-Afghanistan, 1365/1986), pp. 85–86.

13. Ghubar, *Afghanistan dar Masir-e-Tarikh*, p. 631.

14. Hafizullah Emadi, "Radical Islam, Jihad, and Civil War in Afghanistan," *Internationales Asienforum* 30, nos. 1–2 (1999): 5–26.

15. Hafizullah Emadi, "Exporting Iran's Revolution: The Radicalization of the Shiite Movement in Afghanistan," *Middle Eastern Studies* 31, no. 1 (January 1995): 1–12.

16. Emadi, "Exporting Iran's Revolution," pp. 1–12.

17. For details see, Hafizullah Emadi, *Repression, Resistance, and Women in Afghanistan* (Westport, CT: Praeger Publishers, 2002).

18. For details see, Hafizullah Emadi, *Afghanistan's Gordian Knot: An Analysis of National Conflict and Strategies for Peace* (Honolulu: East-West Center, 1990).

19. Field trip to Khorog, Tajikistan, July 30, 1996, made by Shafik Sachedina, then president of the Isma'ili National Council for Britain; Taj Mitha, coordinator of Interagency Relations in Aiglemont; and the author; Shughnan, Afghanistan, 30 July 1996; Another field trip to Shughnan, Darwaz, Ishkashim, Darayam, Yamagan, Faizabad of Badakhshan Province, Afghanistan, 17 November-1 December 2003.

20. Field trip to Balkh, Samangan, and Baghlan, 21 February 2000.

21. "New Mobile network launched," *The Kabul Times* 37, no. 28, Sunday, 29 June 2003, p. 1.

22. Field trips to Kabul, October 2002; July–December 2003.

3

Literature and the Arts

Afghanistan's literary history, like its physical history, reflects centuries of influence by neighboring countries and scholars and writers of invading countries, yet the product in its final form is altered, and is made unique by the counter influence of the people who absorbed and learned it and then changed it to fit their chosen style of expression. In addition, a unique and pervasive theme found in poetry and literature, regardless of its style or the period, is the remarkable strength and resilience of the people described in verse and prose. Afghanistan's literature, arts, and music celebrate a people who persevere, are always adapting to the world around them, and who will survive.

HISTORICAL PERSPECTIVE

Invading tribes and communities brought their culture and traditions to Afghanistan, although much of the cultural heritage of the past has been destroyed recently due to successive wars among feuding tribes and empires. In ancient Afghanistan, literature was heavily influenced by religious thought. The Veda, which means sacred knowledge, is the earliest religious literature, produced by the Aryans who lived around the Oxus River. The Veda, which dates to about 1200 B.C., contains 1,028 songs, which were sung by a group of individuals known as the *Rishis*. With the migration of the Aryans into the northern parts of India it became the sacred religious literature of the Hindu community there.

The Veda songs are considered to be the origin of literary works in Afghanistan, and it consists of four volumes: Reg-Veda is the oldest literature, and deals with religious rituals, rites, and ceremonies, including daily events. Sama-Veda is an appendix to Reg-Veda, with the chants making an important aspect of the literature. Yajur-Veda is a collection of hymns sung while performing rites and rituals related to sacrifice. Atherva-Veda contains songs related to magic and incantations. Vedic literature was produced in an era in which tribal warfare constituted a major aspect of primitive communal societies, and the scripture encouraged people to fight hostile tribes and required them to endure environmental and physical hardships.

Vedic literature reveals the existence of social classes and sheds light on various aspects of the people's social, cultural, and economic activities of that period. The Avesta, which is regarded as canonical religious scripture, also contains devotional songs, which were memorized and orally transmitted from one generation to the next. The word Avesta means foundation and principle, and the scripture consists of five parts, the Yasna, Visperd, Vendidad, Yascht, and Khorda Avesta. Most such literature and artistic heritage of this period had been destroyed when invading armies of powerful tribes conquered the region and promoted their own literature.

When the Greeks established their domination, Greek art and culture flourished in Afghanistan for over two centuries, and Greek became the official language of the court. Excavation of the historic site in the Aikhanum Region (the word means "Lady Moon" in the Uzbeki language) in the northern areas of the country revealed Greek architecture, script, and cultural heritage. When ancient Afghanistan came under the influence of Buddhism, it became a stronghold for the propagation of Buddhist civilization, evidenced in the building of Buddhist monasteries and shrines in the valley of Jalalabad, Bamiyan, and several other regions.

MUSLIM CONQUEST

Consolidation of Islamic rule paved the road for the expansion of Arab arts, literature, and civilization. Islam did not sanction the destruction of the arts and cultural heritages of others and in this spirit of tolerance, worked to adopt and refine some of the ancient traditions to suit the needs and requirements of the new Muslim community. Arab domination of the country caused writers, poets, and scholars to use Arabic language in expressing their ideas and thoughts, and Arabic became the medium of communication in the administrative domain. Although writers and scholars wrote in Arabic, common people continued to speak their own native languages. The Arabic and Persian languages and literature mutually influenced each other and enriched their respective vocabularies by borrowing words from one another. The Persian language adopted the use of Arabic script and it is chiefly due to this reason there are no written documents in the Persian language during this period.[1]

Arab domination lasted over two hundred years until nationalist movements put an end to its influence. During this period, the Persian language gradually established its dominance to the extent that various rulers promoted the Persian language as the medium in their courts. Religious precepts served as guiding principles for the development of literature and arts, and efforts were made to translate Arabic literary works into Persian.

LITERARY DISCOURSE

Poetry

Poetry constitutes one of the highest forms of literary expression and is highly regarded by the people. Poems with themes related to religious and historical events, love, romance, jealousy, war, patriotism, and national pride are particularly favored. A poem must have three fundamental elements: meaning, rhyme, and meter, which determine the type of the poetry. Persian poetry is classified into four styles: Khurasani, Iraqi, Hindi, and Modern. The first three styles are named after the geographical region where they developed and gradually established their influence beyond its original place. The Khurasani style began in the middle of the fourth century and lasted until the middle of the sixth century. It uses few Arabic words except for religious terminology such as *namaz, zakat,* and *haj* and has a meter. The concept of meter in poetry prior to Islam was based on verses that did not have equal syllabi. Another distinguishing feature of the Khurasani style is simplicity of words, adjectives, and similarities. The Iraqi style started at the beginning of the seventh century and lasted until the end of the tenth century. In the Iraqi style, poetic expressions are complex and use more Arabic words instead of Persian. Poets often include the element of date in their poetry and poems with ethical, religious, and spiritual themes expanded during this period. Poets often include their name or pseudonyms in their poems so that readers will know it is their work. Well-known mystic poet Abdullah Ansari wrote:

The way to God is achieved by means of two *Kaabas*
One is the building and the other is through the heart
Until you can, make a journey through the heart,
One heart is greater than a thousand *Kaaba.*[2]

The Hindi style developed around the tenth century and continues to the present day. In the Hindi style, tender, delicate, imaginative thought and ideas are profusely used in poetic expressions. Modern style is gaining recognition, and most young writers prefer the modern style of poetry. It is based on expressing new ideas and thoughts in classic as well as in modern forms of poetry, where poets are free from the constraints of the traditions of rhyme and meter.

Persian poems are generally classified into *Dubaiti, Rubayi,* and *Ghazal. Dubaiti,* which is also known as *Fard,* consists of a couplet with rhyme and its complete meanings. *Rubayi,* a quadruplet, has similar rhyme and rhythm, and its first, second, and fourth stanzas end with similar rhyme. *Ghazal* has longer verses and deals with love stories, either imaginary or genuine, and has rhyme and rhythm and succeeding verses follow the rhyme of the first two verses. Early Persian poetry is attributed to Abu Hafs Hakim bin Ahwas Sughdi Samarqandi, dated 300 years after Prophet Muhammad settled in Medina. He wrote:

How does the wild deer run in the mountains
How can he run without a companion.[3]

Hanzala Badghisi was an acclaimed poet who died in 220/841 and worked at the court of Tahirid rulers (205–295/826–916). His poems stress the theme of bravery and heroism. He wrote:

If greatness lies inside the jaws of a lion,
take the risk, snatch it from the lion's jaws
Your fate will be crowned with honor and glory
Otherwise welcome death with valor.[4]

Reciting poetry is common both in the private as well as in the public domain. People of all classes love poetry, and memorize and recite them for hours when entertaining guests and family. Professional and semiprofessional minstrels recite poetry when they entertain people at occasions such as weddings and holiday festivities. Poems with themes of bravery and heroism are found within the literature of every ethnic community. Proestablishment writers depicted the Pushtuns as warriors who honor the promises they make and do not harm the enemy if they take refuge in their houses. The concepts of love, jealousy, war, heroism, and the like run through the literature of the Hazaras, Baluchis, Uzbeks, Turkmens, and others. Lack of rigorous efforts at research on literature of the non-Pushtun minority communities has resulted in many scholars becoming oblivious to the full scope of their own literary heritage.

Folk Poetry

People appreciate folk poems that are especially intimate with their day-to-day lives and are usually sung on special occasions. A special form of folk songs are known as *nakhta* and are generally sung by women when they mourn the death of a dear one or a hero. Another form of folk songs, the lullaby, was sung by a mother when she rests her baby in a cradle, her arm, or lap and sings to put the baby to sleep. A special form of folk song is called *landay*, common among the Pushtun tribes. *Landay* is composed both by men and women. Many hundreds of folk songs have been transmitted orally from one generation to the next. Scholars familiar with *landay* maintain that the first line of *landay* usually consists of nine syllables, while the second line is longer, about thirteen lines. The following is a translation of a *landay*.

Your face is a rose and your eyes are candles;
Faith! I am lost. Should I become a butterfly or a moth?[5]

Prose

Nonpoetic literary works emerged about a hundred years after the development of poetry and further developed at a later period. Persian literature is classified into five distinct styles that emerged at different historical periods. Literary works during *Dawra-e-Nakhust* (Early Period, 300–432/921–1053) were characterized by its simplicity of words and sentences. During *Dawra-e-Duwum* (Second Period, 432–617/1053–1238) writers used quotes and verses to substantiate their views. By the time of *Dawra-e-Sayum* (Third Period, 617–920/1238–1541), literature became more complex because writers not only used frequent quotes and verses to prove their arguments but also gave preference to grandiloquent words over substantive meanings and content, and Arabic words were frequently used to refine literary expressions. *Dawra-e-Chaharum* (Fourth Period, 920–1319/1541–1940) is characterized as the degradation of Persian prose writing in which Arabic, Turkic, and other foreign words were frequently used in Persian literary works. During *Dawra-e-Panjum* (Fifth Period, 1940 to the present), Persian literature again stressed simplicity of words and meanings.[6]

Literary works consist of various types, such as the novel, short story, literary criticism, drama, dialogue, autobiography, folk and satirical literature, and others. Storytelling covers a wide range of topics, such as tales on religious events, ethnic stereotyping, and ethnic humor. It is intended to entertain an audience and relieve the tedium of idle time. Folk literature had been orally transmitted from one generation to another, usually by parents, elders of the family, or a cleric *(mullah)* who teaches religious classes. Although individuals created all of Afghanistan's folk literature, the authors generally remained anonymous.

LITERATURE DURING THE GHAZNAWIDS AND AFTER

Persian literature flourished during the Ghaznawid rule and after. Acclaimed female poet Rabia Balkhi (d. 940 A.D.) composed poems in the Arabic and Persian languages that encouraged defiance against rigid social and cultural norms. Balkhi fell in love with Baktash, one of the slaves working at her brother's palace and her brother, Haris, not only disapproved Balkhi's choice of marriage but also denied her an opportunity to marry Baktash and imprisoned her when she refused to honor and submit to his order. Balkhi died in prison and prior to her death she wrote the following poem with her blood on the prison wall that reads in translated form:

I am caught in love's web so deceitful
None of my endeavors turned fruitful,
I knew not when I rode the high-blooded steed.
The harder I pulled its reins the less it would heed.
Love is an ocean with such a vast space.
A true lover should be faithful till the end.
And face life's reprobated trend.
When you see things hideous, fancy them neat,
Eat poison but taste sugar sweet.[7]

Literature, particularly poetry dealing with ethics, morality, and glorification of the dominant powers, gained popularity across a spectrum of social classes. Ghazni became the center of the literati community where King Mahmood employed an estimated 900 scholars, including 400 poets at his court. Renowned poet Abdul Qasim Firdawsi compiled his major epic work, the *Shahnamah,* or Book of Kings, containing 60,000 couplets that cover historical tales related to heroism and bravery over four ancient dynasties. Firdawsi dedicated the work to King Mahmood in anticipation of greater financial reward. When he received a pittance of what he expected, he rewrote the introduction into a satire and then fled Ghazni to avoid persecution and died in exile around 1025. *Shahnamah* intended to do away with domination of the Arab culture and its influence on the Persian language. It encourages nationalist sentiments and people read it with great interest. The Persian language became a dominant medium of discourse at the Ghaznawid court and Persian literary works established its influence in India during the eleventh and sixteenth centuries and became the official language of the court there.

Scholarship dealing with science, philosophy, mysticism, gnosticism, and the like was further developed during the Ghaznawid period. Well-known writer and religious mystic Abdullah Ansari composed a number of devotional prose and poetry works. Abu Ali Sina (980–1037), who came from an Isma'ili background and became known as Avicenna, produced numerous works, and his major writings in the medical field are known as *Ketab al-Qanoon fi tib*, the Canon or Book of Medicine and *Ketab al-Shifa*, Book of Healing. Sina criticized the rigid social and political environment that did not support free and innovative thinking. In a poem he stated that:

Bah! These small deluded men imagine
in their ignorance, they are the wisest men on earth
It is better to be a donkey because this ignorant community
Pronounces those not like them to be infidels.[8]

Literary works produced by Nasir Khusraw, a celebrated poet and writer, were imbued with philosophical arguments. His poetry was widely read by the people who were introduced to a new way of thinking about the cosmos. His contribution is that people who read his works developed a deeper appreciation of knowledge beyond the immediate self. Khusraw was born around 1003–1004 in Qubadian, Balkh, and was employed as a revenue collector in Marw, which gave him access to the Ghaznawid court. He went to Cairo to meet the Fatimid Imam and to further his knowledge of the Islamic world. Khusraw wrote:

I made cushions and beds from rocks
And made shelter and tents from the clouds
Like camels carried loads on my back
And sometimes labored like beasts of burden
Inquired as I went from town to town
Inquisitively searched this ocean to the coast.[9]

Khusraw embraced the Isma'ili faith and was appointed representative of the Fatimid Imam in Afghanistan. After he returned home he began to propagate the Isma'ili doctrine and encountered opposition by conservative Sunni clerics who persuaded the public against him, causing him to flee to Badakhshan. Khusraw spent the remaining years of his life composing prose and poetry dealing with theological and philosophical issues. He died around 1073–1074 and was buried in Yamagan, Badakhshan. Khusraw refused to glorify tyrant rulers in his works and maintained that they are not worthy of the respect and veneration bestowed by verse. He stated:

I am not one who casts at the feet of swine
These precious pearls, the words of Dari.[10]

Khusraw's poems reflect his views of the cosmos and man's relationship with the universe and the creator, with a clear message that people must love and help one another and refrain from harming the poor.

If you cannot assuage a person's pain
Add not to his suffering and pain
Stab not a man with a dagger
Irritate not if you cannot help
Love human beings as you are one of them
Be with them for there is no gain in being a demon.[11]

Persian literature evolved during the Timurid era to the extent that the Timurid era capital, Herat, was transformed into a center of learning and civilization, with learned men traveling from far distances to work there. Nasiruddin Abd al-Rahman Jami was one of those acclaimed scholars. He composed more than 40 volumes of works dealing with romantic poetry, mysticism, theology, and similar topics. A renowned poet of the court, Mir Nizamuddin Ali Shir Nawayi (b. 1441 in Herat) was a major patron of Turkic literature and used the Turkic language as a medium of discourse for composing prose and poems. Other known Turkic writers and poets at a later period included Mohammad Biram Khan, murdered in 1561; Makhdom Quli Feraghi (1733–1798); Mohammad Wali Kamina (1770–1840); and others.[12]

Much of the country's literary works had been destroyed when Genghis Khan's army invaded the country. Mongolian domination led to the development of resistance literature and epic poetry. A renowned Pushtun poet Khushhal Khatak defied Mongol domination of his homeland and composed poetry that reflected his aspiration for freedom. Khatak was born in 1613 and was imprisoned by the Mogul ruler Awrangzib. When he was released he expressed contempt to Awrangzib in a poem translated here that states:

Was I an eagle or a falcon in the sight of Shah Jahan
That to Awrang as a Crow or Sparrow—I should be?
The life that before it sees but its own dishonor,

He who leads it, at such a life astounded am I.
Fire takes their titles and their service then I say,
Since in the Mughul's eyes and understanding I am despised.
Maddened now am I that my name and honor are in question,
Though no care is mine for the gain or loss of countless wealth.[13]

When Khatak died in 1691 at age 78 his last words were to bury him where the shadow of his enemy would not fall on his grave.

Literary works of both poetry and prose that deal with religious and historical events continue to inspire people. Music is often played during recitation of poems, epics, and stories related to romantic love affairs. Ethnic groups show great interest in poetry and prose that deal with the community's history and distinguished national and local heroes. Intellectuals of the Hazaras, Baluchis, and other ethnic communities have played a major role in the development of literature of their own respective communities. For example, Mullah Musa Hazara, who lived in the period of the Moghul reign, is the author of *Kashf al-Ayat,* an explanation on Quranic verses and Jam Durrak is a renowned Baluchi writer of the eighteenth century.

RESISTANCE LITERATURE DURING BRITISH COLONIALISM

Two types of literature emerged during the colonial period: proestablishment and anticolonial. The rulers backed by the British imperialism promoted literature that served their vested interest. The anticolonial literature encouraged rebellion against the British-backed rulers and their patrons. For example, when the British invaded Afghanistan in 1839 and installed Shuja to the throne, a Pushtu folk poem reviled Shuja, calling him a puppet leader. In the poem Shuja is also referred to as an Armenian who served the interest of British-India Company. The poem reads:

Coined on gold and silver Shah Shuja, the Armenian,
  Who is the sweetheart of Lord Burns and the true servant of
    Company.[14]

Folk poetry promoted themes that ranged from noncooperation to armed insurrection. Poets glorified the anticolonial armed struggle and hailed Mohammad Akbar Khan as a hero who taught the British a lesson that they would remember for eternity. A portion of the poem reads:

To British lords and magistrates
You tossed them bones from century to century.[15]

Literary works thrived after the establishment of state-owned printing presses and publication of the first paper, *Shams al-Nahar*, in 1873, which provided space for literature, poetry, and essays on ethics, morality, and other such topics. Prior to this period, literary works were either hand copied or printed in India. Although there was no private paper to publish alternative news, reformist and patriotic intellectuals had to work their way into the bureaucracy and surreptitiously used government printing facilities as a means to propagate reformist programs and ideas.

Anticolonial writers and poets composed poems encouraging people to participate in the war of liberation when the British again invaded Kabul in 1879. Folk songs were composed that praised local heroes and demonized the British army General Frederick Roberts. One of the Persian folk songs reads:

Mohammad Jan Khan is a legendary hero
Ayub Khan is a ferocious roaring lion
Mir Bacha Khan is the leader of leaders
Liberation is Afghan's honor
Bald Roberts [Frederick] is the biggest idol
O brother, Come and eat grapes.[16]

During a battle in Maiwand, Qandahar, in 1880 it is suggested that a young woman named Malalay participated in the battle. She carried the standard of a dying soldier to rally others to continue the fight. A Pushtu folk song is attributed to her when she cried loud to encourage anticolonial fighters to resist.

I make a beauty spot on my forehead from the blood of my martyred
    love
To put the roses in the garden to shame
If you are not martyred in the Maiwand battle
Then God save you from shame.[17]

Scholarship

Although the ruling elite in the state apparatus was reluctant to support education and literary works, progressive, liberal, and patriotic-minded intellectuals of middle-class families fought for social and political reforms. These intellectuals also produced works that chronicled political events that unfolded in Afghanistan. One such a work is *Seraj al-Tawarikh* (Torch of Histories), written by Faiz Mohammad Katib (1861–1931) that covers developments in Afghanistan from 1747 to 1929. Writers who advocated reforms used the media to express their ideas on a wide range of social, cultural, and political issues. Mahmood Tarzi is one of the figures who spearheaded the reform movement and founded *Seraj al-Akhbar,* Torch of News, a private paper published in October 1911. Tarzi urged intellectuals and the masses to embrace modernity and technological advancement and worked to keep the public informed about local and international events. He invited writers, essayists, and commentators to contribute poetry, short stories, and send letters to the editor concerning modernity, independence, and freedom from colonial rule. Tarzi did not attribute backwardness as a manifestation of religious beliefs but as a result of reluctance on the part of people to change themselves according to the requirements of the time. One of his poems reads that:

The black smoke rising from the roof of the fatherland
Is caused by us.
The flames that devour us from left and right
Are caused by us.
The disunity and weakness of Islam was not caused by Christ or the
     Church
But was caused by us.[18]

Tarzi is credited for translation of a number of Turkish books and literature into Persian. Such works provided opportunities for intellectuals, writers, and scholars to become familiar with the works of their counterparts in Turkey. He imported a number of books from Iran, encouraged authors to engage in the creation of literary works, and strove to print the works of renowned local scholars. The publication of the collected works of Abdul Qadir Bidel was regarded as a significant step toward the development of literary works during this period.

One of the major characteristics of literary development during this time is the epic poem. Poets admired individuals who gave their lives for the cause of the people and liberation and hailed those whom the pro-British government executed because of their anticolonial sentiments. One such individual is Mullah Mohammad Sarwar Khan, principal of Habibiya School who argued passionately for constitutionalism that limited the powers of tyrant rulers. Prior to his execution he wrote the following poem:

Sacrificing the property and one's life
Is the first step toward constitutionalism.[19]

Abdul Rahman Khan was another such individual who advocated constitutional rights and freedom and was executed. Another advocate of constitutional rights was Mirza Mohammad Husain Raqim. He received a rudimentary education at home, became a commissioned officer in the army, and later was promoted to the rank of clerk and was imprisoned for nine years due to his critical ideas. The following poem reflects his passion for modern education.

> O Muslims, gone are the days of indulgences
> Hurry, the time of negligence has passed
> People are busy learning science and arts
> Alas, the life that is spent in ignorance.[20]

LITERATURE IN THE POSTINDEPENDENCE PERIOD

Persian and Pushtu literature were further developed in the postindependence period. Writers, poets, and scholars used private and state-owned newspapers and journals to express new ideas with regards to building a modern civil society with its corresponding culture and politics. Publication of the bimonthly *Aman-e-Afghan* and several other papers were used as a means to disseminate progressive ideas and to encourage the public to integrate themselves into the lives of the new era. Another aspect of literary development was an effort by radical and liberal writers to expose the treachery and regressive politics of those who opposed modernization. Publication of *Haqiqat* (Truth) in 1924 was intended to counter a barrage of propaganda by conservatives and clerics viewing modernization as a threat to their interest. The paper exposed the politics of the antistate rebellion aided by the British in order to overthrow Amanullah.

Establishment of other papers such as *Ghazi* in Paktiya, *Itifaq-e-Islam* in Herat, *Setara-e-Afghan* in Jab al-Seraj, *Itihad-e-Islam* in Balkh, *Islah* in Khanabad, *Tulo-e-Afghan* in Qandahar, and *Irshad-e-Niswan* in Kabul had to a great extent contributed to the development of literary works. Similarly, the founding of journals dealing with education, the army, health, and economics, not only played a role in the development of literary works but also served as the instruments of dissemination of new ideas and consciousness to mobilize people toward building a modern society.[21] Writers and intellectuals concerned with modernization established independent papers such as *Anis, Nasim-e-Sahar,* and *Naw Rooz* to encourage people to support modernization and development in the twentieth century. Poetry received special attention, and poets and writers reflected upon topics such as patriotism, humanism, and religious mysticism. Prominent poets were Abdul Ali Mustaghni, Obaidullah Qari, Ismail Guzook, Mohammad Anwar Bismil, and others. Qari compiled numerous literary texts for school students, Guzook composed short and long satiric poetry critical of bureaucratic officials, and Bismil defended liberal and constitutional ideas in his works.

The repressive political environment since the fall of King Amanullah in 1929 was not conducive for expression of critical ideas and radical literary works. State-owned papers, weeklies, and journals adopted conservative politics. Commissioned writers and scholars produced literature that encouraged submission to the state and discouraged initiatives and critical thinking. Individuals who advocated for the freedoms of the press, of association, and of expression were harassed and jailed. Critical scholarship was banned, and access to foreign literature was restricted only to those who were in the leadership position in the state bureaucracy. In spite of the state's repressive measures, the struggle for democracy, freedom, liberty, and equality continued. Progressive and liberal democratic writers and scholars were forced to express their ideas subtly, using indirect references while working for the state institutions. *Anjuman-e-Adabi-e-Kabul,* the Kabul Literary Association, which was founded in July 1931, had a number of progressive and liberal-minded figures, such as Mir Ghulam Mohammad Ghubar, Mohammad Sarwar Joya, Sarwar Goya, and others. The *Anjuman* sponsored publication of a monthly journal, *Kabul,* focusing on historical research. By 1932 the *Anjuman* sponsored the publication of *Salnama-e-Kabul,* an annual gazette that served as a reference to scholars, students, and literati community. Similar literary institutions were established in a number of other provinces. Pushtu literature was further developed when the state founded *Anjuman-e-Pushtu,* Pushtu Society in 1931 in Qandahar to conduct research on the Pushtu language and literature. The society intended to promote the Pushtu language as the national language to replace the dominance of Persian as a medium of communication within and outside the government.

LITERATURE IN THE POST–WORLD WAR II PERIOD

Literature after World War II was largely influenced by the writings of Muslim scholars in India, Middle Eastern countries, Turkey, and Bukhara of Central Asia. Scholars of wealthy families received further training at institutions of higher education in these countries and upon returning home they engaged in scholarship that followed the style and methods of writing of the schools they attended. The government printing press published the works of scholars and writers whose writings were compatible with the policy objectives of the ruling elite. These scholars and writers remained on the payroll of the state, promoted to key government posts inside and outside the country, and their works were made available for public consumption. These scholars did not reflect the suffering and misery of the majority of the people, who labored to make ends meet. Intellectuals, scholars, and poets who reflected the suffering of the poor were deprived of the means to make their works widely available to the public.

Proestablishment scholars described the lives, culture, history, and traditions of non-Pushtun ethnic communities as filtered through Pushtun nationalism. In 1935 the Pushtu Society transferred its office from Qandahar to Kabul, and in 1937 it merged with the *Anjuman-e-Adabi-e-Kabul* forming one research institution, the *Pushtu Tulana,* the Pushtu Academy. The academy published books, dictionaries, and literature, both in prose and poetry, targeting students at schools, colleges, and universities with the intention to promote the use of the Pushtu language and for its culture and traditions to be emulated by other ethnic communities.

State-owned research institutions such as *Anjuman-e-Tarikh* (the Historical Society), *Dayirat-al Maarif-e-Aryana* (the Aryana Encyclopedia), and others published articles on Afghanistan's ancient and contemporary history, geography, and culture. Proestablishment intellectuals at the forefront of modern literary expression included figures such as Abdul Rahman Pazhwak, Khalilullah Khalili, Abdul Raouf Benawa, Siddiqullah Rishtin, Sayed Qasim Rishtiya, Mohammed Ali, and others. Dominant themes of their literary works ranged from the lover/beloved, the garden, the images of roses, the nightingale, and wine to spirituality, morality, and nationalism—topics that were detached from the reality of life of the majority of low-income and poor people. For their services to the ruling class they were rewarded with top government posts. When these dissemblers fell from position of authority they decried political oppression, posing as nationalists and champions of the rights of the poor. For example, Khalili wrote.

> I have no homeland, thrust away from my mother's breast
> Sitting amidst fire and swimming in blood
> I am a leaf thrown around by the winds and
> Events scatter me like dust upon every doorstep.[22]

Nooruddin Rawnaq Naderi, son of the Isma'ili chief Nader Kayani, is another poet who was coddled from the day he was born, with maids and servants looking after him. He neither decried the suffering of poor Isma'ilis nor did anything to improve their lives but vociferously condemned societal injustices when he was imprisoned on charges of murder in 1967. He wrote:

> We are the victims and it is not something new
> If you open our heart you won't find anything but pain
> Not a day passed that has joy and cheer
> The universe above our heads is nothing but a black night

Our shoulders bow with grief
The burden of oppression cannot be measured in mere pounds.[23]

In the 1960s, antiestablishment writers, poets, and scholars intensified their activities to transform the status quo. Continuation of the struggle for a free and democratic society eventually paved the road to a new liberal era, when a new constitution was promulgated in 1964. A number of literary works, that is, poems, novels, short stories, and articles, were published during the constitutional period (1964–1973) that focused on social realism. Literary works that did not defy the legitimacy of the ruling class expanded when a republican regime was established in 1973. The regime promoted proestablishment intellectuals, writers, and scholars and awarded them prizes for their works, which were considered to have contributed to the development and expansion of Persian and Pushtu historical and modern literature. The ruling elite did not make efforts to support and encourage the development of literature in the languages of other ethnic communities, and instead forced them to read literary works in the Persian and Pushtu languages.

LITERARY DISCOURSE AFTER THE APRIL 1978 COUP

Radical literature became widely available after the promulgation of the 1964 constitution that permitted formation of political parties. Two types of radical literature emerged: pro-Soviet reformist and literature that stressed people's revolution and partisan struggle. When the pro-Soviet *Hizb-e-Demokratik-e-Khalq-e-Afghanistan* (the People's Democratic Party of Afghanistan, PDPA) seized power in 1978, it encouraged writers, poets, and scholars sympathetic toward its policies to reflect on ideas aimed at strengthening its base of support. It published the works of Noor Mohammad Taraki, President and General Secretary of the PDPA, and distributed them to bookstalls and libraries, and civil service employees were obligated to purchase copies. In so doing, the regime intended to artificially build Taraki's cult of personality. Party literature often mentioned that Taraki and the PDPA are body and soul that cannot be separated. Artists and screenwriters produced shows that demonized former rulers, and their works were displayed and shown at theaters in Kabul and in provinces. The main objective was to convince the public that the ruling party supports the cause of the people and defends their interests against those who exploit them and wish to reestablish their leadership.

Prominent writers within the pro-Soviet group were Asadullah Habib, Mohammad Hasan Bareq Shafii, Sulaiman Layeq, Akram Osman, Karim Misaq, Latif Nazimi, Azam Rahnaward Zaryab, and many others. They held key posts in the state bureaucracy and avoided condemnation of the subsequent Soviet occupation and their loyalty to the Russians earned them sobriquet "Soviet stooges." Although in their works they reflected the interests of the poor and blue-collar workers, in practice they repressed laborers, peasantry, and others who did not agree with state development policies. When the regime jailed and executed hundreds of intellectuals, poets, writers, and others, pro-Soviet writers depicted these people as reactionaries and antirevolutionaries.

Revolutionary and progressive literature defied coercive social measures and called for radical transformation of social, political, and economic structures. They exposed repressive state development policies and exploitation of the poor and dispossessed and urged the public to take matters into their own hands. A Pushtu folk poem expressed people's hatred toward Taraki and his regime for brutalizing the people. A portion of the poem reads:

O Taraki! May your grave catch fire,
Because you set our beloved country on fire.[24]

The regime arrested and executed individuals suspected of producing revolutionary literature. Prominent revolutionaries who were executed included Abdulillah Rastakhiz (1949–1979), Haidar Lahib (1947–1978), Abdul Majid Kalakani, and others. Kalakani was a partisan who devoted much of his time to revolutionary activities and admired self-sacrifice and revolutionary zeal in his writings. A portion of one of Kalakani's poems reads:

Toward dawn I draw a line from my blood
Oh! my destiny is tinged with this lovely Red
It is a message that conquers the night and guides travelers
It is the song of the spirited messengers.
I am a wounded eagle and you can kill me
But it is impossible to tame me for a second.[25]

The works of Wasif Bakhtari (b. 1942) have made a major contribution in the field of modern literature. Bahktari obtained a bachelor's degree in literature from Kabul University in 1966 and his master of arts degree from Columbia University in 1975. He remained in Afghanistan and neither condemned Russian imperialism when it invaded and occupied the country, nor denounced the perpetrators of the civil war that claimed the lives of many people and destroyed much of the country's infrastructure. The following poem shows his artistic expressions.

It is written on the leaf of every corn-poppy
Do not pick this flower

Do not snatch this pampered child from his
Mother's breast
But alas, the winds
Cannot read.[26]

LITERATURE DURING THE SOVIET OCCUPATION

Writers affiliated with the union of writers worked to rewrite the county's political history based on the political ideology of the ruling party. Efforts were made to discredit the works of independent and radical scholars and writers who did not agree with government policies, and the state called them enemies of the "revolution." Literary works from the Soviet Union and its bloc countries were made available to bookstores in Kabul and in major urban centers throughout the country. Articles, essays, poems, and cartoons were produced that demonized opponents of the regime (i.e., clerics, religious leaders, revolutionary and patriotic intellectuals). Scholars and writers who did not support cultural and artistic policies of the regime were arrested and jailed and some were executed. This situation forced many others to seek refuge in neighboring countries as well as in the West.

Sovietization of Afghanistan constituted one of the major preoccupations of the puppet regime. Literary works that did not conform to the established policy were purged from bookstores and the regime made concerted efforts to seek cooperation of scholars, writers, and artists to produce new genre of literary works that defended the regime's development policies. The publication of state-owned papers led to elimination of independent papers and literary works by the pro-Soviet *Tudeh* party of Iran that was made available to bookstores and libraries throughout the country.

Sovietization programs also led to the establishment of cultural and literary institutions that promoted the traditions, costumes, and cultural legacies of minority ethnic communities. In so doing, the regime intended to win the support of the minority ethnic communities. *Kanun-e-Farhangi Nasir Khusraw*, Nasir Khusraw Cultural Center, founded in Kabul conducted research on the history, literature, religion, and cultural legacies of the Isma'ili community that were denied recognition as a religious community in the past. The *Gharjistan* magazine published essays, poems, and research on the Hazaras, and intellectuals of other ethnic communities were provided with financial means to publish papers in their own languages.

RESISTANCE LITERATURE

Literary works that defied social and political oppression significantly flourished in the 1980s. Poets, artists, and writers who fought for liberty and human rights composed works that glorified those who opposed and fought the Soviet forces and the puppet regime. A Pushtu folk poem characterized the Soviet-installed leader Babrak Karmal as a traitor. A portion of the poem reads:

> O Babrak! Son of Lenin
> You do not care for the religion and the faith
> You may face your doom and
> May you receive a calamity, o! son of a traitor.
> O! son of Lenin.[27]

There were two types of resistance literature: religious oriented and secular. The former appealed to religious sentiments and called upon Muslims to oppose the Soviet-installed government and support Islamic fundamentalist parties in their *jihad* to establish an Islamic order. Secular resistance literature called upon the people to participate in the war of national liberation, appealed to people's nationalistic sentiments, and lauded individuals who gave their lives for the cause of the country's liberation. Nationalist, patriotic, and secular political groups and individuals promoted national unity and supported the establishment of a political structure that assured equality of ethnic communities. A poem by Nasir Nasib reads:

> What a day it will be when Pushtuns and Hazaras
> Do away with the bigotry once and for all
> Hazaras, Uzbeks, Pushtuns and Tajiks
> Be like intimate friends and comrades.[28]

Literature produced by Sunni and Shia political parties consistently promoted the concept of *jihad* and the establishment of an Islamic system of governance. Scholars and writers belonging to different ethnic groups focused exclusively on the study and research on history, costumes, traditions, cultures, and socioeconomic and political development of their respective communities. Radical and progressive literatures debated on what type of political structure would ensure political equality of ethnic communities, however, most literature published by Islamic fundamentalists opposed propagation of critical ideas concerning formation of a secular political structure and condemned such a trend as anti-Islamic. When the Soviet-backed regime collapsed in April 1992, Islamic militias fought one another for domination. Revolutionaries, liberals, and secular groups wrote their condemnation of the Islamic militias for the war that destroyed much of the country's infrastructure and claimed the lives of thousands of people.

Visual Arts

In ancient Afghanistan, arts and paintings were under the influence of Greco-Bactrian culture. Greek arts at its earlier stages was symmetrical and depicted Greek deities as full of strength and vigor. During the Buddhist period, arts and paintings were more reflective of human spirituality and ethical dimensions. Two of the world's tallest Buddha statues, 53 and 35 meters in height, had been carved on the face of a mountain cliff in Bamiyan and are among the most significant cultural and artistic legacies of Buddhism. The statues are called *Salsal,* symbol of a tall man, and *Shahmama,* meaning sturdy and strong woman or mother respectively by residents of Bamiyan. Paintings around the head of the statues are a reflection of advanced artistic works of the time. In February 2001, the Taliban militias destroyed the two statues considering them as anti-Islamic in nature. Representation of Buddha was symbolic at the beginning, just composed of a foot, a handprint, and so forth, but at a later time Buddha was portrayed in full human form in most works of art.[29]

When Islam came to Afghanistan it did not eliminate existing cultural heritages but adapted, refined, and integrated Greco-Bactrian and Buddhist arts, culture, and traditions. Artistic activities included miniature painting, engraving of epitaphs, and calligraphy. Calligraphers copied manuscripts in the *Kufi* style, which later evolved into *Nakhsh* supplemented by the works of illuminations that emerged in Herat. Artists used geometrical designs such as branches and leaves as headings in the first and last pages of a book chapter, and later on books' margins were decorated with illuminations such as flowers, animals, and human figures. The artists used gold, blue, and crimson colors for illuminations and lapis lazuli as the background color. Illuminations were later applied to chinaware, rugs, and carpets. The works of illuminations were divided into pre-Mughul, post-Mughul, and the Herat School of the Timurid era. The latter assumed a reputation for its miniature paintings that gradually established its dominance in the works of art. Behzad is the prominent artist of his time whose works are admired and serve as a source of inspiration for contemporary artists. However, these pieces of art and paintings failed to depict the lives of the poor, laborers, and marginalized groups that comprised the majority of the country's population.

Art and painting did not flourish until the sixteenth century because of the lack of material and facilities essential for production of such works and because the ruling class did not exhibit a keen interest in promoting and supporting the profession. People were poor and could not afford painting materials, even when they were available. Working under such conditions with no financial support made it difficult for impoverished artists to make ends meet. Calligraphy and miniature paintings were one of the few forms of artistic activity that continued to produce works because they did not require expensive materials for their production. In the early twentieth century, King Abd al-Rahman commissioned well-known artists and sculptors such as Mir Zamanuddin and Yari Baig who designed his two palaces, Koti Baghcha and Bostan Sarai, and decorated them with precious and semiprecious gems. A well-known artist Ghulam Mohammad visited Germany in 1921 and received training in lithography.[30]

In the 1930s, *Maktab-e-Sanay-e-Nafisa,* School of Fine Arts, was founded in Kabul by Ghulam Mohammad to train modern artists, painters, and sculptors. After his death in 1933, a renowned artist Abdul Ghafoor Brishna who added lithography, architecture, sewing, pottery, and tile making to the curricula headed the school. The School of Fine Arts received technical and professional support from Germany, while UNESCO and the United States provided funds for the Creative Center for Arts attached to the Teachers' Training College.[31] The state sponsored art shows and invited foreign artists residing in Kabul and local artists to exchange ideas about their works. Works of the artistic community were mainly oil paintings, watercolors of nature, human beings, and events related to significant religious or historic importance and some were displayed at a number of private art galleries.

The tradition of sculpting dates back to the Greco-Bactrian Buddhist period. Wars of conquest by invading tribes and empires destroyed much of the ancient arts, paintings, and sculpting. Modern sculpture emerged in the immediate post–World War II period when a number of students were sent to study in the West, the Soviet Union, and its bloc countries. Their artistic works did not gain public recognition except among the ruling elite and foreign expatriates. Modern sculpture did not have an immediate impact on the lives of the poor and the low- and middle-income families. Some of the works included sculpted birds, animals, jewelry boxes, ashtrays, and the like, made from marble and lapis lazuli and were largely promoted to foreign visitors.

The pro-Soviet regime encouraged artists and painters to produce works of art that were sympathetic to the cause of the working class. Artists and painters who did not abide by state policies were jailed and many were forced to leave the country. In exile, the artists produced works that depicted the suffering of the people both inside the country as well as in refugee camps in Pakistan and Iran. An intrepid group of young artists had embarked upon concerted efforts to revive calligraphy and miniature paintings because of the resurgence of renewed interest in these paintings that once embellished religious scriptures, mosques, and their religious institutions.

When the Islamic parties seized power they discouraged painting on the grounds that this activity drew people's attention away from spiritualism. The

One of the world-famous Gandhara Buddha statues that were destroyed by the Taliban regime in early 2001; only its 53-meter tall niche remains, Bamiyan, 2004.

Taliban militia destroyed most of the modern paintings and drawings that depicted human faces and removed them from the Kabul Museum and art galleries. Taliban religious leaders maintained that depicting human faces go against Islamic principles, and Taliban enforcement officers punished artists and painters who did not abide by their rulings.

PERFORMING ARTS

Performing arts existed in Afghanistan long ago in the courts of kings, where individuals sang songs, narrated jokes, and performed various acts and plays to the delight of the palace courts. Modern theater did not establish in the country until the twentieth century. The earliest form of public entertainment was the narration and recitation of epic poetry by individuals known as *Sadus*. These individuals used public places such as streets and parks to entertain people and relied on donations to continue their profession. This form of public entertainment gradually declined when a number of carnivals and theaters were built, and professionals called *Sayins* entertained the audience by performing plays often critical of the social and political environment. Fearing that continuation of this profession could negatively impact political stability, the ruling elite discouraged and censored such artistic and creative activities and did not provide the needed financial support that would ensure its survival.[32]

Families discouraged their children from pursuing such a career, and women were not allowed to perform in public because conservatives viewed women's engagement in such professions as a flagrant violation of the Islamic code of conduct, so male performers played female roles as needed. Performers and entertainers were often males who lacked professional training. Working in such a field was not rewarded with much remuneration, and people did not view the performing arts as an honorable profession.

Afghanistan is known for its vividly painted trucks, adorned with bright colors and designs. Favorite designs include landscapes, birds, flowers, and the moon, a significant Islamic symbol. This truck was parked on a roadside near the *Eid-gah* mosque in Kabul, 2003.

Performing arts was encouraged in the postindependence period when the state built a theater for women in Paghman, Kabul in 1921, to entertain housewives and help them relieve the tedium of their isolation. It also provided women with the opportunity to take time out from their daily routine of household chores. The theater was closed when conservative clerics opposed Amanullah's modernization programs and rebelled against him in 1929, viewing his policies including women's liberation as anti-Islamic. In the late 1930s, reformist intellectuals within the state apparatus decided to revive the theater and devise policies to support the performing arts. Their struggle yielded results when a group of artists participated in theatrical shows in Qandahar, Herat and Balkh.

The performing arts received a major boost in 1941 when the state built the *Pohani Nandari,* Theater of Education in Kabul, which remained under the censorship of the Ministry of Information and Culture. The state supported plays that reflected on themes such as the struggle for freedom and independence and plays by local writers with occasional performances of the works of French playwright Moliere. In 1947 a new theater, the Municipal Theater, was founded in Kabul[33] and a few years later the state built a theater in Qandahar and in Herat, and the number of theaters increased in subsequent years to the extent that most provincial centers had a theater. Local plays and films imported from India, Iran, the Soviet Union, and the West and were made available to the public. The state closely censored the shows in order to cut out scenes that they believed would be an affront to Islam and tribal cultural values and antagonize conservative clerics and religious leaders. As early as 1950s, a significant number of men and women performed in the public and gradually gained recognition as the social environment became conducive for their involvement in the domain of performing arts.

MUSIC AND DANCE

Music and dance constitute an integral part of the community's culture and traditions. Generally, music implies the use of instruments and song refers to poetry. Early music was basically in the form of hymns and sacred chants, the focus was on the underlying text, and so it was often classified as literature, not music. The concept of music as including instruments, musicians, and nonreligious lyrics developed as more secularized elements into society. During the Kushanid reign (ca. first–third centuries A.D.) music was accompanied by some dances and rituals associated with religion and when Alexander invaded the region the music assumed the mirthful form characteristic of the Greek life style.

The conquest of Afghanistan by the Arab Muslims led to the development of an unfavorable attitude toward music and musicians. Clerics associated music with the *Shaytan* (Satan) and musicians as Satan's agents who encouraged worshiping the devil. The end of Arab domination paved the road to the revival of monarchies that ignited changes in music to the extent that during the period of Ghaznawid rule, new requirements dictated the return to folk, court, and epic music. However, consolidation of reactionary trend toward music at a later time made the environment less conducive to music and caused many musicians to flee to India. Music flourished in India because the Indian culture was more receptive to its development and clerics had little or no control over people's lives. King Shir Ali (1868–1879) relied on the British for support against his internal rivals seeking Persian and Russian aid to seize power and initiated the entry of Indian music into Afghanistan. He provided musicians with all manner of support, which enabled them to achieve an artificially elevated status in society, which had a negative impact on the local community of musicians. Already burdened with the stigma attached to musicians by the people, local musicians struggled to survive, some altered their music style to be similar and some changed their names to mimic Indian names.[34]

In the nineteenth century there were two genres of music, Punjabi and Kabuli. The Punjabi style was introduced when a number of musicians from Punjab were brought to perform at the court of the kings in Kabul, and the Kabuli genre adopted the ragas of Indian music with a Kabuli version. Kabuli music was further developed in the 1920s as the liberal political environment provided fertile ground for its development. Renowned local singer Ustad Qasim sang Kabuli *ghazal* at Amanullah's court, and *ghazal* gradually assumed popularity to the extent that it established its influence as a popular art in several major cities such as Balkh, Herat, and Qandahar where musicians from Kabul performed and were applauded by the audience. These performers also trained a number of young local men in these cities to continue the tradition. A prominent singer of this school who commands considerable respect and recognition is Sarahang.

In the past, musicians and singers were men because strict local tradition prohibited women from playing musical instruments, singing songs, or dancing. Women could play musical instruments such as the *chang*, Persian harp also known as Jew's harp, and the *da-yereh*, commonly pronounced as *daira* (tambourine), during weddings and may sing songs, but only in women-only quarters. Musicians were invited to perform and entertain the audience at weddings, engagement ceremonies, and fairs. However, most people did not prefer their children to choose music and dance as their career because the profession was viewed as a trivial pursuit rather then an occupation that would support a family and some others even regarded it as a sinful activity. Musicians generally held a low position on the social scale, and very few members of the upper classes held or entertained musical ambitions. The distinction between professional and amateur musicians usually rested upon whether music was performed for compensation or for one's personal enjoyment, not upon skill or talent levels.

In the distant past, musicians generally were members of the barber community who also performed circumcisions. The occupation was regarded as lowly, and for this reason they were called by a variety of names including the derogatory name *dallak*. Musicians who played reed instruments were particularly despised because the reed is placed in the mouth in order to play instruments like the *sorna,* aerophone, and thus both the reed and the entire instrument were viewed as fowled with the musician's spittle, a concept highly offensive to society. Only professional musicians play the reed instruments, amateurs tend to shy away from them. Despite such negative attitudes, a small community of the Sufi order of Islamic mystics held favorable views of music and used musical instruments to accompany religious rituals.

People's attitude toward music changed considerably when it was broadcast by radio in the late 1950s and 1960s. The government honored outstanding local musicians and supported greater involvement of others in the profession. In the late 1960s, female singers such as Rukhshana, Parwin, and others who came mainly from upper-middle-class families became popular throughout the country.[35] Their entry into the field not only paved the road for other female singers and performers to pursue this career as their profession but also changed the public perception toward music and singing as a profession. The rise of pop singer Ahmad Zahir, son of Prime Minister Abdul Zahir—himself of a prominent Pushtun family, further contributed to the enhancement and public acceptance of music as a noble profession leading to the establishment of the Music School in Kabul in 1974. Prominent musicians include figures such as Mohammad Husain Sarahang, Abdul Ghafoor Brishna, Ghulam Husain, and many others. Well-known music composers are Salim Sarmast, Nainawaz, Arman, Nangialai, and others.

INSTRUMENTS

Musical instruments and technique vary along tribal and geographic orientation. Common musical instruments include the *dutar* which is a lute with a bowl-shaped body made from mulberry wood, a long neck, and two strings that are plucked when played; the Herati dutar commonly has three strings. The *dambura* is also a lute with a bowl-shaped body, long neck, two strings, and no frets. This instrument is also made from mulberry wood. The bowl is carved from a single section of the wood. The *tambur* is a long-necked lute with frets and metal strings. In Badakhshan this instrument is called *setar* and has only three strings. The *rabab* is a short-necked lute and has a waist like a violin, which is made of mulberry wood. It has three main strings of nylon and one of catgut. The *ghichak* is a distinctive instrument, because its body is typically made from a large metal tin can. It is a two-stringed fiddle played with a horsehair bow called a *kaman*. It is common to the central and northern regions of the country. The *soorna* is a cross between a flute and a clarinet, one that utilizes a double reed. When played it is usually accompanied by the *dohl,* double-headed drum. The *daira* or *daf,* is a tambourine, it only sometimes has the typical jangling metal pieces attached. The *zirbaghali* is a single-headed drum that has a body made of wood or pottery. It is shaped like a goblet with a wide drumhead and a tapered base.[36]

The most common instruments used to accompany Pushtun songs are the *harmonium, rabab, sarinda,* and *dohl.* Although all communities may use the same instruments, they distinguished themselves by developing unique techniques and modifying instruments to suit their purposes. Turkmen use two end-blown flutes such as *tuiduk* (a Turkish word that means reed) and the smaller and thinner *dili tuiduk* (tongue reed) known as *ney* in Persian. Turkmen musicians also play the *ghichak* and their version of the *dutar,* which is smaller than the typical *dutar.* Popular instruments among the Uzbeks include the *dambura* and the *ghichak.* Women and children play the *daira* and *chang.* Amateur Tajik musicians favor the Herati *dutar* and Tajik musicians in Badakhshan play the *dambura* and *tula,* wooden flute, as well as the *ghichak.* Hazara musicians play the *dambura* on occasions such as festivals and weddings. The Baluchi musical instruments include end-blown flutes, the *rabab,* and the *dambura.*

WESTERN MUSIC

Western music established its influence in the early 1960s when a number of students returned from studying in the West and foreign tourists visited the country in large numbers, mostly young Americans who did not want to fight in the Vietnam War. Western music largely catered to the interest of foreigners and Western-educated members of the upper and upper-middle classes. There were two bands, the Stars and the Four Brothers, playing Western music, rock music at the Khaybar Restaurant and Hotel and the Inter-Continental Hotel and later at private parties and during picnics held at Paghman, Kabul. Other popular Western music forms such as jazz and rock and roll were played in exclusive restaurants and Western music enthusiasts

Pottery salesman plays a Tabla, a musical instrument made of clay and animal skins, to entice his customers, Jada-e-Maiwand, Kabul, 2003.

built clubs known as M and M, the Discotheque, the 25 Hour Club, and the No. 9 Club in Kabul.[37]

Public Dancing

Public dancing is common among all ethnic communities, and it is performed on special occasions such as weddings, festivities, or fairs. For example, Hazara women perform a dance known as *peshpo* when they welcome a new bride. In some Pushtun settled areas, men and women dance in celebration of a wedding when they leave the bridegroom's house and proceed toward the bride's house. *Atan* is a special type of dance performed by a troupe of 50 to 100 dancers who wave red scarves in the air while musicians beat drums. This dance is common among the Pushtuns and the ruling elite promoted it as a national dance of Afghanistan.

Dancing by men and women together increasingly gained momentum among the educated and upper- and middle-class urban families in the 1970s and afterward. The pro-Soviet regime encouraged young men and women to defy traditional values and participate in these public activities. Men and women members of the ruling party and its sympathizers performed dances in public that were widely broadcast via television. Dancing, whether at the private home or in the public, was prohibited when the Islamic parties seized power and severely punished those who defied the ruling, as they regarded dancing to be against Islamic values. The Taliban's religious police beat those caught playing music and dancing at weddings and other celebratory occasions. After the United States launched a military offensive that toppled the Taliban and installed Hamid Karzai as head of the state, warlords and remnants of hard-line conservatives who still dominated the state bureaucracy continue to oppose women singing and performing in the public.

CINEMA

In 1946, Afghanistan's first film, *Eishq wa Dusti* (Love and Friendship), was produced. Abdul Rashid Latifi wrote the script and local actors Abdul Rahman Bina, Abdul Latif Nishat, along with a number of Indian actors produced the film in India and then showed it in a theater in Kabul. Fourteen years later, the Ministry of Information and Culture founded the Afghan Film Department, which produced short documentaries on local events and played at theaters just before the main show. *Roozgaran* is the first motion picture produced by the Afghan Film Department. In the mid-1970s, Nazir Film, a private film industry, began its operation in Kabul and produced *Rabia Balkhi*. Other private film industries at this time were Aryana Film, Shafaq Film, Gulistan Film, and Qais Film. Young actors and actresses competed for stardom. The state did not provide needed support to independent film industries, and it was responsible for importing foreign movies. The pro-Soviet regime instructed the state-owned film industry to produce shows that glorified the struggle of the ruling party in building a new society. A number of professionals who were forced to leave the country and sought refuge in the neighboring countries and the West produced shows and plays that depicted people's inspiration for freedom and their struggle to reform rigid social contracts that inhibited free thinking.

NOTES

1. Mohammad Haidar Jobel, *Tarikh-e-Adabiyat-e-Afghanistan* [History of Literature in Afghanistan] (Kabul, Afghanistan: Maiwand Publication Center, 1382/2003), pp. 28–38.

2. *Afghanistan* (Kabul, Afghanistan: Aryana Encyclopedia, 1955), p. 200.

3. *Afghanistan*, p. 166.

4. *Afghanistan,* p. 167.

5. A. Benawa, "Landay," in *Afghanistan,* ed. Louis Dupree (Karachi, Pakistan: Oxford University Press, 2002), p. 90.

6. Naghat, "Shiwaha wa dawraha-e nasr-e Farsi" [Styles and periods of Persian prose writing] *Adab* 10, no. 4 (1341/1962): 11–12.

7. K. Habibi, "A Glance at Literature: A Box of Jewels," in *Afghanistan,* ed. Louis Dupree (Karachi, Pakistan: Oxford University Press, 2002), p. 78.

8. Hashmatullah Riyazi, *Gulha-e az Gulistan-e Shair-e Farsi: Az Rabia ta Parwin* [Flowers from the Persian garden of poetry: from Rabia to Parwin], vol. 1 (Tehran, Iran: Nashr-e Pardis, 1380/2001), p. 31.

9. Nasir Khusraw, *Diwan-e-Ashar-e Hakim Nasir Khusraw Qubadiyani Ba Zamima-e-Roshnayinama, Saadatnama, Muqtaat wa adabiyat-e Mutafariqa az Roye Nuskha-e Tashih shuda-e Marhoom Taqizada Hamra-e Sharh-e-Hal wa Tahlili Tarikhi wa Eijtima-e Dawran-e-Ao* [Collection of Nasir Khusraw Qubadiyani's Poetry including his works, Roshnayinama, Saadatnama, short poems and miscellaneous articles produced from the printed copy edited by the late Taqizada with his biography and socio-historical analysis of his time] (Tehran, Iran: Nashr-e-Chakama, 1361/1982), p. 242.

10. Nasir Khusraw, *Diwan-e-Ashar,* p. 36.

11. Nasir Khusraw, *Diwan-e-Ashar,* p. 667.

12. Mohammad Salih Rasikh Yaldram, *Tarikh wa Farhang-e-Turkman-ha* [History and culture of Turkmens] (Kabul, Afghanistan: Anjuman-e-Farhangi Makhdum Quli Feraghi, 1381/2002), pp. 158–181.

13. Hakim K. Taniwal, "The Impact of Pashtunwali on Afghan Jihad," *Writers Union of Free Afghanistan, WUFA* 2, no. 1 (January–March 1987): 11.

14. M. I. Negargar. "Afghan Folk Literature after Soviet Invasion," *Writers Union of Free Afghanistan, WUFA* 2, no. 2 (April–June 1987): 80.

15. Faiz Mohammad Katib. *Seraj al-Tawarikh* [Torch of History], Vols. 1–2 (Kabul, Afghanistan: Ministry of Education, 1331/1952), p. 177.

16. Mir Ghulam Mohammad Ghubar, *Afghanistan dar Masir-e-Tarikh* [Afghanistan in the path of history] (Tehran, Iran: Entisharat-e Jamhoori, 1995), p. 624.

17. Ghubar, *Afghanistan dar Masir-e-Tarikh,* p. 638.

18. Cited in Vartan Gregorian, *The Emergence of Modern Afghanistan: Politics of Reform and Modernization, 1880–1946* (Stanford, CA: Stanford University Press, 1969), p. 167.

19. Ghubar, *Afghanistan dar Masir-e-Tarikh,* p. 718.

20. Khal Mohammad Khasta, *Yadi az Raftagan: Mushtamil bar biyugrafi edda-e-az Shuara-e-Kishwar* [Remembering the passed away figures: Including biography of a number of the country's poets] (Kabul: Ministry of Press and Information, Government Press, 1344/1965), pp. 33–34.

21. Mohammad Kazem Ahang, *Sayr-e Journalism dar Afghanistan* [Chronology of Journalism in Afghanistan] (Peshawar, Pakistan: Maiwand Publication Centre, 1379/1999), pp. 139–219.

22. Riyazi, *Gulha-e az Gulistan-e Shair-e Farsi,* vol. 2, p. 355.

23. Nooruddin Rawnaq Naderi, *Armaghan-e-Zendan*. Handwritten collection of Naderi's poems by Ewaz Akif (Karachi, Pakistan, 2000), p. 39.

24. Negargar, "Afghan Folk Literature after Soviet Invasion," p. 88.

25. Abdul Majid Kalakani's poems have not been published but copies are available with Kalakani's friends.

26. Nimat Husaini, *Sima-ha wa Awa-ha* [Pictures and Sounds], vol. 1 (Kabul, Afghanistan: Government Press, 1367/1988), pp. 79–84.

27. Negargar, "Afghan Folk Literature after Soviet Invasion," p. 85.

28. Ali Dad Lali, *Sayri dar Hazarajat: Tahlil-e Jamia Shenasi-e Mazhabi, Siyasi, Ejtimaei, Farhangi, wa Akhlaqi Jamia-e Tashayu dar Afghanistan* [An excursion to Hazarajat: Sociological analysis of religion, politics, society, culture, and ethics of the Shia community in Afghanistan] (Qum, Iran: Ehsani, 1372/1993), p. 272.

29. Ghubar, *Afghanistan dar Masir-e-Tarikh*, pp. 32–58.

30. Enayatullah Shahrani, "The History of Fine Arts in Afghanistan," *Afghanistan* 26, no. 3 (December 1973): 20.

31. Shahrani, "The History of Fine Arts in Afghanistan," p. 20.

32. M. Ismailpur, "Tiyater dar Afghanistan [Theater in Afghanistan]," *Dur-e-Dari* nos. 9–10 (Spring and Summer 1378/1999): 91–94.

33. Gregorian, *The Emergence of Modern Afghanistan*, p. 358.

34. Hiromi Lorraine Sakata, *Music in the Mind: The Concepts of Music and Musician in Afghanistan* (Kent, Ohio: Kent State University Press, 1983), pp. 83–84.

35. See also, Hafizullah Emadi, *Repression, Resistance, and Women in Afghanistan* (Westport, CT: Praeger Publishers, 2002).

36. For details on musical instruments, see Sakata, *Music in the Mind: The Concepts of Music and Musician in Afghanistan*.

37. Louis Dupree, "It Wasn't Woodstock, but the First International Rock Festival in Kabul." *The American Universities Field Staff, AUFS* 20, no. 2 (May 1976): 1–11.

4

Architecture, Housing, and Settlements

Architectural style as seen in Afghanistan's structures, homes, and monuments is a result of mutual influences. Public architecture in Afghanistan demonstrates the country's unique position as a crossroads of ancient cultures and the successive visions of domestic and invading rulers, as well as the gradual and pervasive influence of Islam that altered centuries of secular and other religious influences. Domestic architecture, both rural and urban, reflects the history and lifestyles of the many types of people who reside in the country, and they in turn were influenced by the country's climate and geography and the need to adapt to survive.

PUBLIC ARCHITECTURE

In Afghanistan, public architecture, as expressed in the country's monuments, places of worship, and other public structures, was formed over the centuries as a succession of cultural traditions established their dominance, as immigrants and invaders built grandiose palaces and tombs, quietly dignified mosques, and vibrant gardens that reflected various architectural styles and building techniques. In contrast, domestic architecture (residential homes, teahouses, public baths, etc.) developed in a more consistent manner, reflective of a simple lifestyle and more attuned to climate and geography, and subject to the availability of building materials and the builder's skills. These factors exerted a stronger influence than customs prevailing at the time, as new settlers shared their design skills and methods with their neighbors, and building techniques were developed to adapt to environment and climate, enabling Afghanistan's architecture to evolve into having unique character and meaningful form.

INFLUENCE OF ENVIRONMENT

Immigrants and invading armies followed rivers and marched through valleys to reach different areas in the country and left their traditions and lifestyles in their wake. The northern region of the country reflects the cultural influence of Central Asia, while ancient Persia and Gandharan India left their own stamps on the politics and culture of the Kabul River Valley. Greco-Bactrian influences during 200 B.C.–400 A.D. also contributed to the evolving architectural styles in these areas. Bamiyan is the site of the most famous examples of Gandharan art, reflected in its monasteries and temples, although almost none have survived intact to the present day. The remains of two giant Buddha statues in Bamiyan stand in niches carved out of the massive sandstone cliffs—one 35 meters and the other 53 meters in height. The geometric shapes of the niches and cavernous assembly halls cut into the rock and extending almost two kilometers throughout the cliffs are all that remains of the building techniques of ancient Gandhara (now eastern Afghanistan and the northern Punjab), which was itself influenced by Greco-Bactrian and Sassanian styles.[1]

Architectural monuments from other traditions can be found elsewhere in the country, from Greek columns in Aikhanum, Buddhist stupas (shrines) and monasteries in Jalalabad, Samangan, and Minar-e Chakari, south of Kabul, as well as Persian minarets and public gardens, and the famous *Bala Hisar* fort. Islamic influences can be seen in such famous structures from the period as the Lashkari Bazaar (Lashkargah) and the 1,000-year-old Great Arch of *Qalah-e-Bost* in Helmand, the two "Towers of Victory" in Ghazni, the ancient mosque of Herat, the famous mosque of *No-gunbad* and the mausoleum of Ali in Balkh, the *Chel Zina*, Forty Steps in Qandahar, the tomb of Babur, and the mausoleum of Timur Shah in Kabul.

The minaret is a major architectural tradition in Afghanistan. A minaret is a tower that is erected near a religious building for the purpose of making that structure noticeable from a far distance. The word comes from the Arabic "minar," lighthouse, in which a fire "nar" would burn to guide ships. Minarets are usually circular or conical in shape (very early Persian versions were square), and there are minarets in Ghazni that are star-shaped. The gigantic, three-story, conical minaret of Jam built by the Ghorid king Ala al-Din in 1149 rises two hundred feet high out of a deep gorge. It is covered with stucco and deeply carved with the floral and geometric patterns typical of Persian design. This ornamentation is interwoven with bands of Arabic calligraphy in a style known as *Kufic,* inscribed with an entire chapter of the Quran. While portions of its platform have broken away, the minaret is still standing today.[2]

Housing

Afghanistan's unique domestic architecture takes two distinct forms: clusters of indigenous mud-walled houses and cotton and wool tents that reflect their Central Asian origins. The tents that stand on hilly grass-covered plateaus overlooking agricultural fields were made of wool, felt, or goat's hair, depending on the location and ethnicity of its occupants. Pushtun nomads, also known as Kochi, favored the black goat's hair tents. White cotton tents were typical residences of seasonal migrants from eastern Afghanistan known as "Sheikh Mohammadi." Sturdy, felt-covered yurts built by Central Asian migrants stood against the elements in the cold northern areas. Houses were built with mud-brick walls, and wooden frames supported mud-covered roofs. Mud houses in Kabul may also have an intervening sheet of heavy

Traditional family compound in Shibar, Bamiyan, 2004. Typical of housing in rural areas in Afghanistan, the *pakhsa* walls of this home were constructed in the 1950s.

plastic underneath the mud to make the roof waterproof. These structures are found in abundance along the major riverbanks and valleys and at the foot of mountains. Walled compounds constructed of mud and stone are found in the desert lands, houses in the mountainous areas of Jalalabad are formed almost entirely from stones or carved out of caves in Bamiyan, and clusters of wood frame dwellings perch precariously on the edges of steep cliffs in Nooristan.

Housing construction styles at the village level did not vary significantly over the centuries because the methods and styles that were developed suited the environment and took advantage of locally abundant building materials. Newly introduced building techniques that were retained over time tended to improve on existing designs. The *memar,* master builder or architect, adapted his work to meet the challenges posed by the diverse, vast, and often-severe environment of Afghanistan. The thick-walled mud houses common to Afghanistan were not only cost effective to build, with abundantly available materials, and did not require specialized masonry skills to construct, they also served to insulate occupants against heat in the summer months and kept them warm in the winter. (See also further sections on housing in this chapter.)

THE ARCHITECT

Well-known Muslim historian Ibn-Khaldun (1332–1406) described the ideal architect *(memar)*. In his view, the architect is a combination of artist, designer, builder, mathematician, urban planner, and lawyer. To make homes and buildings comfortable to live in, he must be able to control, leverage, or repel the elements: light, air, humidity, dampness, dryness, and temperatures that fluctuate between freezing and baking. The *memar* must be able to foresee the effects of natural calamities such as earthquakes and floods, and plan and design structures that will stand regardless. In crowded cities, the man-made obstructions that accompany population density intrude, and the *memar* must design structures that provide access to rights of way, natural light, and privacy for its inhabitants. The *memar* must be able to plan, design, and build, while considering myriad constraints and incorporating available building materials. His profession requires an intimate familiarity with all the structural components of the buildings he designs, as well as the culture and lifestyles of the people who will live within these buildings. A home for one group of people in an area with heavy commercial traffic, like that of Shor Bazar in Kabul, may require rooms that can not be viewed from a doorway, or a mesh structure constructed at an angle that allows a view to the outside but not of the interior, in order to provide privacy to the women of a family

View of the Shah-e-Dushamshirah mosque in a busy intersection next to the banks of the Kabul River, Kabul, 2004.

while still affording them a view of the outside. Another building may require lightweight construction to accommodate multiple stories so that extended families can reside within, or homes may be designed so family members can work on their roofs, and so on. An architect must be able to account for the local climate and fulfill the basic needs of the human inhabitants with his work, while using available and affordable tools and materials. Architects are also responsible for planning, designing, and supervising the construction of structures that require elaborate design and craftsmanship and are intended to house, serve, or accommodate an entire community or class of people, such as mosques and other religious centers, palaces, government and commercial buildings, bridges, and caravanserai.[3]

Various artisans and tradesmen in Afghanistan that engage in architectural design and construction are members of a longstanding guild system for the skilled trades. They elect one of their own to serve as their liaison to the local state functionaries and to take care of administrative details while they pursue their trade. The veterans in a particular trade who have achieved the highest skills and knowledge of their craft, are known as master *(ustad)*. Generally, masters own their own shops and will train their sons or immediate family members as apprentices, which is why certain skills may run in families.

Those who no longer actively practice their trade become teachers and mentors, imparting their knowledge and wisdom to instill discipline and professional ethics into succeeding generations of tradesmen.[4]

RELIGIOUS AND SECULAR ARCHITECTURE

As Islam spread through the country, building mosques *(Masjids)* replaced the Persian palaces and Buddhist monuments as the new cultural foci for the country. Mosques are designed and built to welcome and serve all Muslims, whether a dispossessed wanderer, farmer, merchant, or a wealthy chief. The mosque is not only a place of worship but also provides a basic educational institution in the religious school *(madrasa)* and libraries that are usually found attached to larger mosques. The most recognizable mosque shape is the pavilion, which, at its most basic, consists of a domed roof over a square chamber. Other common shapes include the barrel vault or open *diwan,* which resembles an elongated arch, and the "Arab plan," an open court surrounded by arcades, which are lines of arches supported by pillars or columns.[5] All mosques have a prayer niche indicating the direction to Kaaba in Mecca, as well as a minaret from which a *muezzin* gives the call to prayer. Larger mosques also have a pulpit used for Friday sermons. Inside the open courtyard of mosques there is always a fountain for people to perform ablutions, older mosques may have a pool or other water source.

The Timurid leader Shah Rukh (1405–1447) and his wife Gawhar Shad were behind the first ambitious construction of a mosque and a *madrasa,* the Gawhar Shad School, outside the city of Herat. The school had a large library and a guesthouse. The building had high walls and minarets decorated with colorful enameled tiles and illuminations. What is left of the ruins of the complex is a domed structure that residents of Herat refer to as the Green Dome.[6] Another Timurid leader, Sultan Hussain Bayiqara (1470–1506), built a covered bazaar, a hospital, and a *madrasa* in Herat in 1504. This series of complexes had courtyards in their center and were surrounded by arcades and hallways crowned with domed and vaulted ceilings. Four minarets rose from a marble base, covered with colored and glazed tiles and topped by domes crowned with stone or marble stalactites.

Public architectural activity was not confined to religious monuments and palaces. Highly skilled specialists also built impressive constructions to serve the local needs of commerce and industry: bridges, bazaars, fortifications, gardens, and the uniquely Persian caravanserais. Caravanserais were multipurpose structures that usually contained a toll or customs house, amenities such as kitchens and baths, and, at the more remote frontier locations, defensive structures. These were built with recreation in mind as much as security and transit, and great attention was paid toward planning for the movement of people and their pack animals. Travelers could stop for rest, refreshment, or entertainment.[7]

Caravanserais were necessary to stimulate trade and to protect caravans in Afghanistan traversing the long distances between major commercial centers and towns. The dangers to merchants and other travelers included the harsh natural climate and windstorms as well as threats of bandits and other marauders. A secure site was needed for stopping and resting, and fortified, semicircular, manned posts at the corners of the caravanserai were established for defense of the local population and to shelter caravans in exposed territories. Such structures were built in a time when economic life, dominated by individuals (farmers, herdsmen, merchants) occurred in a domestic environment, and human activity and commerce was the chief design concern.

A caravanserai plan is either square, round, or octagonal, with defensive towers at the angles. It varies in size but is essentially concentric, with a thick outer wall allowing access through a single gate. Just inside the peripheral wall is the stable, which is only accessible by a series of passages intended to prevent easy access to the animal quarters. Every effort is made to protect a guest's pack animals because their theft would mean a loss of transportation, and effectively death to their owners, especially in remote areas. The central court was surrounded by open arcades, up to two rooms deep, and contained fireplaces for cooking or to provide heat. Sleeping quarters for travelers were located near the center and were elevated several feet above ground level, also for security purposes. There may be luxurious rooms on the roof and overlooking the main entry gate for housing wealthy travelers. The massive outer walls are made of stones, while interiors walls were usually made of fired brick or sun-dried brick, sometimes combined with stone, if available in the area. A layer of plaster applied over the brick to smooth it out may also be decorated with painted murals or enameled tiles.[8]

ORNAMENTATION IN BUILDINGS

Structural ornamentation is rendered in different materials: stucco, wood (often carved into intricate and beautiful geometrical patterns in railings and ceilings), precious and semiprecious metals used for window gratings and ceremonial doorways, and mosaic faience, a technique which employs colorful tiles and tile fragments.

Stucco as architectural ornament was extensively used in Afghanistan. The carving process is not easy, it involves wet plaster applied to a wall and worked on by the artisan who must carve out the mostly geometrical patterns (combinations of triangles, circles, squares) before the plaster dries and hardens.

After drying, the plaster is cut and polished until it resembles marble. The stucco carver must work quickly and work in sections before the plaster hardens. The most intricate work involves deeply cut patterns, giving the surface a three-dimensional look, built up in separately worked layers.[9]

The use of enameled tile and mosaic faience for decoration is a uniquely Persian technique that emerged in the twelfth century, first used mostly to decorate the prayer niche and later the entrance gate of mosques (expanding in use and peaking in popularity in the fourteenth and fifteenth centuries). Mosaic faience employs tiny pieces of tiles, individually baked and painted, and was originally used as a method for making decorative pottery and decorating the archways of niches, but gradually developed into an art form that covered entire mosques and monuments.

The process for creating mosaic faience is painstaking and complex. Tile patterns are first drawn to exact scale on heavy paper or on a flat table of plaster, and the artisan decides on the different colors to use. Clay tiles are painted and baked to his exact specification, and then cut by chisel, sanded, and individually fitted into the design, set colored side downward on the pattern, after which the tile backs are covered with stiff plaster. When light shines on a finished piece, it reflects at every angle and affects the perception of colors in each tile differently.

It takes a skilled artisan to work in this art form. The colors in the tiles when fired shine at different temperatures, and determining the best temperatures to bring out just the right level of vivid color is a skill learned over time and practice. Early mosaic tiles generally employed colors of blue, white, and turquoise, and they do not fade in the unforgiving Central Asian climate because of their sources. For example, the particularly striking azure blue color is made from grinding the semiprecious stone lapis lazuli. The harsh dry and severe cold climates in Afghanistan have much less deleterious effect on the colored, baked tiles than they would on a painted decoration, so this art form is used for external application. Whole buildings when covered with these brilliantly colored tiles look as if the designs were painted on.[10]

DOMESTIC ARCHITECTURE

Domestic architecture in Afghanistan provides shelter, security, and a place for work and social life for families and clans. Structures and arrangement of their interiors reflect the lifestyle of the community. A distinct regional architecture evolves as experience with the physical environment determines what techniques and methods will and will not last. Climate and geography determine whether air circulation or heat conservation must be a design priority, while cultural traditions determine how buildings and rooms are configured and whether the house is to be a permanent or a temporary, portable structure. Within tradition are variations that are influenced by the context of ethnicity, income, and social status. Central commerce hubs, where different groups interact frequently, may serve to disseminate new design and construction methods to emulate.[11]

BUILDING MATERIALS AND TECHNIQUES

Afghanistan's architecture does not follow a single tradition or take its influence from a single culture, but variations in construction style are relatively few, in large part because of constraints like availability of suitable construction materials. Basic infrastructure building styles generally take three forms: *pakhsa,* thick walls of mud that are mixed with hay and compressed, common in villages because it is affordable; *khesht-e-kham,* sun-dried bricks of pressed mud, common in the country; and *khesht-e-pukhta,* fired bricks, most often found in modern buildings in the cities throughout the country.

Widespread use of the *pakhsa* technique in wall formation was due as much to the abundance of heavy clays in the country as well as its simplicity: soil is mixed with water into a mud mixture and then trod underfoot until it is thickened, then is pressed firmly onto a foundation in a series of separately dried layers. Typically, pits are dug near the construction site and the mud mixture is created a day or two before construction begins so that it will be of the right consistency.

Erosion from groundwater is a serious problem for mud-based structures, so as an added measure to ensure the strength of the *pakhsa* walls, a solid foundation of stone is laid. Builders will begin by digging a trench about half a meter deep and filling it with stone to just above ground level so that the wall stands above the ground. The walls are built in a series of layers, each of which is allowed to dry before the next layer is added. Chunks of mud are pressed or thrown with force onto the stone foundation until it forms a horizontal tier about half a meter high. The mud is shaped with a shovel as needed and then it is left to dry. More horizontal tiers are added; each is allowed to dry before the next one is formed, until the wall reaches about three meters in height. Each wall is topped with a poplar pole along its length, and additional poplar poles are laid across the walls and nailed to the pole to form the base of the roof. Reed mats or thin tree branches or sticks are laid over the poles and they in turn are covered with several layers of the claylike mud. Flat-roof construction is not entirely so—to prevent rainwater from collecting on the roof, it is actually built with a slight slope so that water will slide off. The mud layers offer moderate protection from the elements but require diligent maintenance to prevent damage from snow or standing water. Normally, each spring after the snow has melted and the spring rains have ended, people put another layer of mud on the walls and the roof. Some do this before the next winter comes. It is labor intensive but less costly than replacing the wooden roof supports.[12]

Pakhsa is also used in constructing the peripheral walls of the fortified compound *(qalah)*. A *qalah* is usually square or oblong in shape, and typically members of a single extended family or clan build their homes within a *qalah*. This is different from a walled village, which comprises an irregularly shaped cluster of closely built houses whose outer walls join together to create a common barrier to the outside and which lack defensive towers, which are a distinctive and integral part of a *qalah* and are to be found rising above each corner. There are very few that still remain standing, and they are not constructed anymore. The traditional *qalah* was constructed in a time when villages had small populations on average, and long distances separated these communities from commercial centers and from each other. As modernization encroached and populations grew, there was an accompanying lack of space within communities and increased need for building materials. It became less practical and more expensive to build a fortress, even for a large family. The single front entrance in smaller modern compounds is the remaining vestige of security features common to the once-imposing fortress homes.

Qalah construction begins with the outer walls built in the *pakhsa* style and the digging of a trench for its stone foundation. The mud chunks that form the successively built layers are shaped with shovels and left to dry. The perimeter of a *qalah* is built thicker at its base, usually a little more than a meter thick, and gradually decreases in thickness as it is built upward so the walls have a tapered look. The defensive towers at the corners also serve to stabilize the walls. A layer of thin stones that are cut to have sharp edges are laid on top of the last mud layer and project slightly at the edge, an additional measure of protection for the compound. A final layer of mud covers the tops of the walls, it is shaped in rounded fashion to prevent damage from erosion. Inside the *qalah,* major supporting walls are also built in the *pakhsa* style, while walls for interior rooms may be built of sun-dried bricks held together with mud. When these walls and their roof supports are completed, a thick layer of wall plaster, comprised of water, clay, and lukh (part of a locally grown marshland plant), is applied on it that makes the wall surfaces smoother and amenable to ornamentation. The final step is construction of the roof, which is usually made from wooden poles, branches, and reed mats and finished off with layers of mud.[13]

Despite the ease and affordability of building flat-roofed homes, they are not ubiquitous across the country because wood, necessary for roof support, is scarce in some areas. In areas where wood is scarce, domed and vaulted ceilings may outnumber flat roofs in some areas because these structural types do not require wooden beams for ceiling and roof support.[14] Domed roofs may also be a personal preference, even when wood is available, as is the case in Mazar, Balkh. In Paktiya, Logar, and Kabul regions, the flat roof is preferred because wet conditions and snow is only a structural challenge in winter. The walls themselves may still be built with the less expensive *pakhsa* technique for more modest homes, but the ceilings and roof will employ bricks, which are lighter and more flexible than heavy clumps of mud and are better able to support a curved form.

Domes and vaults are similar in construction, but they differ most in the dimensions of the structure they are built upon. Both structures originate from the basic arch form. An arch rotated in a circle forms a dome shape, and an arch that is extended or elongated until it looks like a tunnel or long curved roof supported by two walls is a vault. Domes are built to sit on walls of square shaped buildings and vaults are used on structures with a rectangular shape. These brick-based structures offer advantages in desert climates, where temperatures climb on hot days and plunge on cold nights. In hot weather the higher curved ceilings within allow warm air inside the dwelling to rise above the occupants and escape through a small opening in the top of the dome, and thus keep the dwelling cool. The thick walls that support the curved roofs also serve to incubate a home against heat loss in cold weather.[15]

Construction of domed and vaulted ceilings begins at the corners where the four main walls meet. Masons create squinches (a small arch made of bricks) to serve as a base that supports the layers of bricks in the ceiling. Several arches are arranged on each corner, with the smallest arch at the corner and inclining outward until it looks like a kind of half shell. The remainder of the dome consists of layers of bricks arranged in a circular pattern that gradually decreases in circumference until they meet at the rounded top. A vaulted roof is built in much the same way, beginning with a squinch at each corner, but since the walls are in a rectangular shape, the infilling of bricks is slightly different. Instead of a series of shrinking circles of bricks, the bricks are arranged in a series of extended arches beginning at each short end of the rectangle, and arches are added as they meet in the middle. When completed, the roof is covered with additional layers of a mud plaster mixed with pieces of straw that give added protection.[16]

To achieve the perception of a flat roof in a structure with domed or vaulted ceilings, a construction technique called *khancha-poosh* is employed that involves adding plaster to the sides of the vault or dome, covering it until a square or rectangular flat outer roof is visible inside. This construction uses fired bricks to create the vault, which is more expensive but more resilient and able to support the extra weight of the plaster in the flat roof. Builders will create these higher-grade fired or "burnt" bricks by making sun-dried bricks and then firing them in a kiln. This design requires meticulous measurement and calculation of weight and stress, so only the most skilled architects can employ this form.

Stone is a common building material in areas along rivers and on mountain slopes where it is found in abundance. In other areas where it is less abundant, it is used primarily for building foundations. Stone is durable, but it is also difficult to transport and cut to shapes, so the use of brick construction and masonry is more common in more parts of the country.

The higher altitude mountainous regions experience severely cold winters and the large amounts of snow and ice would be very destructive to mud-based dwellings. Stone is the abundant building material and is used to make thick-walled houses (the spaces between the stones are filled with clay) that insulate its occupants from the cold. Wood and clay roofs are built with a slope to prevent water from pooling but still require a lot of maintenance and must be replaced every two to three years.[17]

In the regions where mountains are thickly forested, post and beam construction is used in the wood and stone buildings common to the area. Homes are precariously perched on cliffs and do not allow for use of larger or bulkier tools, which must be carried to the building site. In Paktiya, two-story houses are constructed and roofed with slate. They are built close together and stacked, like a series of terraces. Ladders are needed to climb from roof to roof.

Wood-frame houses are a good choice for urban areas with dense population, as these light-weight constructions are suitable for vertical building. A popular method, known as *senj* construction, is a wood-frame building system that employs cross-braced beams and sun-dried brick infillings, which combine to create a lightweight, flexible structure that can tolerate growth in the form of added rooms or stories. In *senj* construction, most of the frame construction is done on the ground, then all pieces are assembled. The roof is made of wooden boards and brush is placed at right angles to the joists, next its covered with layers of reeds, and then the entire roof is covered with several layers of mud. Although it is generally flat, the roof is built to slope slightly so that snow and water will not collect but rather run off the edge. [18]

Cave dwellings may be found in regions with sandstone, which is stable but can be cut and large openings can be carved out with hand tools. These types of dwellings are not usually used for homes. Occasionally, caves have been known to serve as residences in the Hazarajat Region in Bamiyan, and in the prewar years they were increasingly used only to house farm animals. More recently, some poor families in the area have taken up residence in caves after their homes were destroyed in the country's long civil war.

ARCHITECTURE IN MAJOR URBAN CENTERS

Modern influences and traditional ways often meet in major urban and commercial centers because of the diversity of the traffic and the higher average income of its residents, which allows more expression of cultural preferences. Kabul, Afghanistan's modern capital, follows somewhat the pattern of traditional provincial centers that were built as fortresses, although instead of a perimeter of massive walls, the surrounding mountains served as the city's primary defense perimeter, and seven gates controlled access to the city; however, none of them remain standing today. Bala Hisar was the center of old Kabul and the nearby *Mandawi bazaar* was the main commercial center. The British destroyed the *Charchata* bazaar in retaliation for the murder of their envoy William Macnaghten in 1841.[19] At least one place bears the name of its traditional gate, *Lahori Darwaza*, "Lahore Gate." Kabul was informally divided into an old section and new section, and the old section reflects traditional housing construction patterns, including bazaars with two-story buildings, with a store on the ground floor and housing on the upper floor.[20]

Houses in the contemporary section of Kabul follow a grid pattern, with rows of structures of varying size and shape, with mostly flat roofs, and walls two to three meters in height made primarily from fired brick. Just inside the main entryway there is a reception room where men will greet guests. The reception area may in some cases open out into a spacious courtyard. The women of the family are hidden from casual view in another room toward the back of the home, and a small kitchen with a fireplace is the third major space in a typical home.

The city started to expand in the 1940s. New districts such as Shahr-e Naw, Karta-e-Char, and other areas were planned. In 1953, Jada-e-Maiwand was constructed with three- and four-story apartments on both sides of the street, and by 1962–1964 the first master plan of the city was designed. In the 1970s, a number of five-story apartment buildings known as Microrayon complexes, boxy structures of Soviet design, were constructed. Occupants of those complexes were mainly middle-class families. Building materials were prefabricated in factories outside the city, near the mountains to the east, and then delivered to the building site to be assembled. Plumbing and ductwork systems for providing water and heat to the apartments, as well as a sewage system for removing waste, were also part of the complex's design. The units did not have private patios but some may have communal courtyards. Except for the Microrayon district, multiresidential buildings were not common structures in Afghanistan's cities. In the 1980s, a number of high-rise buildings were built in Kabul to house businesses, and the city expanded considerably, building wider roads and rotary intersections to alleviate the traffic congestion that quickly followed on the heels of modern transportation.

The older sections of Kabul consisted of Shah Shahid, Shor Bazar, Chindawul, Murad Khani, and Deh-Afghanan. Houses in these older areas were arranged in irregular patterns, on lots of varying size, and their general look is one of numerous small compounds: thick exterior walls approximately two meters high that were made from mud or sun-dried bricks that rested on a stone foundation and enclosed the rooms centered around a courtyard. Roofs were composed from a mud and straw structure supported by wooden beams. Newer buildings substituted concrete for the mud walls and tin for roof construction.[21]

Structures in the old sections are densely packed together, to the extent that the eaves of roofs meet over the narrow streets so that some parts of the city seem like a dark network of tunnels and passages. These houses are also smaller, as space is at a premium, and the once-spacious courtyards are small and cramped, if they are present at all. The flat roofs double as an extra working and recreational space, affording women both space and privacy when they do their work outdoors. During summer, the evenings are cool and frequently families will bring their bedrolls up to the roof to sleep.

The disposal of waste and sewage remains a major problem for the city, since in the older areas of the city human waste may simply be emptied directly onto the streets outside, into an open sewer that runs along the side of an alley. Residents typically had to develop their own methods of dealing with the open sewage. When the city used to be surrounded by agricultural lands, the resident farmers there set up an informal waste-management system, entering the city regularly to collect the waste and use it as fertilizer for their fields. As the city expanded and farmlands disappeared to make room for urban growth, the farmers decreased in number, even as waste production increased, and those residents who could afford it would pay men from lower classes to collect waste and dispose of it.[22] These waste collectors were called *kharkar,* donkey worker, because they typically used these pack animals to carry the waste out of the residential areas. Much of Kabul's old section was destroyed during the civil war in 1992–1996.

In Qandahar the climate is dry and hot, and wood is scarce. Houses with domed and vaulted ceilings are common here. Burnt brick is the most popular wall-building material because it helps keep homes cooler in hot weather, and it is relatively easy for people to both create the affordable sun-dried bricks and then have them baked in shared or rented kilns.

The ancient city of Herat resembles a giant *qalah* more than a standard city because of its peripheral walls and five access gates that lead to its two main internal streets. The intersections of the access roads and the main streets physically divide the city into four quadrants. The inner streets were built before the advent of wheeled transportation so they are extremely narrow and winding. Housing within the city generally consists of small, densely packed homes mingled with the larger, professionally designed houses complete with spacious courtyards and gardens for Herat's affluent residents. Water is channeled to the city from nearby streams and is stored in brick cisterns, dome shaped structures as many as 20 meters in height. Communal baths can be found throughout the city. These simple brick structures were as much of a social and communications center as teahouses are still. Another unique type of housing is found in the villages outside Herat's walls, two-story homes built so closely together they seem to share a single roof. The lower part of the house consists of a single room that will typically house animals and extra supplies, as well as a single access door. Stairs within lead to the upper floor and the family's living quarters.[23]

Centuries ago, vertical windmills dotted the landscape of western Afghanistan, and the most famous among them are the windmills of Herat. These structures do not resemble the well-known Dutch form. The base of these windmills is square, it consists of a room with four mud walls, with two of them built taller and stand parallel to each other. Within the walls are the millstones that turn and grind the wheat. A wooden feeder built into the wall channels the grain from the storage bin into the stones. A wooden pole rises from the center of the millstones, and the two taller mud walls rise on either side of this pole. Six pairs of reed mats are attached as sails to the pole, and as they catch the winds they are spun around, turning the pole, which in turn moves the millstones. As the grain is ground into flour, it drops from between the stones into a long trough for collecting. These windmills only operate during a short period when the winds blow their strongest, from June to September, and it is known to local residents as the "wind of 120 days." It is during this period that wheat was harvested in the area, and the mills operated day and night for that entire period.[24]

VILLAGE SETTLEMENT PATTERNS

Geography and climate govern the lives and movements of seminomadic dwellers. Villagers developed their migration patterns to take advantage of the warm and cold regions. In the summer they move from their winter camps to summer camps and pasture regions in higher and cooler areas. When the weather is cold, they abandon the summer camps and return to the winter camps. The availability or lack of water for irrigating agricultural land also influenced settlement patterns. Communities with a ready supply of agricultural laborers were more likely to develop adjacent to irrigation networks that divert river water to agricultural fields.

Village settlement patterns were also affected by the need for defense. Houses of wealthier families with possessions to protect are designed to serve as fortress-like compounds for its residents, containing within its walls individual homes with separate structures for stables, tool and storage sheds, and small granaries. In some cases of poor families, all the rooms and structures are built under the same roof. Villages without protective walls were clustered around larger towns in a nuclear pattern among the surrounding fields, resting on nonarable ground.[25] Every village contains a mosque and some villages also have a place for social gatherings. For those that didn't, the mosque also serves that function. Usually a village's inhabitants are members of the same clan or tribe.

Villages in Nooristan stand apart architecturally in their house construction as well as the terraced and stacked arrangement of homes, which cling to sheer mountain cliffs. Most of them are only accessible via a network of ladders and neighbors' rooftops. The Nooristani house is comprised of post and beam construction, with wood and stone used as the primary building materials, because they are abundant in the area. Dwellings there are typically two or three levels high. Structures are crowned with flat roofs that double as patios, and wooden ladders connect the roof and the living area below. Water distribution is accomplished by a series of hollowed wooden logs constructed to carry the water from one location to another. A typical settlement in Nooristan is densely packed together and has two- or three-story houses closely juxtaposed on every piece of available ledge space on the steep hillsides. This close arrangement is possible because the homes do not have traditional entrances and exits. A single door exists to the ground level room that can be secured from the inside. This room usually houses the family's animals and also holds a store of firewood and other supplies. A ladder and trap door in the corner provides access to the upper floor and main living area. Another ladder and trap door provides interior access to the rooftop that also doubles as a work and recreational area, and is also closely adjacent to neighbors' rooftops.[26] In contrast to the high, thick outer walls and segregated interior rooms of a traditional village settlement, there is little privacy in a Nooristani community. Houses hold tight against the mountainside and to each other, and all significant movements, recreation, work, and socializing takes place on the open roofs. Resources and tools are usually shared because of their scarcity as well as the difficulty in transporting significant amounts of supplies up the steep slopes, and there is also very little available room to store many supplies.

In contrast, privacy and security are a high priority in the fortress-like *qalah*. These structures are typically home to the wealthy extended families, usually feudal landowners or tribal chiefs, who can afford to build them. The thick walls enclose gardens and individual dwellings, and protect inhabitants from bandits and the occasional violence resulting from tribal hostilities or rivalries over water rights and land ownership. A room for guests is built above the single arched gate of the *qalah,* it is considered a place of honor and affords the best view of the owner's fields. Business between host and guest is conducted in the guest quarters so that people not directly related to the family can be kept separate from the women, and this is reinforced by the separate entrance and stairway located directly inside the arched entrance that leads a visitor upstairs without ever seeing the family's living area of the *qalah.* Even the entrance to the family quarters is a twisting passageway, so that no one in the passageway can see into the court when the door is opening or closing. This extra feature makes it easier for women to retreat to inner rooms if they hear someone unfamiliar coming through the passageway toward the family quarters.[27]

In Kabul, Qunduz, and Salang Pass areas, villages use their natural surroundings as fortification. The steep mountainside creates a natural defensible barrier to invaders. Houses are typically arranged in a terraced fashion along the slopes, with some distance between homes. Stone is abundant in this area, so most of these houses are built of stone and have pieces of wood, if available, or mud that seal the openings between the rocks. The roof is made of wooden poles topped with layers of reeds and then covered with layers of mud. The mud-based layers of the roof wear out quickly under rain and snow conditions and must be replaced every couple of years. Unlike in Nooristan, where the closely interconnected housing pattern imparted a sense of community and sharing, the housing in Salang, with thick walls, and very small apertures in them, reflects a more solitary and isolated mood, and privacy is valued among these families. The heavy stone walls can be as much as a meter thick at the base, and while it is good for conserving heat in cold weather, its thickness and weight prevent the easy creation of windows.

Traditional heating fuels are wood, charcoal, vegetable wastes, and dried manure. Electricity and coal have been introduced with the advent of developments in transportation and the construction of hydroelectric dams, although they mostly benefit larger urban areas. Rural areas continue to rely mostly on traditional, hand-gathered fuels. In many rural homes and *qalahs,* and in some village mosques, that are located in areas where winter cold is severe, some people have created innovative construction methods to protect from the cold and damp conditions, such as the building of complex trenches or channels that wind their way under the floor and serve to circulate air throughout the home. This under-floor network of channels may also be used for *tab-khaneh,* a system of using a single cooking fire in one room to heat the rest of the home. The oven that contains this fire is called the *tanoor.* It is a cone-shaped oven that holds hot coals covered with a fine coating of ash to make the heat dissipation more uniform. A small tunnel is built that leads from the oven and draws the hot air draft from the fire into the under-floor channels. The hot air is thus channeled throughout the home.

A round metal plate is placed inside the *tanoor* and is used to regulate the heat flow through the channels by obstructing the flow when it is too warm. Some families may have a water container built into the rooms in the path of the under-floor channels, which the heated air will warm as it passes through. Small village mosques may use this system to heat the floor before people congregate to say their prayers. In places where cold weather is not as severe in the winter, such as Jalalabad and Qandahar, people use simpler methods of heating, such as a charcoal fire in a container in the middle of the room or warm blankets. *Char Kheshti* is a simple heating method that involves a square pit dug in the middle of the floor, with charcoal burning inside.[28]

PORTABLE AND TEMPORARY DWELLINGS

Tents are the dwelling of choice for nomads who move continuously, and seminomads will favor tents, yurts, or huts as portable housing when they take their animals to distant pastures in the late spring and summer seasons, and when repairing their permanent mud, wood, or stone homes for the rest of the year. Tents may be built with frames or with tent poles as the central support and are popular because they are lightweight, easy to assemble, and break down and load on pack animals as a caravan moves along its seasonal routes.

There are three types of tents: black tents, usually found in the south and west; white wool or cotton tents, common in the east and north; and the barrel-vaulted tent found mainly in Baluchistan. They are not the small structures one would picture for camping trips. The average tent is designed and built to house a family or small clan, and a series of them grouped together would form a community containing an entire extended family. A tent will usually cover about 25 square meters, and its main support may be a wooden frame or, if unframed, a set of centrally placed tent poles that serve as the main centrally based support for the rest of the tent parts, unlike permanent structures, with thick peripheral walls that provide the primary means of structural support.

Ropes are used extensively as the means to fasten together the various parts of a tent; nails would be inconvenient for securing pieces because they would have to be pulled out repeatedly, which would damage the wood over time as well as lengthen the time it takes to break down or set up a tent. A major and the most visible building material is the tent cloth itself. The black tents are made of thick goat's hair, which is durable but cheaper than the wool used for the white tents. These materials are woven into long, thick strips that can be fastened together and hung off the wooden frame or tent poles to form the ceiling and walls of the tent. Wooden sticks are driven into the ground and secured with strips to the frame by means of ropes. A strip at the front is left to hang loose to serve as a door. The sides of the tent are also loosely secured in warm weather so that they can be rolled up as necessary to let air circulate though the structure.

The black goat's hair tents come in two styles: vaulted or peaked. Ghilzai Pushtuns and Brahois prefer the peaked tents, which consist of tent poles with the woven cloth strips attached and tied down to form a ceiling and walls. The vaulted style that is favored by Durani Pushtuns has a ribbed wooden frame, with woven cloth strips stretched over the frame.[29] The Taimani tribes use a rectangular-shaped tent that is created by willow poles inserted into the ground about a meter or so apart. A series of additional poles are laid diagonally against the vertical poles and lashed together to give the walls more strength and make them better able to support the cloth that will cover it. Two forked poles slightly taller than the vertical wall poles are inserted at each far end of the structure, and a single pole that measures the length of the entire long wall is laid into the fork, and serves as the central point for attaching the tent cloths that then drape across the frame and are tied down at ground level. Doors are lightweight, made of woven reeds, and attached to cover the main entrance.[30]

Seminomads require housing that is portable but more stable than tents, because they tend to reside in them continuously for longer periods before moving and also may remain longer in regions with more severe weather. Yurts fulfill this purpose and are popular in the colder northern regions, and huts, a sturdier descendent of the nomadic tent, are also common in areas where semi-nomadic farmers divide their residences between winter and summer homes.

The yurt was brought to the country long ago by immigrants from Turkmenistan and is most popular among Turkmen, Qirghiz, and Uzbek herdsmen and seminomads who travel the region seeking pasturelands for their animals in the colder northern areas, and who favor this warmer and sturdier structure. These structures can be erected with ease near fields where they work as farmers or pastures where they herd their animals, usually in the warmer summer months. As winter approaches they break down these structures and take them along back to their mud homes to wait out the winter months.

The basic yurt consists of a domed or conical wood frame, approximately 3 meters in diameter, covered with layers of felt. It requires skilled artisans to construct its precisely curved domed frame and so is more expensive to build than any other tent, but once built it is very easy to assemble, disassemble, and transport, and this is a major factor in its popularity. The wood used for the frame is usually willow tree branches, which are acquired while still green and then bent into curved rods to the artisan's painstaking specifications, because it is important that all the curved rods used for a single yurt be exactly the same length and curve the same. The curved green-wood rods are then baked in a specially constructed cylindrical brick oven. When they are cooled they retain the curved shape permanently.

The rods are the central feature of the structure and provide stability for the entire structure. The domed form is more stable against strong winds than the looser tent structures, and the thick felt covering that is applied after the frame is constructed and standing also contributes to its ability to withstand severe weather. Stakes driven into the ground around the outside are tied to the structure to further anchor the yurt against strong winds. A wooden door with elaborate carvings is attached last, and is as much a signature feature of the yurt as its domed shape.[31]

Another type of portable dwelling is the hut, a longer-standing version of the nomadic tent used largely by agricultural laborers who lead a seminomadic life working on the fields of different landowners. While the permanent homes of sedentary farmers are sturdy with thick walls, these huts are lightweight and are constructed of available materials to keep costs down. They can be disassembled so that seminomads who work on other people's farmland in the harvest period, for example, can easily migrate from one place to another, and set up their portable homes at the sides of the fields they will be working on. At the end of the harvest season they normally return to their permanent homes, but if they are able to find extra work, they may stay longer and even into the winter season, which is why it is important that these huts are able to withstand the cold weather. The basic hut structure is a round, polygonal, or oblong freestanding frame with a curved roof and a wooden door at the single entrance. The frame is usually made from wood, but when it is scarce or expensive, bundles of reeds are a common substitute. Layers of mud cover the structure and seal openings between the wood or reed parts. Tree branches are usually used for the roof.

Round huts come in three basic types: *lacheq, kapa-e-chamshi,* and *chapari.* The *lacheq* is a lightweight structure that is inexpensive to make and does not require a high level of skill. Walls and roofs are made of flattened reed mats or grass woven into strips and arranged in an overlapping pattern that gives the structure an overall stability and strength almost comparable to that of a yurt. This is a popular summer hut among the Uzbeks, Arabs, Tajiks, and Turkmen, who may bring their entire families with them to live by the side of

A summer tent inside a family compound in Surkhak Tamas Village, Doshi district, Baghlan, 2004.

pasturelands during the warm summer months. The *kapa-e-chamshi* is made entirely of reeds. If tied together tightly, the reed structure offers some protection from the cold, but it is not very useful against rain or wind, and this structure does not disassemble easily so is not very portable. In some cases it may simply be abandoned after it is no longer needed, and left for salvage or disposal or for the next seminomad laborer to take residence.[32]

The third round hut type is the *chapari*, which consists of a circular pattern of wooden poles set into the ground with walls made of woven reed mats tied to the poles. Straw or felt pieces are used to make the roof. This type of hut is popular among the northern Hazaras who take their animals from their northern winter residences to mountain pastures and reside there in the warmer spring and summer months.[33]

The polygonal huts come in two types, the *kapa-e-Arab* and the *chubdara*. The *kapa-e-Arab* consists of a set of wooden poles tied together and wrapped with walls made of reed mats and is used by nomadic shepherding Arabs when they travel to pastures in Badakhshan for grazing purposes. The frame of the *chubdara* is made of wood, and the walls and roof are made of tightly packed reed bundles. The reed bundles are set vertically deep into the ground, with additional horizontal reed bundles secured to them for added stability. The roof descends from a ridgepole to the top of the wall. This structure is not used as a residence, but is built to store supplies and house animals.

Oblong huts include the *kodai, kodik* (tamarisk hut), and *kapa* types. *Kodai* are commonly used by Pushtun villagers as summer dwellings. The *kodik* hut is made from tamarisk boughs, which are abundant along the lower course of the Helmand River and are popular among Baluchi residents. Where tamarisk boughs are not plentiful, reeds are a suitable substitute. The *kapa* is popular among Tajik residents and consists of poles set into the ground at equal intervals in an oblong shape and covered with reed walls. These huts are not very sturdy and are only suitable in mild climates, such as that found in Badakhshan in the summer. The portability and low cost of huts also make them popular for use by merchants, who will set up temporary seasonal teahouses and shops along the trails commonly crossed by nomads and other travelers.[34]

THE INFLUENCE OF REPATRIATION

Over the past decades, invasions and civil wars have again caused movement of people, and architecture in the country is again undergoing a gradual assimilation of influences. This time the new methods and techniques are brought in by expatriates who are returning home after years spent in other countries: Pakistan, Iran, India, and the West. Residents bring new preferences, and architects and builders bring with them new techniques and building methods. Most of the nomadic caravans and seminomadic communities are gone, many of them had to flee to refugee camps and spent many years away, those that return find the mined and warlord-controlled lands too dangerous for travel and for isolated living. Traditional building materials are also affected, since so many of the country's natural resources were destroyed or looted, and are slow to replenish, imported materials are also making their way into the cities, and as the architects and builders adapt to these new conditions and rebuild the country's infrastructure, it is inevitable that Afghanistan's public and domestic architecture will once again evolve to adapt and express new artistic nuances and innovative construction styles that reflect as well as alter the influences of their international neighbors near and distant.

NOTES

1. Banister Fletcher, *A History of Architecture*, 18th ed. (New York: Charles Scribner's Sons, 1975), p. 119.

2. Fletcher, *A History of Architecture*, p. 96.

3. Arthur Upham Pope, *Persian Architecture: The Triumph of Form and Color.* (New York: G. Braziller, 1965), pp. 264–265.

4. Stanley Ira Hallet and Rafi Samizay, *Traditional Architecture of Afghanistan* (New York: Garland STPM Press, 1980), pp. 171–173.

5. Pope, *Persian Architecture*, p. 78.

6. Sarwar Goya. "The Green Dome or the Mausoleum of the Timurid Princess," *Afghanistan* 1, no. 1 (January–March 1946): 16–17.

7. Pope, *Persian Architecture*, pp. 236–237.

8. Pope, *Persian Architecture*, p. 238.

9. Pope, *Persian Architecture*, p. 147.

10. Pope, *Persian Architecture*, pp. 165–166.

11. Albert Szabo, Thomas J. Barfield, and Eduard F. Sekler, *Afghanistan: An Atlas of Indigenous Domestic Architecture* (Austin: University of Texas Press, 1991), p. 10.

12. Szabo et al., *Afghanistan*, pp. 135–137.

13. Szabo et al., *Afghanistan*, p. 141.

14. Szabo et al., *Afghanistan*, p. 135.

15. Szabo et al., *Afghanistan*, p. 121.

16. Szabo et al., *Afghanistan*, p. 119.

17. Szabo et al., *Afghanistan*, pp. 145–147.

18. Szabo et al., *Afghanistan*, pp. 115.

19. Hafizullah Emadi, "Kabul," in *Encyclopedia of Urban Cultures: Cities and Cultures Around the World*, vol. 2 (Danbury, CT: Human Relations Area Files at Yale University, Grolier, 2002), pp. 438–439.

20. Hallet and Samizay, *Traditional Architecture of Afghanistan*, pp. 175–177.

21. For more details of housing units in Kabul, see Bashir A. Kazimee, *Urban/Rural Dwelling Environments: Kabul, Afghanistan, Case Studies, Proposed Model* (Cambridge: Massachusetts Institute of Technology, 1977).

22. Hallet and Samizay, *Traditional Architecture of Afghanistan*, p. 187.

23. Hallet and Samizay, *Traditional Architecture of Afghanistan*, pp. 147–149.

24. Louis Dupree, *Afghanistan* (Karachi, Pakistan: Oxford University Press, 2002), pp. 140–142.

25. Szabo et al., *Afghanistan*, p. 20.

26. Hallet and Samizay, *Traditional Architecture of Afghanistan*, p. 87.

27. Hallet and Samizay, *Traditional Architecture of Afghanistan*, pp. 127–129.

28. Abdul Shukoor Raji, "Traditional Dwellings: Domestic Heating Systems of Afghanistan" (Master's thesis, University of Newcastle Upon Tyne, 1986), pp. 70–78.

29. Szabo et al., *Afghanistan*, pp. 30–31.

30. Szabo et al., *Afghanistan*, p. 49.

31. Raji, "Traditional Dwellings," p. 24.

32. Szabo et al., *Afghanistan*, p. 73.

33. Szabo et al., *Afghanistan*, pp. 83–85.

34. Szabo et al., *Afghanistan*, p. 87–95.

5

Social Customs, Cuisine, and Traditional Dress

Afghanistan is home to different ethno-linguistic and tribal communities and each group adheres to and cherishes its unique traditions and way of life. Although the civil war had destroyed much of the country's infrastructure, life went on as people began to rebuild their homes. People socialize in teahouses (*chai khanahs,* popularly called *samawar* from the Russian "samovar") and restaurants in Kabul and other major urban centers, organize picnics, and participate in festivals and sports, and play games. Amid the rubble and ruins in Kabul one sees the vitality of life on the streets. Music blares from tape players, the aroma of dishes from restaurants and *chai khanahs* permeates the air, the ice cream shops are doing robust business, and the fragrance of sweets and bakeries appeals to both locals and visitors. The bazaars are crowded with people who work hard to make ends meet, while customers and vendors negotiate the prices. Juxtaposed with this are the jarring images of the physically disabled and war-affected men, women, and children who beg passersby for money.

Although the country remained poor due to years of neglect on the part of the leadership to devise policies to improve the economy and build a modern society, it is slowly but surely returning to the modern world despite outward appearances of life in the Middle Ages. A handful of people who trade on the streets, work in *chai khanas* and restaurants, and manage stores, also own the latest cellular phones and use them to communicate with friends and relatives abroad. Modern technology has brought the past and present together and has combined tradition with modernity, evidenced in the installation of satellite dishes on the rooftops of bungalows owned by warlords as well as on the roofs of a number of mud-walled houses in the outlying neighborhoods of Kabul. See also Chapter 7 about life in rural and urban areas.

CUISINE/CLOTHING

Afghanistan's social activity centers largely around food. Afghan cuisine is a unique blend of influence and resourcefulness. Fruits, grains, nuts, and vegetables are available either in abundance or not at all, depending on where a family resides. The energy and activity of nomadic traders affected and was itself driven by the cuisines of each region. Severe climates and limited windows of agricultural productivity are the norm in many areas, and so cookery is taken seriously by Afghans. Special occasions also center around food and are a major occasion for donning costumes that demonstrate the spectrum of the country's ethnicity.

ETIQUETTE AND MANNERS

There are unwritten rules and codes of conduct that govern interpersonal relations. These codes deal with issues such as pride, honor, hospitality, respect, virtue, and morality. These traits, which demonstrate the values of a society, are general characteristics of all ethno-linguistic communities of Afghanistan, and individuals are conscious of their behaviors, which may negatively or positively affect their status and the status of their family and tribe.

References to such ideals are found in literature and folktales, and themes such as *Sadaqat wa Imandari* (honesty and integrity); *Mehman Nawazi* (extending hospitality and invitation to friends and strangers); *Dosti* (making friends and maintaining and nurturing these relationships); *Ghayrat wa Namus* (safeguarding and defending personal and family honor and property); and *Wafadari* (remaining loyal to family and friends and keeping one's pledges) are essential ingredients of Afghanistan's cultural values, and they are not taken lightly. A common thread running through all of these is one of responsibility. Being a good guest is considered to be as important as being a good host. Loyal friends watch each other's back and family and clan honor is fiercely protected.

Hospitality is extended to friends and strangers alike. People greet each other, acquaintances and strangers, with handshakes, saying *Salam*, Peace (Be Upon You). Close friends embrace and kiss each other on the cheeks when they greet. Men often hold each other's hands while walking, which expresses affection and friendship; however, men are not allowed to touch or shake hands with women who are not related to them.

CULINARY TRADITION

Afghanistan's strategic location (situated between Asia and the Middle East) served as a converging point where numerous major cultures and traditions from countries such as ancient Persia (Iran), the Middle East, Greece, Central Asia, China, and India interacted with one another. As various dynasties emerged and fell, traders, merchants, and new settlers brought with them exotic goods and merchandise, including spices, teas, and cooking techniques and utensils. People in Afghanistan gradually absorbed and adapted the cooking techniques of the new settlers and nations. The blending of the cooking styles and dishes of these settlers and nations with the vernacular traditions resulted in the emergence of a unique and original cuisine in Afghanistan that reflects these cultural diversities.[1]

Food serves as a factor of social cohesion. For example, food is consumed when two opposing parties successfully conclude negotiations and resolve a dispute. Food in such cases is served to seal the agreement reached between

Butcher slaughters a sheep, goat, calf, or a cow and displays the cuts for customers, Kabul, 2003.

the parties. Food is also regarded as passion, art, and joy. When families invite friends, relatives, or guests, they spend considerable time preparing a sumptuous meal to express their respect and goodwill. The tradition of hospitality has both cultural and religious origins, and the cuisine and dining practices have adapted to the generous quantities and elaborate care in preparation and cooking that this exceptional solicitousness of guests demands. The guest of honor is always accorded special treatment in terms of the seating area in the guestroom, and others are seated according to status and age.

Families often eat at home, and food is served without table settings. The host never knows for sure how many people may actually sit down to a meal. Invited guests may bring extra friends, and so in a typical party with a dozen invited guests the host will usually prepare enough food to feed three times that many. Even the poorest families will extend great generosity to guests, even if it means going beyond their means to prepare a sumptuous meal. The tradition of dining in restaurants is not common, but dining out does occur when people conduct business, such as trading in a market place.

Sikh national of Afghanistan in his spice shop. The signboard reads "Spice store of Darmandar Singh Soorbizada Delsooz," Kabul, 2003.

Islam has influenced the country's cuisine. It forbids the consumption of pork and alcohol. The common source of meat is beef, sheep, goats, poultry, and game animals but even with these meals Muslims strictly adhere to the dietary standard of *halaal*, which requires that specific procedures be performed when slaughtering animals for food as well as for preparing the food afterward. The word *halaal* means slaughtering according to "Islamic law." The procedures stress that the person who slaughters the animal must use a sharp knife so that by one strike of the knife the three major blood vessels of the animal's throat are cut and he must recite *Allah Akbar* (God is great) three times. The slaughtered animal will be cleaned of blood, which is considered unclean, before the meat can be processed.

Basic home cooking utensils include a mortar and pestle for grinding spices and herbs, a large pot and pan for cooking soup and stew as well as rice, a colander for draining washed rice and vegetables, and a clay oven *(tanoor)* is for baking bread *(nan)*. Cooks use a wide variety of spices in preparing meals that are not that spicy and yet have a sweet taste. Families often purchase large quantities of spices and keep them whole, as they last longer, and grind them using a mortar and pestle as needed. The following are the most commonly used spices.

Hel (Cardamom): While it is the intensely flavorful seeds that are the spice, their tough outer pods also have a use: they can be chewed to relieve indigestion or to freshen the breath, and when used to flavor tea, usually the entire pod is crushed and dropped into the boiling water. Cardamom comes in three types: Green and white seeds are ground and used as ingredients for *pilaw* (pilaf) and desserts and to flavor tea, and black cardamom seeds are much stronger and in ground form are one of the ingredients of the spice mixture called *char masala* (four-spice).

Shanbalelah (Fenugreek): The rhombic-shaped seeds of this plant are the spice, although some cooks also like to use the fresh leaves. This spice is aromatic and slightly bitter, like celery, and dry roasting can enhance the flavor of the seeds and reduce the bitterness. These seeds are used for flavoring spinach and to sweeten rice dishes, as well as for making a lemon pickle dish called *tursh-e-limo*.

Char Masala (four-spice): This spice combination is used to flavor *pilaw* (pilaf). A family may develop its own combination, but the most common spices, which are ground together in equal parts, include cinnamon, cloves, cumin, and black cardamom seeds.

Zireh (cumin): The fruits of the plant are the spices, although they are usually called seeds. This strongly aromatic spice is usually used to flavor rice, and is one of the four ingredients of the *char masala*. It is also a popular medicinal remedy for indigestion.

Anisum, Bodiyan-e-rumi (anise, aniseed): Although they are referred to as "seeds," it is actually the fruit of the plant, a member of the parsley family, which is used as a spice in cookery and as a medicinal remedy (it is considered an effective aid to digestion and cure for flatulence). It is sweet and aromatic and is used to flavor biscuits and *roht* (a sweet baked bread).

Darchin (cinnamon): Cinnamon is an ancient spice and is the stem bark of the tree Cinnamomum zeylanicum. It may be sold in ground form and in the form of tightly rolled sticks, called quills. It has a strongly aromatic scent and a sweet flavor. Sticks are inserted whole into stews to flavor them, and in ground form cinnamon is part of the spice mixture *char masala*.

Mikhak (cloves): Cloves are the dried flower heads, or buds, of the clove tree. Mikhak means "little nail" in Dari, which is what the dried cloves resemble. In ground form it is one of the four ingredients of *char masala*. Cloves have a strongly aromatic and intense fragrance as well as a strong, almost overpowering and sometimes bitter taste.

Women like Sanam still spend most of their time in the kitchen preparing meals for their families, 2003.

Meals

Women traditionally prepare family meals, and young girls begin learning how to cook as early as 10 years old. The family eats together on the floor; segregation is only necessary when male guests who are not close relatives are present. After all have washed their hands, the meal commences. All the dishes are brought out at once in platters laid upon the *daster khan,* a cloth placed on the floor around which people sit cross-legged while eating. Each person has a plate but no fork, and knives and spoons and bowls are provided if soup or stew is served, but in urban settings, a spoon is used for rice. Otherwise, all food is eaten with fingers. A typical meal includes tea, *nan,* rice, and a meat dish (chicken is the most common and abundant of meats) accompanied by pickled vegetables and chutneys. Summer time beverages are water, lemonade, and buttermilk.[2]

Chai (tea) is an important part of people's social life and is a ubiquitous drink of hospitality and communication. People drink green *(chai-e-sabz)* and black *(chai-e-siyah)* tea both at home and in *chai khanahs,* which dot the country. *Chai* is usually served in a glass, so that its beautiful amber color can be admired, and it is seldom mixed with milk because milk is expensive, but sugar is a popular addition. A sugar cube may be dissolved in the tea before it is drunk. Tea with sugar is called *chai-e-shirin* and without sugar is called *chai-e-talkh.*

Chai is usually flavored with green or white cardamom—the pod is crushed and then dropped, with the seeds, into the tea mixture before boiling water is poured over it. After steeping for a minute or so, the tea is ready to be served. Tea is the first thing offered to visiting guests as soon as they arrive, and tea glasses are continuously refilled throughout the visit, unless the guest turns his empty glass over as a signal that further refills are not desired. Host and guest can chat and do business over glasses of tea while the main meal is being prepared. If the host can afford it, a variety of sweets may also be served with the tea: *nuql-e-nakhud* (sugarcoated chickpeas), *nuql-e-badam* (sugarcoated almonds), and *nuql-e-pistah* (sugarcoated pistachio nuts).

Qeymaq-chai is a specialty tea that requires elaborate preparation and is more costly, so it is normally only served at formal occasions such as engagement ceremonies and weddings. *Qeymaq* consists of cream that surfaces after the milk has been boiled and is added to the top of glasses of green tea. The qeymaq gives the tea a slightly salty taste. In *chai khanah,* tea is served from a samovar that dispenses constantly boiling water. *Chai khanahs* serve tea in small teapots for each customer, along with tumblers or small porcelain bowls for drinking the tea. An extra bowl is served with the tea to hold the dregs.

Scene from a typical teahouse *(Chai Khanah)* painted by artist Ghulam Sediq, Kabul, 2003.

As refills are made, the customers wash out the dregs of the previous cup with a bit of hot tea and deposit it into a cup called *awkash*. This action serves to clean and warm up the cup before more tea is poured into it.

Nan (bread) is served with all types of meals and it is also used generally to refer to food. No person, regardless of ethnic group or income level, could imagine a day without *nan*. It is very versatile and methods of making it range from simple, flat-baked *nan* to elaborate sweetened and stuffed *nan*. *Nan* is made most commonly from wheat or barley. Bread is baked in the *tanoor* (in-ground clay oven), which is heated by burning wood and then by charcoal. The prepared dough is flattened on a board, put on a cushion stuffed with coconut fiber, and slapped against the inner walls of the *tanoor*. The vast majority of families do not have their own ovens. Most buy *nan* from bakeries. Families also bake *nan* on a heated stone or circular iron plate (originally from India, it is used in many homes in the eastern part) that rests on or near hot coals, the dough is turned over occasionally until it is baked. People treat *nan* with great respect, to the extent that it is considered a serious breach of social etiquette to drop bread on the ground. It originates both from religion, to respect God-given food, and from the shortage of food. Passersby have been observed coming upon a piece of nan left in the road, to pick it up and carefully lay it down on a ledge, a wall, or other out-of-the-way location, so that it will not be trod underfoot by street traffic.

Traditional cuisine in Afghanistan has been based on animal and dairy products like meat, cheese, yogurt, and buttermilk. To this, fresh fruit are added during summer, and dried fruits and nuts are added during winter. Common fruits include grapes, melons, apricots, mulberries, cherries, apples, and plumbs. Dried fruits and nuts are also popular snacks and form a substantial part of the average diet. Walnuts, almonds, pistachios, and pine nuts are the most abundantly available nuts and are popular in plain and sugar-coated form. Simple sweets include sugar-baked nuts, raw sugarcane or sugar beets, *gur* (lumps of molasses), and *jelabi* (deep-fried twists of wheat and sugar covered in syrup).

Popular dishes are mainly *pilaw* and *kabab*. *Pilaw* is the most integral dish and families often prepare it to treat a guest of honor. The most common

Bakery in Kabul displays bread while customers in the front wait for their turn to pay, 2003.

pilaw consists of long grain rice, or basmati rice, meat (usually mutton) in the center, and a side dish of vegetables to supplement the meal and to give added flavor. This dish is not unique to Afghanistan, but the combinations of spices and cooking styles make this dish stand apart from dishes elsewhere.

There are several varieties of *pilaw,* such as *Qabli Pilaw,* an Uzbeki rice dish that is studded with raisins, almonds, pistachio nuts, and shredded carrots; *Narenj Pilaw* is covered with dried orange peels; *Murgh Pilaw* is made with rice and chicken; *Sabzi Pilaw* consists of rice with spinach; *Masheng* (Mashee) *pilaw* is rice with green peas; *Landi Pilaw* is rice with dried jerked meat; and *Banjan-e-siyah Pilaw* is made with eggplant. *Yakhni Pilaw* contains rice and mutton; the mutton is cooked and then steamed together with the rice. The resulting broth seasons the rice in the process.

Kabab is another major dish served mainly in urban areas. It consists of lean bits of cubed meat on a skewer *(sikh),* sometimes interspersed with pieces of raw vegetables such as onions, tomatoes, and small pieces of fat. The *kabab* is broiled over a charcoal fire and served on the skewer, sometimes the cooked meat is seasoned with salt, ground red pepper, and dried, ground, sour grapes called *ghorah.* Kabab comes in varieties such as *koftah kabab* and *karahi kabab.* For example, *koftah kabab* is made with ground meat, packed around a skewer, and broiled over charcoal. It may be served as a side dish with *pilaw. Karahi kabab* is fried in oil.

A typical meal is soup *(shoorba),* and a family might gather around a communal meal where one to three persons share a single bowl of soup (depending on the size of the bowl) and break bread for dipping and soaking up the soup and eating with fingers or with a spoon. *Kala-Pachah* is another common dish and consists of a sheep's head including eyeballs and feet, and served with rice and bread. *Shulah* is a thick gummy pudding dish that consists of a mixture of meat, rice, cereal, and ghee (clarified butter). *Aash* is made of noodles, sour cream, and butter or ghee. Chicken and eggs are widespread across the country, and guinea hens, ducks, and turkey are also eaten in areas where they are plentiful.

Yogurt has a multitude of uses: as a tenderizer and marinade for meat, as an ingredient in rice dishes, and as a beverage either salted or sweetened with sugar or honey. It may also be served alone or as an accompaniment to a main dinner course. Most rural families keep sheep to provide milk, and yogurt made from goat's milk has a slightly saltier taste then that from a sheep. *Qurot,* dried yogurt, is a popular condiment in rural area. The process involves taking unsalted yogurt made from skimmed sheep's milk (which lasts longer) or curdled milk that has been boiled. After draining the water it is left to dry. It becomes a hard mass and takes on an off-white, bone color. *Qurot* has a sour taste, and it is convenient to store or to carry around and is easily reconstituted by breaking into chunks and soaking in water for several hours. Liquefied *qurot* can be used as a thickening agent in stews and soups, or in its original form as yogurt dish.[3] A dish made of *qurot* is called *quroti*. Rice is served in a plate and a well is made at the center and filled with liquefied *qurot*, fried onions, and clarified butter or ghee. There is no tradition of eating dessert after a meal, and fruits and sweets may be provided with tea.

Tobacco products are consumed frequently and a common form of tobacco product popular in Afghanistan is *naswar,* a mixture of tobacco and lime. *Naswar* is kept in the mouth for a few minutes and then spat out. It is popular among a wide spectrum of the population, and families often provide a spittoon for a guest who uses *naswar.*

Since the Soviet invasion of Afghanistan in December 1979, an estimated five million people of all ethnic groups were forced to leave the country and many settled in Pakistan and Iran. Although the refugees integrated themselves into their new environment by adapting certain features of the host country's lifestyle, their diet remained relatively unchanged.

CLOTHING AND FASHIONS

Dress in Afghanistan does not merely serve the utilitarian purpose of protecting one's body from different climates, it is also indicative of social status and cultural identity. Religious beliefs, to a great extent, have influenced people's style of clothing. It generally stresses modesty in women, who lead largely secluded lives under gauzy veils or shrouded long dresses, and simplicity and ease of movement for men. Daily clothing in societies generally tends toward the practical, but it also sends a message to observers. It is a point of pride for a family or a tribe to demonstrate its place in the larger society and within their immediate community.

While Islam is a basic unifying factor in style and dress in the country, everything diverges at times vividly and creatively, as the influences of ethnicity, geography, and climate come to bear. People largely dress and change their mode of dress on individual basis or in reaction to trends or both, and this will also change over time, but in Afghanistan clothing and accoutrements are also a symbol of their identity and their membership within their communities.

Peerahan-toonban (also called *kamis-shalwar*) is the most recognizable garment throughout the country. *Peerahan* is a loose-fitting cotton slipover shirt, which has a long knee-length tail and is secured with a button over one or both shoulders and falls over *toonban* (baggy pants held together with a drawstring). The fronts of the shirts may be plain or elaborately embroidered, with threads of the same color as the shirt, or with colorful threads and intricate

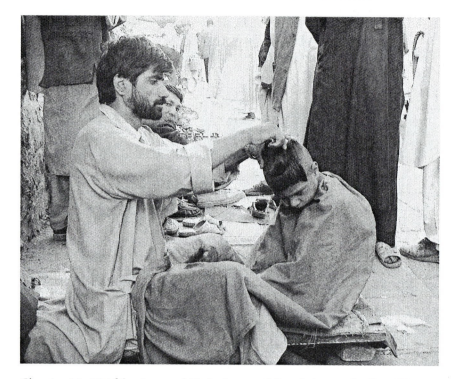

Charging 10–15 Afghanis, a roadside barber can deliver haircut styles from Western to local tastes, Jada-e-Maiwand, Kabul, 2003.

patterns. In Qandahar, shirtfronts may even have small mirrors and beads sewn into intricate designs. The *peerahan-toonban* is generally light colored (only *mullahs* and *Sayyeds* wear white). This outfit is comfortable and versatile; a man who needs to labor on a farm or in construction can tuck away the loose ends of the shirt into his trousers. Wearing layered garments over and under the shirt helps a person to keep warm in colder weather. A sleeveless vest *(waskat)* is worn over the shirt, and is usually embroidered. In the northern areas men wear form-fitting trousers that are representative of their Central Asian heritage and are also more practical than the loose, baggy trousers for riding a horse, which is common in the region. Most men carry a *patoo,* a lightweight fold of cloth resembling a shawl, over their shoulders. It has many functions: it can be used as a prayer mat or a rug as well as a towel.

In Nooristan, where communities live at colder and high altitudes in houses packed against cliffs accessible by steep winding paths, the men wear a loose-fitting drawstring shirt that falls to the knee, topped with a thick wool shirt. Heavy coats are common. Some are made of wool and sheepskin *(pustin)*. The *pustin* is lined with fleece; the *kusay* is a short-sleeved wool coat, the *paysawoi* is a cloak worn over the shoulder; the *chapan* is a quilted cotton or silk coat and it is sold widely in cities. The *gopichin* is similar to a cotton poncho and is buttoned over two shoulders. Turkmens and Uzbeks usually wear it. Western-style wool coats and vests are also popular apparel in cities and villages, worn in juxtaposition to sandals and turbans or other headwear, which themselves contribute to expressing group identity.

Men in the northern and central regions usually keep their hair short. Some friends and relatives will get together and shave each other's heads, usually once a month or so; others will seek the services of a part-time or itinerant barber. In eastern and southern Afghanistan, men wear their hair longer in a bob style that extends down to their earlobes. Beards are regarded as a sign of masculinity and wisdom and are particularly popular in rural areas and towns. Modern urban men tend more toward mustaches if they choose to grow facial hair.

Headgear is very distinctive among the ethnic groups. Traditional headwear items are *dastar* or *lungi* (a turban) and *kolah* (skull cap). Turban cloths are usually a few meters long and wearing a turban is regarded as a symbol of manhood. *Mullahs* and Sayyed of the Shia community often wear black turbans while other mullahs wear white. Black, gray, and brown are common colors except among nomads, who are more likely to use black cloth for turbans, which is easier to hide dirt. The *Kolah* is placed on the head and serves as the base around which the turban is wound, and the style of tying the turban clearly identify the wearer's region of origin. For example, Pushtuns leave some of the end of their turbans, known as *shamlah,* suspended over one shoulder. Hazaras wear the turban with its *shamlah* hanging to the left side, behind the ear. The Qandaharis have longer *shamlah* than men in southern and eastern regions. The custom in some other regions is to tuck the *shamlah* into the wound turban. For example, the Turkmen only leave the *shamlah* hanging down when they say their prayers. The turban is functional headgear as it protects against any hits to the head and its suspended end can be pulled across the face during sandstorms or cold and freezing winter.

The *kolah* are usually made of felt and are elaborately embroidered in distinctive ethnic patterns, although some people in the north tend to leave them bare. In Qandahar, the small mirror beads sewn into shirts are also sewn into the *kolahs*, along with elaborate beading and sequins. These caps are generally round. Men from the eastern region may have *kolahs* made of straw, a tradition they share with the Pushtuns in Pakistan. In the south, the turban has no cap underneath. If there is one, it is made of plain cloth, like a skullcap. The Qandaharis do not have caps underneath. In central areas, the caps are round and made of cotton. Turkmen wear caps of qaraqul wool, which

Mr. Afghan of Shibar wearing a handmade woolen coat and turban common to the Hazara community.

are tall and angular, and Qirghiz men wear felt skullcaps under the lined caps. The *Pakool* cap is another style of headgear. It is now ubiquitous and widely recognized outside of its region of origin, Nooristan, by virtue of television and print-journalism. It is like a long tube sealed at one end. It is placed on the head and the end rolled up so that it resembles a "pork pie," by which it is often referred. The end can be rolled down over the ears in cold weather.

Traditional clothing for women includes *chadar, chadari (burqa)*, and the *peerahan-toonban.* The *chadar*, which is a shawl or headscarf, is the most common head covering for women. It is a long, folded length of cloth that is draped over the head, with one end looped over the opposite shoulder. It is versatile and functional beyond its primary purpose of allowing a woman to cover her face while in public. The chadar shields the head and hair from dust and on special occasions women may also wear embroidered caps under the chadar. Nomad women typically wear a black *chadar* and *toonban* in a variety of colors. The *chadari* is a voluminous garment of pleated rayon, which covers a woman's entire body, with only a latticework panel in front of the eyes so she can see where she is going. Women in rural areas often help men on the farm, so they do not wear the *chadari*, but when they visit cities they may be compelled to wear it. In rural areas, men are more disciplined in self-restraint and families know each other, a situation that makes it less imperative that women cover their face when they go outside their homes or visit family members in a nearby village. If women encounter a stranger, they immediately wrap the *chadar* around their face until the stranger has passed. As Afghanistan entered its modernization period in the late 1950s, the *chadari* began to fall out of use in major urban areas among the educated classes. When Islamic militias seized power in April 1992, they had imposed the wearing of the *chadari* upon all women whenever they left their homes.

Nigar, Shikiba, and Ahmad Khan wear traditional dress in celebration of the *Naw Rooz* (New Year), 2003. Afghan women wear long, baggy clothing and headscarf (*chadar*) but young girls are not obligated to wear a headscarf.

At present, the *chadari* is still worn by many women, less as a desired form of dress than as a precaution, partly to guard against the occasional assault by religious fanatics who harass and beat any woman who walks in public with her face showing.

Women wear *peerahan,* long shirts in floral patterns that are about a few inches above their ankles, and the baggy *toonban* (trousers). Colors worn range from white to the most vividly bright colors, some may have multicolored patterns or bold, flowery designs. On a day-to-day basis, these women will wear the *chadar,* but in winter they wear quilted caps because they are warmer.

Footwear in rural areas largely depends on the availability of materials. In the warm areas, open-toed and open-heeled *chapli* (sandals) are common. These sandals are made of leather and have soles made from rubber tires. Most people wear Western style footwear imported from neighboring countries. Central Asian migrants brought the long boot to the northern region. Boots are common for protection from the cold, agricultural work, and horse riding. Women's footwear is more varied. Sandals and embroidered slippers are typical in mild weather, and more modern urban women increasingly wear high-heeled shoes as well. Shoes and boots are more popular in wet and cold weather.[4]

In the cities, women of affluent families increasingly adopt Western hairstyles. In rural areas, women usually keep their hair long and wear it in a variety of styles, plaited, coiled, or straight, according to their ethnic traditions. For example, Hazara women part their hair in the center and wear it in two braids that hang straight down to their backs tied with a strip of cotton. They will also work a thick, gummy paste called *kitra* into their hair to keep it close to the sides of their heads.[5]

Women who can afford jewelry typically have artisans and goldsmiths handcraft items to their specifications, usually of gold or silver and often set with semiprecious stones such as lapis lazuli or rubies. Those who cannot afford the real article will purchase brass items set with less expensive stones or even colored glass. During festivals and holidays some women may attend covered from head to toe with jewelry and other ornaments such as rings, necklaces, earrings, anklets, and large pendants suspended from chains. Men typically limit their own adornment to one or a few silver rings.

Use of cosmetics is also very popular among women, both married and unmarried. In rural areas mascara, *collyrium,* is used the most, liberally applied to the upper and lower eyeline using a bodkin, or, if not available, a toothpick-sized wood splinter. Village women often use walnut tree bark to whiten their teeth and color their lips. Wearing a mole-sized spot or beauty mark (*khal-e-sabz*) on the forehead, on the chin, or at the cuticle is also common among most village women. Women in the cities frequently apply cosmetics such as lipstick and rouge.

The dwindling Sikh community has clothing that identifies them as a distinct ethno-religious group. They always wear five things whose names begin with the letter K. *Kes,* long hair uncut held with a *kangha,* comb, and a turban, and carry two distinct weapons, *karpaan,* a small sword and a dagger (these diminutive weapons are shrunk from their original size as a sword and a dagger). Other items include wearing a *karra,* a steel bracelet of 5 to 12 inches in diameter on the left wrist, and *kachha,* long underwear. Other accessories worn by the Sikh businessmen is a small silver *karpaan* around their necks as well as a *karra.*[6]

The culture and lifestyle of neighboring countries, mainly Iran and Pakistan, have to some extent influenced the dress and fashion of the communities in Afghanistan since the early 1980s. Refugees who returned to Afghanistan after two decades of exile brought with them a lifestyle they experienced during their long years of residence in Iran and Pakistan. The culture of the neighboring countries had greatly influenced younger generations. Women who lived in Iran often tend to wear a black *chadar* that is common in Iran, and those who lived in Pakistan mostly wear *burqa* and others adapted the Punjabi and Sindi styles of *peerahan-toonban.* The destruction of local textile manufacturing plants since the 1990s also paved the road to an influx of fabrics, textiles, cloth, and footwear from neighboring countries.

FESTIVALS AND LEISURE ACTIVITIES

Of a country that is often severe and unforgiving, the Afghans are themselves strong and resourceful, and possessed of great reserves of energy and ingenuity. The fiercely competitive games commonly played in the country by adults and children serve as both sources of pleasure and an opportunity to hone razor-quick instincts that ensure victory and survival. Leisure is a concept not all that familiar to the large majority of those who live at the subsistence level. An aspect of urban life includes facilities for leisure activity that are not available in most rural areas. Most people are extremely poor, have no time for leisure activity, and have to work from dawn to dusk to earn money to maintain their families. Financial status largely determines what type of leisure activity people can indulge in. Leisure activity includes a variety of indulgences, such as playing games, going to theaters, and so forth. Well-to-do families can afford to organize picnics on weekends, Fridays in public parks, and exclusive resort areas such as Paghman and Istalif, where they barbecue and play games and music. The popularity of national and religious festivals are an example of the joy and revelry that all people are capable of, regardless of the state of their daily lives.

Major religious festivals in Afghanistan are *Eid-e-Qurban* and *Eid-e-Ramazan* celebrated across the country. *Eid-e-Qurban* is also called *Eid al-Azha* and

Eid-e-Kabir or the Big *Eid* and occurs on the tenth day of the month of Zu al-Hijja in the Islamic lunar calendar. On this day, families celebrate the occasion by slaughtering a goat, a sheep, or a cow in memory of Abraham sacrificing his son Ismail, at the command of God. Ismail was spared when God provided Abraham with a lamb to sacrifice instead of his son. The meat is divided into three parts: the family in charge retains one-third for themselves, gives one-third to immediate family members, and then distributes the remaining one-third among the poor. *Eid-e-Ramazan,* also called *Eid al-Fitr* and *Eid-e-Saghir* or small *Eid,* occurs at the end of the month of Ramazan in the Islamic lunar calendar year, when people end their month-long, dawn-to-dusk fasting. There is no fixed number of days for a month in the Islamic calendar because the calendar system is based on observation of the moon by the religious scholars *(ulama).* The *ulama* determine when the month of Ramazan officially begins and ends. It is possible to project within a day or two of the officially declared date. Table 5.1 shows the lunar calendar system.

The rituals involved in celebration of both *Eids* are almost the same. The night before *Eid* several families in a neighborhood congregate in the house of a respected community member and prepare a sweet dish called *halwa.* Everyone shares it, and distributes the remainder among family members. At

Table 5.1
Lunar, *Qamari* Calendar for Year 1426–1427/2005–2006

Month Name	No. of Days	Gregorian-First day of month	Shamsi-First day of month
Muharram	30	9 February 2005	21 Dalw 1383
Safar	29	11 March	21 Hut 1383
Rabi al-Awal	30	10 April	21 Hamal 1384
Rabi al-Sani	29	10 May	20 Saur
Jamadi al-Awal	30	8 June	18 Jawza
Jamadi al-Sani	29	8 July	17 Saratan
Rajab	30	6 August	15 Asad
Shaban	29	5 September	14 Sunbulah
Ramazan	30	4 October	12 Mizan
Shawal	29	3 November	12 Aqrab
Zu al-Qadah	30	2 December	11 Qaus
Zu al-Hijja	30	1 January 2006	11 Jaddi
Muharram	30	31 January	11 Dalw
Safar	—	2 March	11 Hut

Source: *Taqwim-e-Sale-1384/2005–2006.* Kabul, Afghanistan: Ministry of Information and Culture, Baihaqi Publications, 2005.

the end, an elder member of the group recites prayers that God would bless the dead and living souls.

On *Eid* day men, women, and children wear new clothes and visit families who have lost a member of their family. People greet one another by saying *Eid Mubarak*, Happy *Eid*, and men often hug and kiss each other and women only hug and kiss other women. The host family greets the visitors by offering them tea and sweets, followed by a meal at the appropriate mealtime. Parents who have betrothed their son and daughter visit each other's house, and the groom's parents bring some gifts to the bride and her family. Some families exchange gifts and children also receive gifts or cash money called *Eidi*. Families also visit the graves of the dead relatives and pray that God would pardon the dead souls. During the three days of *Eid*, children and boys play games, families organize parties, and individuals go out with friends.

Another significant religious holiday is *Milad al-Nabi*, the birthday of the Prophet Muhammad on the twelfth of the month of *Rabi al-Awal* of the Muslim calendar. Families cook sweet dishes and offer them on plates to neighbors and people on the street to celebrate the occasion. Men attend mosques and other religious centers to say their prayers and listen to sermons by clerics eulogizing the Prophet.

Eid-e-Ghadir, which occurs on the 18th of *Zul al-Hijja* of the Muslim calendar, is a special occasion for the Shia community. According to the Shias, on the day when Prophet Muhammad returned from a pilgrimage in Mecca he asked the Muslims to assemble near the *Ghadir* pool where he addressed them and designated his cousin and son-in-law Ali as his successor.

The tenth of *Muharram* is another significant religious holiday. On October 10, 680, Imam Hussein, son of Ali and grandson of the Prophet, and his 72 companions were murdered by the Umayyad leader Yazid in the desert of Karbala in Iraq. The day is known as *dah-e-ashura*, and it is observed in Afghanistan. To the Shia community, the month of *Muharram* is a period of grief and sorrow. During this period, they decorate the *takyakhanas* with a black flag *(Alam)*, which has the form of an open hand with the crown symbolizing the five persons *(panjtan)*: Prophet Muhammad, Ali, Fatima, Hasan, and Hussein. The Shias congregate in *takyakhanas* to listen to sermons by clerics eulogizing Imam Hussein for giving his life in the defense of justice and righteousness. They organize *Nawhakhani*, in which a person sings poignant, emotional songs lamenting the killing of Hussein causing the crowd to weep, wail, and flagellate themselves to the point of bleeding. During *Muharram*, the Shias postpone any functions and ceremonies such as weddings, engagements, and other merrymaking events.[7]

The Isma'ilis celebrate two special events, the birthday of their spiritual leader, the Aga Khan on December 13 and the *Imamat Day* on July 11, when the Aga Khan assumed leadership of the community. Families prepare sweet dishes and distribute them to neighbors and celebrate at functions held on these days at the *Jamatkhanas*. In the past, they could not hold public functions, fearing that such activities may get them into trouble with dogmatic Sunnis and Shias within and outside the government. Since the promulgation of the 1964 Constitution they held such functions. The Taliban militias that ruled briefly did not allow the Shias and Isma'ilis to practice their faiths and subjected them to the Sunni practices.

Celebration of *Naw Rooz*, the New Year, occurs on the first day of *Hamal* of the solar calendar. It is also known as *Jashn-e-Dehqan* (farmers' festival). It is a major secular festival. The festival is an ancient Aryan tradition celebrating the first day of the spring season and it is believed that the Achaemenid rulers "shifted the *naw rooz* from the summer equinox to the vernal equinox."[8] Table 5.2 shows the solar calendar system.

There is a legend regarding *Naw Rooz*, which is reported differently in various regions of the country. One variation says that an ugly old woman roaming around appears once a year on *Naw Rooz*. If she falls in a river it means the spring will be rainy and if it rains on the *Naw Rooz* day it means that she is washing her hair. Another variation has it that if she falls on the left, the spring will be dry, or to the right, the spring will be wet.[9]

On *Naw Rooz*, families decorate their houses, and men, women, and children wear new clothing. People greet one another saying *Naw Rooz Mubarak*,

Table 5.2
Solar, *Shamsi* Calendar for Year 1384/2005–2006

Month (Arabic variations)	Month (Pushtu)	No. of Days	Gregorian- First day of month
Hamal	Waray	31	21 March 2005
Saur	Ghoiay	31	21 April
Jawza	Ghabargolay	31	22 May
Saratan	Changash	31	22 June
Asad	Zamary	31	23 July
Sunbulah	Wazhay	31	23 August
Mizan	Talah	30	23 September
Aqrab	Laram	30	23 October
Qaus	Linday	30	22 November
Jaddi	Marghumay	30	22 December
Dalw	Salwaghah	30	21 January 2006
Hut	Kab	29	20 February

Source: *Taqwim-e-Sale-1384/2005–2006.* Kabul, Afghanistan: Ministry of Information and Culture, Baihaqi Publications, 2005.

Happy New Year. On this day, women prepare more elaborate dishes to feed visiting friends and family members. One popular dish is called *halwa-e-samanak*, a sweet dish similar to a pudding, which is made from the sprout of wheat grain grown in a tray. The *samanak* is slowly cooked overnight. As it cooks, women tell tales and they take turns stirring the pot. An elderly woman sings the first two lines of what are known as the *samanak* songs; then others sing the rest of the song.[10] A section of the song goes:

> Samanak is boiling and we are stirring it
> Others are gone to sleep and we play music
> Samanak is a vow to the Spring
> It is all night-long merriment
> This delight is once a year
> Oh fortune! Until next year
> Samanak is boiling and we are stirring it
> Others have gone to sleep and we play music
> Dreams will fly tonight
> As Samanak keeps boiling
> The heart will swell with pride
> Oh fortune! Until next year[11]

Families also prepare a special soup dish known as *hafi-miwah*. It is a mixture of seven fruits and nuts that symbolizes the beginning of the spring season.

On *Naw Rooz,* a major festival known as *jandah bala kardan* (raising the flag) is organized at the Mausoleum of Ali in Mazar, Balkh, and in Karta-e-Sakhi in Kabul. When the flag is raised, devoted believers fight to get near the flag in order to be able to touch the flagpole, in the belief that those who touch it first will be additionally blessed. People also visit Mazar to watch and participate at the *milah-e-gul-e-surkh,* a festival held during the short-lived red tulip blossoming season. When the Taliban seized power, they declared such practices to be anti-Islamic and prohibited people from celebrating *Naw Rooz,* but recently these events are being held again.

Jashn (Independence Day) on August 19 is a major secular festival commemorating Afghanistan's independence from the British in 1919. Independence was actually gained earlier after the war in May of 1919, but *Jashn* is celebrated in August because it marks the end of the summer. Offices, schools, and private sectors remain closed during the three days of celebration.

Hindu and Sikh communities organize festivals in Jalalabad known as *milah-e-vaisakhi* (vaisakhi picnic) to celebrate *Naw Rooz* and spring. Other festivals included *deewali* and *janam ashtmi,* where they gather in a temple for prayers and the *lohi* festival that involves fireworks.

GAMES AND SPORTS

Games and sports are an integral part of an Afghan community's way of life and reflect the lifestyle of its people. Popular games vary from one region to another and do not have established rules. Poorer families cannot afford manufactured toy games for their children, so these children play and invent games using natural objects. One such game toy is *bujul* (knucklebones of goats, sheep, or cows) or *chinaq* (wishbones). In one variation of *bujul bazi*, children draw a circle with a diameter of about half a meter and give their *bujul* to one child, who tosses them in the air. If a *bujul* falls outside the circle, its owner is disqualified from the game and the rest continue the game. The first player is the one whose *bujul* falls nearest to the center of the circle and with his *bujul* he hits a *bujul* that belongs to his competitor. If he knocks it out of the circle he wins and gets that *bujul* and continues to play the game as long as his own *bujul* remains inside the circle. If he fails to hit the target the owner of a *bujul*, the child whose *bujul* is nearest the center of the circle gets his turn and plays the game.[12]

Another popular game is *chinaq-shikastan*, breaking the wishbone. When families cook chicken, two people take the wishbone and break it as they

Ten-year-old Aziza enjoys reading picture books and working on her school assignments, 2003.

recite the phrase: *mara yad ast tura faramoosh*, I remember and you forgot. They try to trick each other by offering something and if the person takes it, then the person who handed him/her the object says *mara yad ast tura faramoosh* and wins the game. The game may continue for a day or more, depending on how focused the players are in remembering the bet. Another game is called *jufi-wa-taq* (even and odds) and is played with small objects. For example, a child may hold a few small coins behind his back and ask his opponent to guess whether the objects are even or odd. If his opponent makes a correct guess, then it is his turn to initiate the game. *Tukhm-jangi* (egg-fight) is another common game. Eggs are hard-boiled and decorated with different designs and colors. The game requires two or more players. If a person hits the egg held by his opponent and cracks it, he wins, and if his eggs crack in the process, he loses the game. These are traditional games that do not involve strenuous physical activity, such as running.

Naizabazi (lance game) is a common game that is played on horseback. A rider coming fast has to spear a small object, the size of a shoe, placed on the ground. *Khusay* is a common game among certain Pushtun tribes. The game involves two teams of players, and each player holds one foot behind his back and hops to reach the goal point. A player is automatically disqualified from the game if he drops his foot.[13]

Pahlawani (wrestling) is an ancient sport and is glorified in classic literature. It is popular sport both in rural and urban areas. In rural areas, wrestling is performed on occasions such as a wedding, *Naw Rooz,* or *Eid.* There is one style of wrestling related to Persian and old Indian styles, and another related to the Central Asian traditions. In the northern part of the country, people practice the Central Asian style, and those in Herat and Kabul practice the Persian style. In wrestling it is important to maintain balance. Wrestling has been described thusly:

Usually, the wrestlers grab one another's forearms in overlapping grips, and move sideways in a crab-like, rocking motion, testing each other's strength and trying to catch each other off balance. Often, a man will leap high into the air, trying to toss his opponent with a judo hip-throw. To counter this, the other wrestler will twist in midair and end up behind his opponent with a headlock. Some times only one such move as this ends the match. The whole object is to throw the opponent and pin his shoulders to the ground. When it seems apparent that one man has another pinned, the coach of the winner lifts his man by the waist and runs around the circle of spectators. The victor clasps his hands over his head and the crowd applauds.[14]

Bird and animal fights are also a common pastime. People use the hunting dogs known as *tazi,* falcons, and nets to catch birds for the purpose of games and entertainment. Hunting birds, wild sheep, goats, and predators is an old hobby practiced throughout the country by those who can afford it. When migratory birds cross the regions at special seasons of the year, people use live birds and decoys made of wood or interlaced reeds to lure them on the ponds and lakes nearby. Birds like quail and partridge (male) are domesticated and trained for fighting. Cock fighting in Afghanistan may also include quails, and the owners set rules that require that the birds paired for a fight be of equal size. When they have agreed on the rules, the birds are released from their cages and they begin to fight. Once a bird appears to be losing, its owner immediately places the cage over his bird.

In Kabul and in most urban areas, flocks of pigeons *(kabutar)* are kept in a special room mostly on the rooftops. The pigeons are domesticated and trained for games known as *kabutar bazi.* The owner releases them periodically for exercise and they mingle with the pigeons released by other people and entice them to land on the rooftop of their owner. When they land on the rooftop of their owner he lures them into captivity by baiting, netting, and whistling. If the owner of the captive bird returns and they are friends, they automatically get their pigeons; otherwise they can get them back by paying a modest amount of money.[15]

Popular animal fights for entertainment might involve dogs, rams, and camels. These fights take place on special occasions, such as festivities and national holidays. Dogfights occur at the end of winter, before spring warms the climate. In Kabul, dogfights were organized on Fridays (weekend holiday) in the Qarghah district. Camel fights take place in regions where the animal is abundant. Fights between captured hyenas occasionally occur in Qandahar. Animal fights draw a huge crowd of spectators and some people bet and lose if their animal of choice loses the fight.

Buzkashi is one of the most popular sports and is played mostly in the central and northern regions of the country. In Persian, the term *buzkashi* literally translates to "goat grabbing," a reference to the carcass of a calf that is the centerpiece of the game. A more resilient calf's carcass is actually preferred by players, and a goat carcass is only used as a last resort. The carcass is prepared for the game by having its head and hooves removed. It is also disemboweled, and the carcass is soaked in cold water to toughen it up so it will not pull apart too easily in the course of the game.

The game takes place on flat, bare ground, for instance, a harvested field, with the carcass placed in a central location. The objective is for two teams of men on horseback to compete at grabbing the carcass from its place on the ground and depositing it at the end of the field in a spot designated as a goal.

Children playing marbles on a roadside in Chindawul district, Kabul, 2003. Most recreational facilities were severely damaged during the civil war in the 1990s, causing children to use narrow alleys as playgrounds.

In these most basic terms, the game sounds very simple; however, there is very little that is simple about this sport. The run at the carcasses by players takes place at high speeds, and riders, known as *chapandaz,* and their horses need to act as a single, quick-thinking unit in order to swiftly get close enough to the carcass to grab it, have the strength and skill to lift the heavy burden without losing balance, and then to make their way through several or even dozens of competitors bent on taking the carcass away. Both men and horses train for years before either sees their first match. The best players of both species may go on to compete for decades. A *chapandaz* may own and train his horse, but this is not an inexpensive undertaking, nor are *buzkashi* skills easy to master, so the more typical scenario is a wealthy owner of one or more horses who hires a *chapandaz* to train and ride them or who pays a trainer to develop the horse and then lends it out to a skilled rider who cannot afford to maintain his own horse. When the best riders and superbly trained horses are paired together, they are more like equal partners actively working to achieve a goal than a master riding on an animal to win a game. The horses are trained to actively play the game, not just to act on specific commands.

For instance, during a play the air is typically choked with dust, and visibility is poor. It is often the horse that will come up against the carcass lying on the ground, and in the space of a few seconds, the horse will pause while simultaneously dropping his near shoulder. This is a signal to the *chapandaz,* who will reach down to grab the carcass while suspended only inches from the ground, his entire body hanging off his horse by a single hand, and the horse will instinctively adjust his balance to keep his *chapandaz* aloft, maintaining a high speed, while at the same time avoiding hitting his or other low-hanging riders or other horses with his sharp hooves. Once the rider has grabbed the carcass, his horse will immediately make for the goal; no command or actions are necessary, and in fact the rider may still be righting himself even as his horse races for the goal, with others in hot pursuit. Depending on the kind of *buzkashi* being played, achieving the goal may be straightforward or dangerously complex. In *tudabarai,* once the carcass is grabbed, horse and *chapandaz* race out of the center and to any nearest part of the borders of the game area. If it is *qarajai,* the horse and rider must first run a large circle around the designated flag on a pole before racing back to the specified scoring circle to drop the carcass, all the while other *chapandaz* are trying to wrest the prize away. Even when a man does occasionally fall to the ground, it is rare that he will be trampled. This is also evidence of the horses' training.

Buzkashi originated in the steppes of Central Asia and Mongolia as a training system intended to develop domesticated male horses into combat weapons and to maintain the razor sharp riding and fighting skills of their warriors. It is suggested that these skills were also used in snatching things and kidnapping people from the enemy camps. As people migrated from these regions into Afghanistan, and also when Genghis Khan came with his armies, they brought this game, which eventually developed into the sport it is today. Originally there were very few rules, no standards for numbers of players, size of the field, or carcass, or the length of time for a game. It was a game of skill, teamwork, and honor, and unwritten rules of thumb against unfair practices, such as hitting opponents or actively trying to knock a rider off his horse, were honored without the need of referees or judges. A loose set of rules regarding team and playing field size, game length, and playing time was eventually established for *buzkashi* matches that now commonly take place during popular organized events such as the *jashn* and *Naw Rooz* festivals, so that risks of injuries can be minimized.

Outside of these organized events, *buzkashi* continues to be played with

Players in a heated Buzkashi game, Darayam, Badakhshan, 2003.

very few rules, and any men who can afford to can sponsor a game and get the word out to attract *chapandaz* and horse teams and spectators. The best *buzkashi* horses are very well taken care of and may eat a better diet than some people: grains (barley and oats), fruit, and occasionally eggs and butter. The horses will eat less and run more in the days before a match to ensure they will be lean and fast on game day.

In some very hard-played games, the carcass may be pulled apart. When this happens, the *chapandaz* ride to their goals, and judges will determine the winner of that score as the player with the largest piece of the carcass. The score is not shared and the game ends when the judges and spectators declare a winner. A *chapandaz* may win token gifts such as rifles or cash, but the real reward lies in the victory and pride in what was accomplished.[16]

Gudiparan bazi (kite flying) is an urban activity and it is not merely a past time involving a boy and his homemade kite. This urban activity is highly competitive and their winners do not become such by flying their kite the highest, but by eliminating and taking the kites of their opponents. The word

Gudiparan translates to flying doll and *bazi* means game. Kite flyers coat their kite's string with powdered glass mixed with a glue made from wheat gelatin or protein-based glue obtained from animal tissue, a mixture that is sticky and will transform the string into a sharp cutting tool. The string coated with powdered glass becomes dangerously sharp. Players will maneuver their kites to rub their strings against the strings of a competitor, to cut the string and win the match. The kite that falls now belongs to the victor. Kites come in various shapes and sizes, ranging from 20 cm to 2 meters. They are usually made without tails, which makes them easier to control and to maneuver against opponents.

Kite shapes can vary but they basically consist of a bamboo skeleton covered with a thin paper shell, designed to be lightweight, aerodynamic, and maneuverable. The string is wound around a spindle usually made of wood so that is also lightweight. A kite game is called a *jang* (fight) and it involves at least two and up to any number of kites. The kites go airborne simultaneously and their players immediately try to eliminate the other kites. A skilled kite player can cut an opponent's string in a matter of seconds, but some competitions may last longer as the competitors jockey fiercely for favorable positions in the air.

The *charkhah* can be a deciding factor in the game. It is made of wood and resembles a small drum with a handle at each end. It holds the kite string as it reels out when the kite ascends, and helps the player to maintain control of the kite. The best-made ones allow the quick unreeling of the string, and the kite that reaches a high spot first is at an advantage, provided the wind is also blowing, because the player can use the tension in the string (caused as the wind pushes against the kite) to slash aggressively at nearby strings. The game can be quite dangerous. The glass and sharp strings may cause injuries, and boys playing this game on rooftops of houses may fall off or fall while they run on the streets and lanes to catch the falling kite.[17]

Upper- and middle-class urbanites indulge themselves in games such as playing chess and cards, and players occasionally gamble. Modern physical sports such as football, volleyball, and tennis are popular in Kabul and in provincial towns and districts because facilities for such sports are mostly available there. Cricket has been brought by refugees returning from Pakistan. The Olympic Association was formed in 1933 and two years later it organized a football tournament in Kabul. Since then, different teams of players organized tournaments and matches at various seasons. The Taliban militia who ruled most parts of Afghanistan prohibited recreational activities that negatively impacted sports and traditional games throughout the country.

NOTES

1. For detailed information on diet and cuisine of Afghanistan see, Asad Gharwal, *Award-Winning, Low-fat Afghani Cooking* (Minneapolis, MN: Chromined Publishing, 1995).

2. For additional information see, Gharwal, *Award-Winning, Low-fat Afghani Cooking.*

3. See also, Helen Saberi, *Afghan Food & Cookery: Noshe Djan* (New York: Hippocrene Books, 2000).

4. Louis Dupree, *Afghanistan* (Karachi, Pakistan: Oxford University Press, 2002), pp. 238–247.

5. Hassan Poladi, *The Hazaras* (Stockton, CA: Mughal Publishing, 1989), p. 305.

6. Dupree, *Afghanistan,* pp. 110–111.

7. Poladi, *The Hazaras,* pp. 140–143.

8. Dupree, *Afghanistan,* p. 98.

9. Dupree, *Afghanistan,* p. 99.

10. Asrari and Amanov, *Adabiyat-e-Shafahi-e-Mardum-e-Tajik* [Oral Literature of the Tajiks], tr. Abdul Qayum Qawim and Mohammad Afzal Banuwal (Kabul, Afghanistan: Publications of the Cultural Council of Kabul University, 1346/1985), pp. 86–87.

11. *Majmua-e-az foklor-e-amiyanah-e-zaban-e-Dari* [A collection of the Dari Language Folklore], (Kabul, Afghanistan: Nashrat-e-Ketabkhanah-e-Kiyumars, n.d.), pp. 39–40.

12. Nico Van Oudenhoven, "Common Afghan Street Games and Child Development." *Afghanistan Journal* JG. 7, Heft 4 (1980): 130.

13. Dupree, *Afghanistan,* p. 222.

14. Dupree, *Afghanistan,* pp. 211–212.

15. "Kabutarbazi." *Akhbar-e-Kabul,* 11 August 2003, pp. 24–25.

16. For detailed information on *buzkashi* see, Whitney G. Azoy, *Buzkashi: Game and Power in Afghanistan* (Philadelphia: University of Pennsylvania Press, 1982).

17. For further information see, David Sahar, "The Art of Gudiparan bazi." http://www.afghana.com/Entertainment/Gudiparanbazi.htm.

6

Family, Women, and Gender Issues

The centrality of family in social life regardless of class and the role of women in modern-day Afghanistan are a study in symbiosis and conflict. The kinship system in Afghanistan centers around the patriarch, and males and females are raised in a family environment that stresses the primacy of the patriarch, and by extension the tribal chiefs and religious leaders, *mullahs,* almost exclusively male. Women as a whole in Afghanistan have experienced varying degrees of gender oppression, both social and political. Their difficulties as they attempt to achieve gender equity in terms of civil rights or education have received the most attention from scholars and outsiders. Not always noticed is the fact that the unique conditions of this physically severe country have resulted in elevated status and influence for some women, mostly those in remote, rural or nomadic communities. Their importance as a partner and a participant in ensuring the survival of a family and of a community is evident when one sees entire communities supported by the revenue from women's handicrafts, such as carpet weaving and embroidery, and women in nonurban areas regularly work side by side with men, related and unrelated.

CONCEPT OF THE FAMILY

Family structure in Afghanistan is primarily based on the patriarchal system. Members of the family defer to the authority of the head of the family, generally the father and the eldest son after the father's death. The entrenched cultural values of such a system stress greater respect for age, marriage at a young age, and a great impetus on the part of young women to become mothers. A major characteristic of every ethnic community is the shared concept of inviolability of the family. An individual's honor, social status, and personal code of conduct are largely determined by the institution of the family. Social values stress the cohesiveness of the family through maintaining the kinship system. Members of the extended family prefer to settle in the same or nearby locale comprising a special neighborhood where families extend a helping hand to one another in times of need. The kinship institution often extends into political institutions where a person rising to a higher position often dispenses favors to kinsfolk and prefers to recruit members of the immediate and distant families if there is a vacancy in the private and public institutions.

The extended family is also an economic unit, where individuals work together on the family's farm, retail business, or estates and support each other, because there are no public services to enable a single family to lead an independent life. Individuals rely on the family's support system and perform their obligations to its members by reciprocating the help that they receive. Although the state established a number of institutions geared to provide services to the family and initiated laws to reform rules pertaining to the family, it did not implement them on any wide scale due to fears of a backlash if it was seen as interfering in family affairs. Social and cultural values prohibit direct intrusion by the state in family affairs. Islamic law and social customs govern family-related business, such as marriage and inheritance.

Most families prefer to marry their children within the extended family, and preferred marriage partners are cousins. If a marriage does not take place within the extended family, the parents look for suitable marriage partners for their children within the clan, the tribe, and people who are remotely related to them. An extended family consists primarily of the father, who is head of the family, his wife, and their children, whether married or single. However, individuals of affluent families prefer to live outside the extended family. The married son's wife and her children within the family compound submit to the authority of the husband's parents. Maintaining family discipline is a cherished ideal, as it gives a man a good name and enhances his prestige in the community. Individuals are encouraged to avoid committing actions that negatively affect the name and status of their families or bring disgrace.

INSTITUTIONS OF THE FAMILY

Each ethnic community has its own culture and customs that help in strengthening the family's solidarity and governs family-related affairs. In a tribal society, people identify themselves with their kinship and trace their lineage to a known ancestor. Members sometimes choose as their last name the name of their kinship group or tribe. Elderly men often remember the name of an individual from whom they are direct descendents and call that person their great grandfather. A lineage can split when families fail to settle disputes or when quarrels develop among them without any resolution. This can affect the recognition of a successor after the death or passing of the head of the group. When a family settles in a far distant region and fails to keep in touch with members of the kinship group, they may gradually dissolve into the new community and lose touch with their family. The new family gradually associates and identifies itself with the new community; however, the family continues to maintain the lineage tradition. Some kinship groups in a particular village have scant or no knowledge of their ancestors. However, the kinship bond among its members remains strong and unites them. Identification and association with a common ancestor is viewed by many to contribute to the maintenance of tribal unity. Genealogy is a crucial factor in passing down knowledge of self and history to the next generation in oral cultures, where there are no literacy traditions. Sometimes people choose a famous person, a charismatic leader, or a warrior as their ancestor, even though there may not be any actual bond.

Polygamy is practiced occasionally among all ethnic groups. However, monogamous relationships prevail among the vast majority of the people. Islam allows a man to marry up to four wives but requires the husband to provide the wives with financial support and treat them equally. Polygamy is practiced primarily by financially well-off individuals who can afford the expenses necessary to keep additional wives. A man usually marries a second, third, or fourth wife when his previous wives did not bear him a son. He may also take an additional wife when the previous wife becomes old, or if the first wife was from an arranged marriage and the second wife is his personal choice. The cowives are referred to as *ambaq* and they share the same living area and live under one roof. Relations between these women are typically characterized as plotting against one another and extreme jealousy toward the other in trying to please the husband. A proverb aptly depicts relations between a husband and his wives as such that " *du zan kardi du gham kardi*," meaning if you marry two women you have created two troubles for yourself.

A small number of poor men also marry more than one wife for economic considerations, especially if the women are skilled and engage in activities such as embroidery or carpet and rug weaving. This happens more often in Northern Afghanistan, and such women fetch a higher bride price because they have special skills. Most polygamous men are generally middle-aged and older and marry younger women with the hope to have more children. The following proverb aptly describes social factors that contributed to polygamous relationships:

May the Lord grant that no person be without a nation,
And that within this nation, no person should be without a tribe,
And that within this tribe no person should be without a community
   of brothers,
And that within this community of brothers no person should be with-
   out a son.[1]

Widowed women are obligated to remarry a person in the extended family, usually the next oldest available male sibling or cousin.

Society attaches greater importance to boys and less value to girls because boys will inherit the family's name and property, while the girl is simply destined to enter another family upon marriage. The harsh agricultural lifestyles also dictate the importance of having a male to provide physical labor in the fields in order to bring food to the family.

Men are dominant figures in the family, clan, and the tribe. The father has absolute authority in supervising and controlling the lives of male and female members of the household within and outside the home. He decides what type of education his children will receive, if any, and what type of profession they will undertake. A father is the primary spokesperson for the family, and he alone makes the decisions that affect the lives of the entire family. In upper and upper-middle classes as well as educated families, a father is more likely to consult with members of the family and seek their support in the implementation of his decisions.

GENDER STATUS

One of the major aspects of tribal social formations is gender inequality and the treatment of women as second-class citizens, depriving them of their basic rights. Women are subordinated to men and are obligated to obey them. The patriarchal system, which is based on androcentrism, maintains that maleness is the natural order of things, and in the Abrahamic tradition, God is male who created the female after man's image. Women, therefore, are bound to submit to men and follow their orders without questioning their merits.

Society and its prevailing culture, customs, and traditions confine women's activities to the domestic realm. Although women of low-income and poor families work outside the homes out of necessity to maintain and support the family, a man is still regarded as the guardian of the family. Writers and intellectuals who support the patriarchical system ardently defend male superiority and their writings have greatly contributed to the perpetuation of this belief system that continues to oppress women. An acclaimed Persian poet

Muslihuddin Sa'adi wrote poems in which he instructed the husband on how to discipline women of the family. He wrote:

Shut the door of joy to a house,
In which women's voices are being heard
You beat the women if she visits the market,
Otherwise you ought to stay home as a woman.[2]

Women are regarded as creatures who have no other social function but to please their husbands, and they are often treated as sex objects. For example, Sa'adi instructed his readers and admirers on how to indulge in pleasure-seeking activities by marrying a new wife. He wrote:

If a woman smiles to strangers
Tell the man to not brag about his manliness
Women eyes must not look at a stranger
They would rather be dead than leave their homes
Oh friend, every spring marry a new wife
An old calendar cannot be of any use.[3]

Women are treated as man's personal property, one that can be purchased and disposed of at any time. The concept of women as a chattel is strong among most tribal communities and some men even tattoo their women with the same mark they put on their animals.[4] In some tribal communities, women are even less valued than animals. For instance, in the northern region, the Turkmen attach more value to their horses than to their wives, because horses are more useful and precious to them. In the past, Turkmen raised horses to launch quick raids on their adversaries and at present their famous stock of horses is an indispensable asset in the *buzkashi* game. A common saying among the Turkmen graphically describes male attitudes and perceptions as they compare their horses with their women: "If you have one day left of your life, take a horse; if you have two days left, take a woman." A similar line of thinking toward women is also echoed among certain nomadic tribes who keep camels as a means of transport. To them "a good woman is like a transport-camel. She is sturdily built, has big, strong legs, a steady gait and is clean."[5]

SECLUSION AND RESTRICTION

Prevailing cultural traditions in Afghanistan support gender segregation and seclusion of women in the public arena. In urban areas, conservative families and husbands demand that their women must observe seclusion *(hijab)* and wear the *chadari (burqa)*, a garment that entirely covers the wearer, whenever they leave the home. The sexes are segregated in most public places such as schools, theaters, and so forth. Women are allotted special seats in the first few front rows of every type of public transportation. Women are not allowed to leave their homes without a legitimate reason, and they must secure permission from the husband or other male members of the family if they decide to visit relatives or their girlfriends, known as *khahar khanda* (adopted sister). Women in Kabul and other large cities are allowed to freely visit the women's public bath and women's hospitals as well as attend wedding and engagement parties of immediate relatives and friends of the family, although these are usually segregated by sexes.

Generally, women are not permitted to socialize with or entertain a guest who is not immediately related to the family or speak to a stranger. However, some tribal communities do not place such severe restrictions on their women. For example, the Hazara Isma'ili women enjoy some degree of freedom of movement and they are not required to be secluded from Isma'ili men even if they are not related to the family. Similarly some Durani Pushtun women "expressed little sexual segregation and women were able to entertain male guests when a man was not present or available to do so."[6] However, women in most tribal communities are restricted from participation in the public domain and their seclusion has been described as follows:

> A [Pushtun] may also invite you to his home, but either he or another man will carry in the food that has been prepared in the women's quarters. The food, in turn, is often the traveler's only clue to the presence of a woman nearby. If the dish is relatively clean and the meal appetizing, it means there is a woman in the adjoining room who cooked it, if the food is inedible, a [Pushtun] man did the deed. A [Pushtun] won't tell you the names of his wife and mother.... Women are as private to a [Pushtun] as his private parts.[7]

Such a conservative view of women is typical of ethnic and tribal communities. One of Afghanistan's most well-known faces is that of a wife and mother in a remote Pushtun community who lives under the absolute authority of her husband. In 1984, a teenage Pushtun girl named Sharbat Gula was photographed by Steve McCurry of *National Geographic* when she was orphaned and living in the Nasir Bagh refugee camp in Pakistan. Her beauty and attitude caught his attention and resulted in a photograph that fascinated nations and became the de facto face of refugees and of women of Afghanistan and their plight in the war-torn country. After 17 years, McCurry returned to Pakistan with a mission to find her and take another photograph of her. After a long wait and many failed attempts and false leads, he found her but had to negotiate with her brother and husband to even meet her again. She was now a mother of three living under purdah in an undisclosed remote area in a Pushtun region of Afghanistan.[8]

Society dispenses severe punishment to women who violate the established social and cultural traditions, even including death by stoning. For example, if a woman is suspected of having a sexual affair, whether proven or not, she will likely be put to death by the men in her family—her husband, her father, and her brothers. In the Muhmand region of eastern Afghanistan, a woman was accused of having illicit sexual affairs and became pregnant while the husband was away from home. Her husband's family regarded her as loose and returned her to her father's house, expecting that he kill her to preserve his family's name and honor. In accordance with tribal customs, the father killed his daughter without any hesitation, and soon afterward, people from neighboring towns and villages came to congratulate him for the deed he performed that was necessary to restore the family's honor. Even the local government administrative officer came to offer his congratulation, instead of issuing an arrest warrant and trying him in a court of law for his actions.[9]

Women have no rights or the means to defend themselves on charges leveled against them, and society looks poorly upon such women who take matters into their own hands and attempt to expose men's brutality. Women can be victimized not only by the husband but also by men of power and authority and have no recourse to fight back. Men who assault women will even kill them without a second thought in order to cover up the crime. For instance, a woman was molested when her brother left her to the care of a trusted religious man in Bamiyan until he would return from a journey abroad:

Shaikh Barsia was a holy man who prayed a lot and therefore was considered a perfectly reliable person. A man going on the pilgrimage wanted to leave his sister, who was very beautiful, with someone trustworthy while he was away, so he decided that there could be no place safer for her than the house of Shaikh Barsia. But while she was staying in the house, Shaikh Barsia noticed her, loved her, and finally took her by force. She became pregnant so he killed and buried her. When her brother finally returned from the pilgrimage the Shaikh told him she had died of a disease.[10]

ENGAGEMENT

Romantic love affairs and courtships are an alien concept in this society, where strict social and cultural traditions are based on segregation of sexes. However, such affairs can occur on occasion among educated strata in urban areas. The strict moral code of conduct does not allow for young men and women to get acquainted before marriage and demands chastity and virginity for men and women. Patriarchal tradition deems women to be creatures who lack the wisdom and judgment to decide their own futures and whom to marry. Parents consult with each other when deciding whom their sons and daughters marry. Typically, the mother will look for and select prospective brides; fathers will exercise greater say in selecting a groom for his daughter.

The tradition of arranged marriage is common in Afghanistan. Young girls are often married at a very young age to wealthy men, regardless of their age. Some Pushtun families have married their children off while they are very young, usually selecting a spouse from the same village or town. Selection criteria for a partner varies from one ethnic community to the other, but most families prefer that suitable mates be related to one another, if possible. There are a number of reasons for arranged marriages and chief among them are economic considerations. For example, any property that the bride is entitled to after marriage remains in the family if she marries a relative. Profit is the main motive for arranged marriages when two families try to combine their landholdings. Another reason for arranged marriages is to reciprocate a favor a man receives during a time of need. He will then arrange the marriage of his daughter as a token of his goodwill to the person who did him the favor or to his son.

An arranged marriage also takes place when two families try to maintain friendly ties or to resolve an existing rift between them. Some engagements are made by force, as when a family may be compelled to offer their daughter in marriage to a man to whom they owe a significant debt. A patriarch may also punish a woman, when she willfully does not obey his orders or tries to marry someone against his wishes, by marrying her off to someone else against her will. Arranged marriages also take place when a man expresses his loyalty to a family and marries his daughter to a member of that family. When a family cannot decide on a husband for their daughter, they often rely on their feelings, assuming that the man they select would prove to be worthy.

When two families agree to marry their children, they are obligated to honor this agreement in all cases. It is rare that these families terminate such a relationship unless they develop major differences at a later time. For example, a family in Herat betrothed their daughter when she was a child. The groom's family left the city and settled in another city without keeping in touch with the bride's family. Social and cultural traditions forbid the young girl to marry another man. This situation forced her family to seek the guidance of a local judge regarding this matter and to find out how long they had to wait prior to marrying their daughter to another man. The judge told them to "hang the young girl's *chadari* on the wall and when it disintegrated and fell off the hook, she should be released to marry someone else."[11] If a girl dies before her marriage, her family is required to give her sister as a replacement or find another girl for the groom to marry.

Another type of arranged marriage that became common since the 1990s is known as "parceled marriage." It takes place between a man who lives in the West and the bride in Afghanistan or within the settled refugee communities in Pakistan, Iran, and elsewhere. The prospective husband sends his photograph and some money to the bride's family, upon which the bride's family will betroth their daughter to him, hoping that their daughter would have a better life in the West. The girl has no choice but to agree to the family's decision and marry the man. However, there have been instances when the husband did not like her later and returned to the West, forcing the woman to live the rest of her life like a widow, unable to marry again. This situation is miserable for the rejected wife but still preferable to the stigma of divorce.

The tradition of matchmaking is fairly common throughout the country and is initiated by the mother, father, immediate family member, or a good friend. It takes place more often in urban areas, where there is a better chance to meet members of the opposite sex who are not relatives. If a boy likes a girl, he tells his mother who will discuss the matter with her husband and then they send a mutual friend as liaison *(ruybar)* to explore what the girl's parents think about it. After the *ruybar* gives the boy's parents leave to proceed, they visit the bride's family and discuss the matter with the girl's parents. The girl's parents will usually stall for time and after a few rounds of meetings they will agree to betroth their daughter to the prospective son-in-law. Educated families do not care much for the services of *ruybar* and will directly discuss the marriage of their children because in most cases the boy and girl already know each other well and have agreed to marry. Disapproval by the bride's family sometimes ends up in an elopement that disgraces the family, so some couples may use the threat to elope to get both sets of parents to agree to let them marry. It is rare for both sexes to refuse the decision of their parents regarding selection of a potential mate. Educated men and women often prefer to choose their mate without any interference by their parents. They value education and believe that their potential mates must have a modern education and do not approve the tradition of marriage within the family networks, preferring to marry someone outside the immediate family circle.

After two families agree to marry their children, the boy's family visits the girl's family, bringing with them a tray of sweets consisting of *qand,* a cone-shaped sugar loaf about 1–2 feet high and about 6 inches wide at the base, wrapped in brightly colored paper. The tray is covered with an embroidered kerchief, and an elder member of the family breaks the sugar loaf with an ax and distributes the pieces among a few guests and members of the family. If the sugar loaf breaks into several pieces, it represents a good sign of a happy marriage. Later, sometimes the two families organize a party called *Shirni-khuri,* at which time they officially declare the engagement of their children. They invite immediate family members and the boy's family brings gifts that include clothes and jewelry for the bride.

The tradition varies somewhat among different ethnic communities and those living in urban and rural areas. Some ethnic communities do not allow the groom to visit the bride until after they are married. However, this tradition varies among other ethnic and tribal communities where the bride family invites the groom and his family for a dinner shortly after the engagement party to enable the groom to freely visit with the bride's family. This situation provides an opportunity for the groom and the bride to get to know each other before getting married.

MARRIAGE

In traditional communities, men generally marry at the age of 17 and some even much earlier and girls are generally married at the age of 16 or younger. In urban areas, educated and well-to-do men often marry after completing their studies and starting a career either in the private sector or in the state-owned enterprises. It is rare to see girls over age 20 and not married. However, the number has increased to some extent as educated girls have to wait longer to first finish high school or university and then find a suitable mate. People also prefer marriage within their own ethnic and faith-based communities. It is rare to see a marriage that transcends ethnic and religious boundaries. However, a significant number of educated people do not attach great importance to such ideas.

The groom's family holds a meeting with the bride's family and both agree on a mutually acceptable date for the wedding. After several sessions, the two families agree on the amount of dowry payments to the bride's family to cover wedding expenses as well as gifts for the bride that include clothing and gold jewelry. The amount of dowry is supposed to be compensation for the girl's care and upbringing before her marriage. The amount of funds given by families varies from one community to another, depending on the economic status of the family. Low-income families often pay a modest amount of cash, goods, animals, and land, and upper- and middle-class families pay cash that ranges from 40,000 Afs. to about 100,000 Afs. or more (U.S.$ = 48.50 Afs. in 2003). Such high wedding expenses force some families to go bankrupt and compel low-income families to delay the marriage of their children until they can afford it. These factors can result in a man marrying when he is past his youth or well into middle age. Individuals who cannot afford to pay a high dowry may be forced into a celibate life. Educated families do not tend to attach significant value to the dowry and are critical of families who seek to enrich themselves by demanding excessive monies for the bride.

When families of the groom and the bride reach an agreement and resolve the issue of dowry, they set a date for the wedding. Before the wedding, the groom and the bride take necessary preparations for the occasion that involves bathing, during which, according to religious rules, they must shave all body hair (the groom is not required to shave facial hair), and the bride is dressed in her wedding gown. It is the tradition among some communities to stain the hands of the bride and groom with henna a day before the wedding. The night before the wedding, immediate relatives of the bride, both male and female, dress in their best finery and go to the bride's house for socializing. Musicians play their instruments and sing songs, and some people dance. The next day the groom rides on a horse (or typically an automobile in the city) accompanied by his best man, friends, relatives, and guests in a procession to the bride's parents' home. Men sit in one room while women are in another room putting makeup on the bride, helping her into her gown, and packing her things to take to her new home. A number of women sing and some dance to entertain female guests congregated around the bride.

After a meal is served, a *mullah* performs the religious ceremony, called *nikah,* in the presence of the fathers of the bride and groom and their guests. The bride is not present at this time; she is sequestered in a separate room. The *mullah* inquires whether the bride is willing to marry the groom. Since the bride is not present, one of her male relatives, a brother, cousin, or uncle represents her and testifies on her behalf. Her stand-in listens for her audible and positive consent before the *mullah* can proceed. The *mullah* then asks the groom's father to specify the amount of *mahr. Mahr* belongs to the bride and is regarded as an insurance to strengthen the position of the woman in case her husband later divorces her so she should not then become dependent on her family. Generally, the husband will control that money; he would only lose it if he divorces her later. After the parents of the groom and the bride agreed on the amount of *mahr,* the *mullah* then recites a few verses from the Quran to bless a cup of water filled with a few pieces of the sugar loaf for the newly wedded couple to drink. He ties the matrimonial knot and offers his blessings, and he hands over the cup to the groom to share it with his bride, which officially concludes the marriage. Male guests shower the groom with sweets and paper money, and people around him scramble to pick up the sweets and money. Before the bride's departure for her new home, the bride's father performs the ritual known as *kamar bastan,* knotting the corners of the bride's veil with a green cloth and handing it over to the groom, an act that symbolizes the bride's purity.

The groom places his new bride on his decorated horse or in his vehicle and brings her home, accompanied by a procession of wedding guests. When they reach the bridegroom's house, a goat or a sheep is slaughtered to honor the bride, and the groom's family prepares an elaborate feast for the guest. During the celebration, musicians entertain with music and songs, while guests socialize and women entertain the bride in her quarters, separated from the men. Friends and relatives then visit the bride and offer presents so she would lift the veil from her face and let them see and talk to her. The ritual is known as *ru-namayi.*

In urban areas, affluent families arrange the wedding to take place in a hotel hall or in a restaurant. The bride may wear the traditional handmade dress or she may choose to wear a Western-style wedding gown, while the groom will usually wear a suit. As the bride enters the hall, accompanied by the groom, her immediate family, and female companions, a band of musicians plays music accompanied by a song called *ahistah buro* ("go slowly"). Immediate family members hold a Quran wrapped in layers of cloth over the bride's head as she slowly walks toward the elevated platform where she and the groom will sit. This act is intended to bring them blessings for a happy marriage. Close female relatives lift off the bride's veil and she and the groom watch people dance. After the meal is served, the groom samples the sweets and then feeds some to his bride. Friends and relatives approach the raised platform to express their good will and offer them presents. After the ceremony is over the bride and groom go home and the band of musicians again plays music and sings the *ahistah buro* song. Immediate family members and relatives accompany the bride and the groom to their home where the celebration will continue for a day or two.

Families attach great importance to virginity, *pardah-e-bekarat* or *dukhtari,* as they regard it to be the symbol of honor. Parents take great pains to ensure that their daughters remain virgin until they marry. Women who are close relatives of the family were once involved in the inspection of the bed the morning after the wedding for blood stains to prove the bride's virginity. In the 1990s, a groom's family in the United States once sent proof of a bride's virginity to her family via Federal Express:

> We happened to come to California for a visit and stayed with our
> paternal aunts. We had met their elder son while we were living in refu-

gee camps in Peshawar, Pakistan. Already at that time we were thinking of him becoming our son-in-law. During this visit our daughter and her present husband got to meet each other and they liked each other, and his family proposed an engagement. The engagement and wedding was all done and we are proud of her being *sar-bayland,* virgin. The groom's family had mailed the blood of her purity through Federal Express to us.[12]

The bride is not allowed to visit her family immediately after the wedding and has to wait for a month or more before she is allowed visit them. In some communities, a woman can frequently visit her biological parents but in some others she is not allowed to do so without the consent and permission of her husband.

CHILD REARING

Families consider children an indispensable asset that maintains the continuity of their lineage as well as supports them in their old age. When a son is born, the family arranges an elaborate feast, depending on the extent of the family's wealth, inviting friends and relatives for celebration. The birth of a girl is not considered important and is sometimes even cause for disappointment. This is not the rule; some families value their offspring whether they are boys or girls. Ethnic communities have their own way of celebrating the occasion. For example, some tribal communities fire guns and beat drums to welcome the newborn baby; others simply throw a party. In urban areas, families celebrate *shab-e-shash* (six nights after birth) and invite friends and relatives who bring presents for the baby.

A few days after the birth, the parents choose an appropriate name for the child. In general, a father chooses the name if the baby is a boy and the mother chooses the name if the baby is a girl. Some families even ask a religious figure to choose a name for their son. Before naming the baby, some parents call the baby by a pseudonym, believing that it prevents the evil spirit *(jin)* from finding and influencing or taking the baby away. A child is typically referred to by his or her name in the context of the relationship with elder family members, for example Abdullah son of Muhammed.

The mother swaddles the baby, carries it, and breastfeeds until it can chew food. A wooden cradle, either left on the floor or hung from a roof or a pole, is used to let the baby lie down and sleep. The baby's older brother or sister takes the baby around as soon as she or he can walk. Boys and girls of the extended family can play together in a playground or on the family compound only until the age of ten. However, children of some extended families or of the same village, regardless of their age, often continue to play together. Girls after age ten are supposed to remain in the home and learn cooking, cleaning, sewing, and other household chores. Mothers often take a keen interest to impart their knowledge and experiences to their daughters so they become excellent housewives. Boys often assist their fathers on the farm in rural areas and help them in their business in urban areas.

According to Islamic tradition, a male child must be circumcised. In rural areas, where there are no medical centers, circumcision is often performed by experienced itinerant barbers known as *dallak,* but in urban areas, families take the child to a hospital. Families celebrate the occasion by organizing a feast and inviting immediate relatives and close friends.

Families make sure that their children get proper discipline from a very young age and inculcate them with Islamic and tribal values that stress obedience to those in a position of authority in the family and in the community. Children also must respect and submit to the older children of the family. Although child abuse is rare among most ethnic and tribal communities, families will punish their children up until adulthood for their offending behaviors, hoping that such measures will cause them to develop discipline and refrain from behaviors unacceptable to family and society. Families expect their children to assume the responsibilities of adulthood by the time they reach age 10 or 12; however, most do not fully enter the adult world until they are much older, unless circumstances are harsh and they are needed to contribute to the family's upkeep. Rearing children is the sole responsibility of the mother because the father works outside the home.

Children are traditionally born at home because women usually prefer the assistance of a midwife to a doctor in rural areas, and many women in urban areas express similar preferences to giving birth at home. During labor, women are generally assisted by older women and an experienced, local midwife. Although various traditions are used to safeguard women in labor, women are taken to a nearby hospital if there are complications. Child mortality is high in rural areas because most families cannot afford to take their women to a hospital, if there even is one in the center of the provincial town. Conservative families do not allow their wives to visit health centers and medical treatment is often conducted in absentia, where a husband describes the condition of the woman to a medical doctor, and he attempts to diagnose the problem and prescribes medicine based on the oral account of the husband. A man's attitude toward his wife has been described as follows:

> The women are the most neglected, the women are the most anemic, the women have the highest level of tuberculosis; the women in general are in pretty bad shape.... Traditionally, the Afghan men get the best of

the food, which is then passed down to the children, and the women eat last, what's left over, if anything. There are certain long-standing taboos: women in some of the tribes won't even eat meat or vegetables, because they think they are bad for them. So what they basically live on is sweet bread and green tea.... You cannot get a husband to donate blood for his wife because if you take his blood you take his life, but if she dies he can always get another wife.[13]

A woman usually gives birth to six or seven babies during her prime fertility years. Abortion is not an option for conservative families as they regard such an act to be against the will of God. In addition, it was not an available service prior to the 1970s. Modern and educated women are more likely to approve of abortion as a way to terminate unwanted pregnancies. They have no objection to the use of contraception. However, in rural areas, women must take locally produced drugs and herbs if they want to avoid having children for whom they cannot provide adequate care.

DIVORCE

According to Islamic and civil laws, a woman is allowed to seek a divorce (talaq) if she is not content with her marriage or if she is mistreated and abused by her husband. In reality it is the man who will usually initiate talaq, without the consent of his wife, and according to the tradition he merely has to proclaim the words "I divorce you" three times in the presence of witnesses for talaq to become effective. Because of the social stigma attached, divorce is still rare and only occurs when the husband and wife develop serious irreconcilable differences. People will look down upon a man who divorces his wife and the word zan-talaq is used as an insult to a man who divorces his wife. In addition he would lose the mahr, the amount of money he agreed to pay the bride when he signed the marriage contract. To avoid public humiliation, and also because of the economic burden associated with the talaq, men often do not resort to divorce.

Fathers will get custody of older children after a divorce, but mothers are entitled to custody of infants until they reach an age where a mother's sole care is no longer necessary. Men are responsible for providing financial support to their children while they are in their mother's custody and can visit them at any time, but once they leave her custody, a divorced mother may not visit her children. If a mother remarries, she loses all custody of her children, and her former husband's family will look after his children until he can find a suitable wife and marry again. Termination of marriage by either party is regarded as a disgrace, and the social stigma attached to it usually compels couples to remain married. In addition, a woman past childbearing age or with children from a previous marriage would have a very difficult time finding another husband. The expenses that accompany the engagement and marriage process may be prohibitive and suitable spouses are more difficult to find. These are among the contributing factors to the relatively low divorce rate in the country.

A woman in an unsatisfactory marriage generally does not initiate *talaq*, even if she is forced to endure frequent physical and verbal abuse by her husband. She would have little to gain in any case, because her family would most likely not welcome her back, and she could not easily remarry. It would be next to impossible for a single woman to find work to support herself, and it is not easy for any single person, and especially a woman, to relocate to another area. The legal system also creates hurdles for women to do so because it requires that women provide two male witnesses to testify in a court of law regarding abuses she sustained at the hands of her husband. She would have great difficulty substantiating her claims regarding irreconcilable differences and mistreatment by her husband. Most women do not have identification cards, and this makes it difficult for them to even prove their identity, much less find two male witnesses willing to testify on their behalf. One witness would have to testify as to her identity and the other has to testify as to the identity of the first witness. A woman who spends much of her time confined into the home finds it difficult, if not impossible, to find a male witness willing to testify on her behalf. She is unlikely to know many people besides her relatives, her husband's relatives, and his close friends.

A woman also encounters further difficulties seeking divorce in a court of law, as the court will still regard her as married to her husband unless he submits a formal divorce application and registers it in court. The husband is unlikely to do so unless he is the one initiating the divorce. Even though the husband may divorce her according to local tradition by proclaiming three times the word *talaq*, "I divorce you," legally the court still considers them to be married.

Reasons for divorce are often cited as an unsatisfactory marriage, lack of love, physical abuse, illegitimate pregnancy, and illicit sexual relations on the part of a woman. Women are usually the victims of such behaviors, and they are punished severely for their own improper behaviors, but society does not harshly condemn a man if he engages in illicit sexual relations. Women who can no longer bear constant physical and verbal abuse by their husbands and find it difficult or impossible to seek legal separation and divorce may find committing suicide as the only option to end their suffering.

Prostitution is illegal and it is prohibited in Islam, and men and women who engage in improper sexual relations are subject to severe punishment. In spite of severe punishment, including stoning to death by the Islamic regime, prostitution continued to survive primarily in urban regions. Underground brothels exist in cities and are managed by both men and women. These places often change locations to avoid trouble with law enforcement officers. Some female prostitutes also prefer to operate independently, and they arrange a time to visit their clients' house. Although homosexuality is forbidden by law and society and subject to punishment, homosexual relations do occur in the country, typically between older men and adolescent boys, and sometimes between men closer in age. It may not always be strictly a matter of sexual preference. The rigid social segregation of males and females may also be a factor in some cases. While such activities are normally carried out away from the public eye, there are occasional recorded instances where warlords fought gun battles over a handsome boy in the 1990s. In July 1994, a marriage between two boys in Qandahar was celebrated with great joy.[14]

SOCIETY AND PERCEPTION OF WOMEN'S EDUCATION

An overwhelming majority of the population is illiterate, and the rate of literacy among the female population is much lower than among the male population. Conservative families do not support education for women because: (a) they do not see any immediate or relevant impact of education to improve the lives of their daughters, and (b) they view modern education to be anathema to the traditional way of life. The more enlightened families do not view education for women to be against Islamic teachings and believe that educated women can and should play a significant role in society's development. The more progressive, liberal, and moderate families not only support education for women but also those who can afford it may even send their daughters abroad to study.

Conservative religious leaders and clerics both in the Sunni and Shia communities oppose education for women, viewing the expansion of modern schooling as a threat that diminishes their own authority as the sole dispensers of Islamic values and possessors of religious knowledge. When confronted with the questions regarding women's equality with men and their education, these leaders often quote a verse from the Quran that alludes to the gender equality in the eyes of Allah. The verse from the Quran reads that God has created men "from a single cell and from it created its mate, and from the two of them dispersed men and women in multitude."[15]

Although there are a number of enlightened Sunni and Shia religious leaders who speak in favor of women's education, they have not worked to create mechanisms to enable women to pursue modern education and participate in public activities. They have not denounced gender inequality in practice, and their positions on women's rights have been limited to mere support for women's right to education. For example, an acclaimed religious leader and political figure, Sayed Ahmad Gilani, made vague references to women's role in Afghanistan, stating that his party "supports social, economic, and political justice, and the participation of the people, both men and women, in the task of development and progress of the country in accordance with the principles of the religion of Islam and acceptable national traditions."[16] Similarly Sebghatullah Mojaddadi, a well-known religious leader and the first interim president of Afghanistan (April–June 1992), expressed his views regarding women's role in the public with these words: "the weakest nations in the world are those that had a woman as a leader. It does not mean that Islam is against women. On the contrary, it respects them and says they are equal to men. But [history shows] that weak nations are led by women."[17] One religious leader who argued passionately in favor of women' education, their equality with men, and their participation in the public domain was the spiritual leader *(Imam)* of the Shia Imami-Isma'ili community, Sultan Mohammad Shah, the Aga Khan III. During a gathering in India he addressed the Muslim leaders, theologians, and clerics:

> How can we expect prayers from the children of mothers who have never shared, or even see, the free [intermingling] of modern mankind? This terrible cancer must either be cut out, or the body of Muslim society will be poisoned to death by the permanent waste of all the women of the nation.[18]

Isma'ilis often proudly quote the Aga Khan, who said that "if a father has two children, one a son and the other a daughter and if he can educate only one of them, such parents, if they were to consult me, I would advise them to educate the daughter first."[19] The Aga Khan believed that by providing the means to educate a man, one educates just one person and by educating a woman, one educates a family. Karim Aga Khan, the 49th and present Imam of the community, continues in this tradition. He instructed his institutions, such as the Aga Khan Educational Service (AKES), to renovate schools in Afghanistan and help in the provision of educational materials to schools and institutions of higher learning. During a speech, the Aga Khan highlighted the role of the Aga Khan University School of Nursing in providing professional training for women as a major step in improving the lives of women, enabling them to become independent. He said that:

> Nursing, primarily a woman's profession..., empowers women and improves their status in their communities. It provides positive role

models for other women, strengthens their decision-making and problem-solving capabilities in the eyes of other, and promotes their personal, professional and financial autonomy.[20]

MODERNIZATION AND THE WOMEN'S MOVEMENT

The struggle for change and modernity in the postindependence period led to radical economic, social, cultural, and educational reforms intended to improve and enhance the status of women. The state built schools for women, established the weekly publication *Irshad-e-Niswan* (the Guide for Women), built the first hospital for women *(Masturat),* and a theater for women in Kabul. One of the major accomplishments of the state in improving the lives of women includes the introduction of *Nizamnamah-ye-Arusi, Nikah wa Khatnasuri,* laws concerning engagement, marriage, and male circumcision in 1924. The statutes prescribed a minimum age for marriage, encouraged girls to freely choose their mate, and take legal action if their spouse mistreated them. *Anjuman-e-Himayat-e-Niswan* (the Association for Protection of Women) was founded in 1928 to defend women's rights and provide needed support toward women's liberation and equality.

Modernization and the women's movement were initiated from the top by the state and intensified in the immediate post–World War II period. The ruling elite intended to integrate Afghanistan into the modern world, and, in so doing, they launched a number of social, political, and cultural reforms, which included recruiting a number of women to work for the state-owned radio station as singers, sending women's delegations to conferences abroad, and employing a few women as flight attendants at the Ariana Afghan Airlines. The ruling elite also resumed the campaign to encourage women to discard their veils. This had failed in the 1920s when the radical measure by King Amanullah failed due to opposition by conservatives who commanded local support. During a celebration of the anniversary of the country's independence in August 1959, the wife of the king and the wives of top government officials publicly discarded their veils. They expected that other women would follow suit.[21] Although conservatives opposed this policy and organized rallies to condemn the unveiling of women, the state used the standing army and suppressed their opposition. Since then, the state vigorously involved more women in the public sector of the economy.

The women's movement to end gender inequality gained momentum after the promulgation of the 1964 Constitution. The Constitution ensured freedom of speech, and of press, and the formation of associations that led to the establishment of a number of political parties. Women participated in politics and fought for equal rights. Women of upper-class families supported the introduction of laws safeguarding women's rights and protecting them against violence by men. *Muassisah-e-Khayriyah-e-Zanan* (Women's Welfare Association or WWA) was established with the prime objective to promote women's welfare. Later, the WWA was renamed *Muassisah-e-Niswan* (the Women's Institute) and established branch offices in most of the provinces. Women of upper- and middle-class families also became active in the political arena. Four women were appointed to the *Loya Jirgah* to deliberate the draft of the 1964 Constitution and another two women were appointed as constitutional advisors. Between 1965–1972 there were two women in the cabinet, four female representatives at the *Shura-e-Milli* (House of Representatives), and two women senators.

Participation in politics was an exclusive domain for men, but women began to challenge them for leadership positions both in urban and in rural areas. In the countryside, tribal chiefs known as *arbab* or *mir* ruled with impunity, were the sole arbiters of social disputes and conflicts, and acted as spokesmen of their respective communities. However, a few women fought their way into leadership positions. For example, Agha Narg from the village of Tagaw Barg of Panjab District of Bamiyan was chosen *arbab* of the community in the 1950s and early 1960s. Another prominent woman, Khadija, was chosen *arbab* of the Anda and Shatu villages in Bamiyan. She often visited the provincial center to discuss issues related to her community with government officials and defended her community's vested interest.[22] Similarly Mah-e-Alam was an influential Isma'ili woman who represented the community of the Dand Village of Zibak District. She frequently visited Faizabad, the capital of Badakhshan Province to discuss with government officials social, political, and economic issues related to her community. She led a celibate life and died at age 30 in early 1970s. People remember her as a leader who cared for the poor and defended their interests.[23]

Women with more radical leanings were not much concerned with reforms, but they were eager to organize their rank and file in support of existing left-oriented political parties. They did not advocate a separate organization for women until a few years later, when they realized that they needed such an organization to focus on issues that women encounter on a daily basis, both at home and in the public.

There were two types of political organizations for women, one is the pro-Soviet *Sazman-e-Demokratik-e-Zanan-e-Afghanistan* (Women's Democratic Organization of Afghanistan—WDOA) headed by Anahita Ratibzad. Ratibzad was born in 1931, attended nursing school in the United States and then the medical college at Kabul University, and became a cabinet member after the pro-Soviet *Hizb-e-Demokratik-e-Khalq-e-Afghanistan* (the Peoples'

Democratic Party of Afghanistan—PDPA) seized power in a military coup in April 1978. The WDOA rallied women in support of building a socialist society based on the Soviet model of socialism and supported the Soviet invasion of Afghanistan in December 1979. Women members of *Sazman-e-Jawanan-e-Mutaraqi* (the Progressive Youth Organization or PYO) advocated radical transformation of the status quo, rejected the doctrine of a peaceful transition to socialism, vehemently condemned the Russian occupation, and participated in the struggle to free Afghanistan.

Pro-Soviet, radical, and revolutionary organizations celebrated Women's Day on March 8 every year by holding public rallies in Kabul, expressing their solidarity with the women's movement internationally. A major women's rally occurred on July 22, 1968, when conservative representatives submitted a proposal to the authorities of Kabul University to prohibit women from studying abroad. This factor galvanized women to protest such a measure and denounce rules that denied them equal educational opportunities. Although conservatives opposed women's involvement in the public activities, women struggle for equality continued. During a women's rally in Kabul in April 1970, supporters of Islamic parties threw acid on female students, which caused severe injuries to and hospitalization of 20 women. During another women's movement protest in October that year, a bicycle-riding man from Herat, Gul Mohammad, assaulted students and when he was arrested he said that he would do it again if he were released. The incident provoked a large demonstration in Kabul where more than 5,000 women gathered in front of the Prime Ministry, the Ministry of Education, and the Ministry of the Interior, demanding that the culprit should be delivered to them so they could punish him. They were shouted, "Give him back to us."[24]

In 1977, revolutionary women headed by Meena formed *Jamiat-e-Enqilabi-e-Zanan-e-Afghanistan* (the Revolutionary Association of the Women of Afghanistan or RAWA). The organization published articles that exposed corruption and nepotism in the government and articulated a radical transformation of the status quo. RAWA intensified its struggle against the repressive policies of the pro-Soviet regime and began to distribute night letters and antiregime pamphlets urging people to oppose the regime and its politics of reform and modernization based on a Soviet model of development. State security agents arrested and imprisoned members and supporters of RAWA as well as women members of other revolutionary organizations fighting the regime. Security agents tortured women activists in order to break their spirit and to obtain information about their organization's activities and agenda.

Women's participation in politics increased substantially after the Soviet invasion. Members and supporters of various radical and revolutionary organizations including RAWA actively participated in the struggle for national liberation. They engaged in political works among students at schools and universities as well as among workers and laborers. RAWA articulated its political programs in these words:

> It is our mission, men and women, to unite and fight for the independence of our beloved country, to establish an Islamic republic, and to build a society in which oppression, torture, execution and injustices must be replaced by democracy and social justice. We will not be able to achieve these objectives until people and all political forces unite and form a united national front.... RAWA, which is comprised of progressive women, fights for women's equality, and maintains that the liberation of the oppressed women is inseparable from the liberation of our oppressed nation.... RAWA will continue its principled struggle for women's rights and liberation after the restoration of the country's independence and freedom from the superpowers and other imperialist powers.[25]

A major anti-Soviet student protest demonstration occurred on April 21, 1980, when the ruling party held a ceremony to replace the country's red-hued flag with a new one sporting the traditional black, red, and green colors. Students marched on streets in Kabul shouting "Long live liberty" and "Russians leave Afghanistan." Protest demonstrations continued, and during the fifth day of the rally, security forces fired upon and killed four students of Omar Shahid High School and one of Habibiya High School. On April 27, female students of Soriya High School organized a major rally and marched toward Kabul University, where students from neighboring schools joined them. Security forces tried to convince them to disperse and return to their classes, but students defied orders and continued to shout "liberty or death," "Russians leave Afghanistan," and "Death to Babrak Karmal." When students tried to leave the campus of the Kabul University and proceed toward downtown Kabul, security forces blocked their way to prevent them from marching toward downtown. Nahid, a junior of Rabia-e-Balkhi School, came forward and shouted "Liberty or death" and encouraged demonstrators to break the blockade and proceed toward the downtown Kabul. Security forces fired on them, killing Nahid and Wajhia, another female student activist.

When the news spread throughout the city by word of mouth, students from other areas organized rallies expressing solidarity with their fallen comrades and condemning the government for its action. When female students passed army officers and soldiers they scolded them telling them to stay home and let them fight the Russian occupation forces. They threw their scarves to army officers telling them that they should wear these scarves and let them fight for liberation of the country. Student demonstrations continued and security forces arrested many of them, and tortured them with the intention to deter others from participating in antistate protest demonstrations. In November 1980, supporters of RAWA distributed a pamphlet in which they denounced the kidnapping of two female students by Russian soldiers and appealed to the public to organize themselves, defend their honor and national pride, and fight for their liberation of the country. Despite the government crackdown, student protests continued unabated, which led to further arrest and torture of radical and revolutionary students.

State repressive policies forced many revolutionaries to leave for neighboring countries of Pakistan, Iran, and India, as well as to the West. In exile, RAWA continued its political activity, published the monthly journal *Payam-e-Zan* (Message of Women), organized people to support the war of national liberation, and exposed the repressive policies and practices of the Islamic fundamentalist parties, especially policies that forced women to refrain from participation in the public domain. Islamic fundamentalists were threatened and angered by women's increased participation in politics. An assassin affiliated with *Hizb-e-Islami* (Islamic Party) lead by Gulbuddin Hikmatyar murdered Meena, the founder and head of RAWA, in Quetta, Pakistan, on February 4, 1987. Meena was a prominent revolutionary who championed women's causes and encouraged women to fight for their rights and equality. She wrote:

I am a woman who has awoken
I have arisen and become a tempest through the ashes of my burnt children
I have arisen from the rivulets of my brother's blood
My nation's wrath has empowered me
My ruined and burnt villages replete me with hatred against the enemy
O! Compatriots, no longer regard me weak and incapable
My voice has mingled with thousands of arisen women
My fists are clenched with fists of thousands compatriots
To break together all these sufferings, all these fetters of slavery.
I am the woman, who has awoken,
I've found my path and will never return.[26]

One of the major achievements of RAWA is the establishment of the Malalay Medical Clinic in Quetta in 1996 as well as building schools for students. RAWA committed itself in promoting welfare programs for women, defending their rights, and exposing policies of the Islamic fundamentalists that harnessed women's initiatives and their participation in outdoor activities. RAWA won international recognition for its consistent struggle to defend women's rights, raise their social and political awareness, and its campaign at the international arena to make the world aware of the plight of the women in Afghanistan.[27]

RAWA continued its struggle for gender equality after Islamic fundamentalists seized power in April 1992. It organized rallies to denounce the Islamic parties for harassing, molesting, raping, and murdering innocent women. It denounced the fundamentalist parties for not allowing women to attend schools, work outside the home, and ordering women to wear the veil. When the Taliban militia seized power in Qandahar in 1994 and conquered Kabul in 1996 and other regions until their rule collapsed in late 2001, RAWA remained steadfast in its condemnation of the Taliban for their regressive policies of social, cultural, religious, and political development. It published articles exposing the Taliban's brutal policy toward women and appealed to the public and international community to oppose and fight for a free Afghanistan.

One of the main slogans of the U.S.-backed government headed by Hamid Karzai was to eliminate rigid rules that suppressed women and prohibited their participation in public activities. Socioeconomic conditions for women remains largely unchanged and will be difficult to remedy in the short term, although the state has appointed two women to cabinet posts. Fundamentalists and warlords who are now part of the Karzai administration continue to harass women who work for the government, private institutions, and international organizations. They are dismayed by women in visible roles, such as anchors on radio and television. For example, Najiyah Hanifi, who worked at a local radio and television station in Mazar, Balkh, was forced to abandon her job.[28] Despite opposition and continued harassment, women are still struggling valiantly to defend their rights and to participate in public activities.

CRAFTS

Weaving *qalee* (pile carpet) and *geleem* (tapestry rug), embroidery, leather, metal, and woodcrafts are common handicrafts in Afghanistan. Leather crafts include making varieties of bags, belts, coats, caps, saddles, shoes, harnesses, and holsters for pistols and guns. This craft is common in most parts of the country. These products are designed and manufactured for domestic use and sales in the markets. Artisans in urban areas make silver jewelry, jewelry boxes, handles for knives and daggers, and trays and bowls with elaborate decorations and inscriptions of verses from the Quran. Precious and semiprecious gems such as lapis lazuli, rubies, and other stones are used in the fine metal works. Herat was known for producing elaborate glassware, but the profession ended in the 1980s. Istalif is famous for pottery with different design patterns. Woodcrafts with colorful designs are found both in rural and urban areas.

Qalee weaving is done solely by women and girls, but in the years since invasion and civil war took a toll on the economy, male family members also have started to weave carpets. The average family cannot afford a loom and usually rents it from someone who has one. The looms come in two forms. Horizontal looms are more common among nomads because they are simple to set up and disassemble. Vertical looms are more common in urban centers. Carpets can be made from silk or wool threads, and a carpet is made up of hundreds of straight rows, each row consisting of hundreds of individually tied knots. The knots are tied on the warp threads, the lengthwise plain-colored wool or cotton strings of a carpet, and as each row is finished, the threads are pushed tightly together with a beater comb that looks like a comb with larger teeth and a handle. A single row of a carpet consists of hundreds of knotted threads, and a typical small carpet will contain almost 3,000 rows of knotted threads. The threads in all the colors needed are rolled into balls

A woman weaving a rug in Surkhak Tamas Village, Doshi district, Baghlan, 2004.

and are suspended from the upper beam of the loom. A well-known Turkmen carpet known as *qalee-e-marw* or moor has about 240 to 280 thousand knots in each square meter.

There are two kinds of knots used in carpet weaving, *Farsi-baf* or *Sehna* also known as the Persian knot, and *Turk-baf* or *Ghiordes* also called the Turkish knot, which is used primarily by the Turkmen tribes. The Persian knot is common in rugs made in town and allows for more intricate detail in design, because these knots are smaller than the Turkish knot. The weavers seem to work without a design or plan and no drawings in many cases. The design patterns were once passed on from one generation to the next and the pattern and color sequence is chanted while the weavers work. Now designs keep changing, indicating new trends and customers' tastes. When the weavers are done, a professional finisher will trim the carpet, still rolled around the lower beam. He will trim the ends of the entire carpet pile with a small scissors with curved blades and then do a second and more systematic shaving with a very sharp knife, moving slowly over the carpet, finally revealing the intricate details and vibrant colors of the design. The final procedure involves trimming to a few inches and knotting the warp threads that remain at both ends of the carpet, which protects the end rows from becoming unraveled and also enhances the appearance. Weavers in every village or town develop their own distinctive local style, in colors used and in weaving or pattern, and carpets are usually named after their town of origin. Carpets were an important part of Afghanistan's market, and now while the economy is struggling, they remain one of the few means of earning a living. While large-sized carpets can fetch thousands of dollars in a marketplace, the families that create the carpets make far less per square foot. A six square meter carpet usually takes between three to four months for a team of three or four professionals to weave. Since the start of the war of national liberation in 1980 and afterward, design patterns with nationalistic and patriotic themes had developed that included weaving a portrait of a commander, map of the country, and war-related portraits. *Geleem* weaving and producing fabrics manufactured from lamb, goats, and camel wool *(barak)* are more common in Afghanistan, and Hazarajat is known for production of fine *barak*. The patterns vary from simple strips to geometrical designs with various colors, with black, red, and golden yellow colors as the most common color.

Embroidery is a common profession for women and young girls, and each ethnic and regional community has its unique style and design patterns: geometric, floral, linear, religious, and so forth. Women and girls work in the home to embroider caps, shirts, vest, handkerchiefs, tablecloths, pillows, belts, bags, gun cases, door hangings, and more. For the most part, works of embroidery are done for members of the immediate and extended family

Example of a traditional *Kamis-Shalwar* with an embroidered front.

and for honored guests. For some families, embroidery also has an economic aspect; if the women are highly skilled it can provide an additional source of income. Embroidered skullcaps for men and women to wear under turbans or shawls are a common item made to sell in a market. Caps come in a variety of shapes: conical, a four-sided square-shaped cap, cupola-shaped, and flat-topped. They come in a variety of colors and design motifs, depending on the traditions and background of its creator. Large multicolored flowers on a dark background, complex cross-stitched geometric shapes, intricate monochrome designs of white or light colored silk threads on fabrics of the same color, and shining mirrors or semiprecious stones stitched onto cotton, silk, wool, or velvet are only a few of the diverse styles found throughout the country. Religious themes, poetic inscriptions, and depictions of animals and mythical creatures can also be found embroidered on cloths and bags, utilizing a vivid array of colors and stitching.[29]

Colorful threads are made of cotton, silk, and wool, and sometimes even gold and silver (actually cotton thread rolled in a fine layer of these previous metals) that is applied onto the background fabric and secured with fine stitches of cotton thread. One stitch tends to dominate in a decoration, but there are also creative combinations that complement the overall design. Common stitches that help create linear designs include a box-shaped stitch, alternating lines to give a ribbed appearance to stitches, and intricate chain and ladder stitches. Variations of the satin stitch are widely used for geometric motifs depicting patterns of triangles, circles, ovals, and stars, such as for same-color embroidery on men's long shirts. Designs often cover the entire expanse of the fabric to stunning effect.

Embroidery is a source of pride among families and communities with skilled practitioners, and aside from its occasional use as a source of income, products are generally kept in the family or given as gifts within a community; it is done to demonstrate skill and to express pride in family, clan, and ethnic heritage.

NOTES

1. Maliha Zulfacar, *Afghan Immigrants in the USA and Germany: A Comparative Analysis of the Use of Ethnic Social Capital* (Munster, Germany: Lit Verlag, 1998), p. i.

2. Muslihuddin Sadi, *Sharh-i Bustan*, ed. Muhammad Khazaili (Tehran, Iran: Sazman-i Intisharat-i Javidan, 1362/1983), p. 327.

3. Sadi, *Sharh-i Bustan*, pp. 327–328.

4. John C. Griffiths, *Afghanistan: Key to a Continent* (Boulder, CO: Westview Press, 1981), p. 97.

5. Anneliese Stucki, "Horses and Women: Some Thoughts on the Life Cycle of Ersari Turkmen Women." *Afghanistan Journal* 5, no. 4 (1978): 140.

6. Nancy Lindisfarne, "Women Organized in Groups: Expanding the Terms of the Debate," in *Organizing Women: Formal and Informal Women's Groups in the Middle East*, ed. Dawn Chatty and Annika Rabo (Oxford, England: Berg, 1997), pp. 211–238.

7. Robert D. Kaplan, *Soldiers of God: With the Mujahidin in Afghanistan* (Boston: Houghton Mifflin, 1990), p. 50.

8. "National Geographic Tracks Down Afghan Girl in Famous Photo," *Seattle Post Intelligencer,* 13 March 2002.

9. Raja Anwar, *The Tragedy of Afghanistan: A First-Hand Account,* tr. Khalid Hasan (London, England: Verso, 1988), p. 128.

10. Robert L. Canfield, *Faction and Conversion in a Plural Society: Religious Alignment in the Hindu Kush* (Ann Arbor: University of Michigan Press, 1973), pp. 37–38.

11. Margaret A. Mills, "Off the Dust and the Wind: Arranged Marriages in Afghanistan," in *Everyday Life in the Muslim Middle East*, ed. Donna Lee Bowen and Evelyn A. Early (Bloomington: Indiana University Press, 1993), p. 54.

12. Zulfacar, *Afghan Immigrants in the USA and Germany,* p. 164.

13. William T. Vollmann, *An Afghanistan Picture Show, or How I Saved the World* (New York: Farrar, Straus, and Giroux, 1992), p. 126.

14. Kamal Matinuddin, *The Taliban Phenomenon: Afghanistan 1994–1997* (Karachi, Pakistan: Oxford University Press, 1999), p. 23.

15. Ahmed Ali, tr., *Al-Quran* [A commentary translation] (Princeton: Princeton University Press, 1984): 73.

16. "Charter of Mahaz-e-Milli-e-Islami-e-Afghanistan." *Afghan Jehad* 1, no. 3 (January–March 1988): 56–57.

17. Cited in *Newsweek,* 11 May 1992, p. 23.

18. For details see, Hafizullah Emadi, "Struggle for Recognition: Hazara Isma'ili Women and their Role in the Public Arena in Afghanistan." *Asian Journal of Women's Studies,* 8, no. 2 (2002): 88–89.

19. Sherali Alidina and Kassim Ali, compiled and trans., *Precious Pearls: Collected Speeches (Farman) of Sultan Mohammad Shah, Aga Khan III* (Karachi, Pakistan: Isma'ili Association, 1961), p. 54.

20. Aga Khan IV, "Speech Delivered at the Development Symposium Held at the World Bank," Washington, D.C., 10 November 1999.

21. *The Kabul Times Annual* (Kabul, Afghanistan: Government Press, 1967), p. 13.

22. Hafizullah Emadi, "Breaking the Shackles: Political Participation of Hazara Women in Afghanistan" *Asian Journal of Women's Studies 6,* no. 1 (2000): 143–161.

23. Discussions with Mohammad Hussain Jalili, an agriculture specialist employed by FOCUS Humanitarian Assistance, Faizabad, Badakhshan, June 2002.

24. Louis Dupree, "A Note on Afghanistan: 1971," *AUFS Reports* 15, no. 2 (July 1971): 17.

25. RAWA, Revolutionary Association of the Women of Afghanistan, *Barnamah, Wazayif wa Asasnamah-e-Jamiat-e-Enqilabi-e-Zanan-e-Afghanistan* [Policy, Responsibility, and Platforms of the Revolutionary Association of the Women of Afghanistan, RAWA], Tabistan 1359 [Summer 1980], n.p.

26. Translation of a part of a poem composed by Meena. *Payam-e-Zan,* no. 1 (1981).

27. For more details see, Hafizullah Emadi, *Repression, Resistance and Women in Afghanistan* (Westport, CT: Praeger Publishers, 2002).

28. "Women Radio Initiative in Mazar," *The Kabul Times,* 37, no. 20, Sunday, 1 June 2003, p. 3.

29. Bernard Dupaigne and Francoise Cousin. *Afghan Embroidery.* (Lahore, Pakistan: Ferozsons, 1993), pp. 12–20.

7

Lifestyles, Media, and Education

Rural lifestyles in Afghanistan traditionally centered around the seasons and agricultural productivity, where success or failure of crops was more often than not a matter of life or death. Nomadic herdsmen focused as intently on the welfare of their flocks, which were, along with their material goods trade, their primary livelihood. Urban life in Afghanistan has revolved around the town and commerce, and social activity took place in markets, mosques, teahouses, and public baths. Decades of war resulted in a new lifestyle that may be a reality for a bit longer: exiled communities. These are expatriated refugees, some of whom have spent more than a few generations living at the subsistence level in tented camps, and internally displaced families who fled their homes in war-torn areas for more remote areas, and are now having difficulty reestablishing their former homes and ways of life.

Freedom of speech and expression has developed in fits and starts as Afghanistan moved from pastoral nomadism to kingdoms under internal and external despots to an independent nation with successive governments that allowed different levels of independence and reacted in varying ways to Afghanistan's intellectuals, who strategized and fought with varying levels of success over the years to make the government accountable to the people. Education, both religious and secular, played an important role in guiding Afghanistan's citizens and preparing them for their role as a nation in an interactive world. Political, religious, and social traditions battled through the forum of the classroom for the hearts and minds of the people, and women in particular have seen their lives transformed as their role in the public arena is established, sometimes without their input, and they are affected, often painfully, as they find their voice.

LIFESTYLE IN A RURAL ENVIRONMENT

The pastoral farmers of long ago engaged in subsistence farming, growing barley, pulses (the edible seeds of legumes like chickpeas, beans, and lentils), and orchard crops such as apricots, pistachio nuts, and others. These products provided even poor farming families with a decent, nutritious diet. However, when the demands of modernization during the 1950s–1970s compelled farmers to move to growing cash crops, it was at the expense of their homegrown produce, because there was no land or time to spare for both, and as a result, the average diet suffered, and families became more and more dependent on consumer markets to purchase food staples they used to grow themselves. Their earnings from cash crops were largely lost to further purchases of seeds and payment of land leases, and many became even poorer as a result. Current developments with farmers moving in increasing numbers to the growing of poppies and harvesting of the sap for the opium market is another example of the limited options left to farmers who wish to survive. Decades of war ravaged agricultural lands and fragile irrigation systems and destroyed precious stores of seeds for future crops. Poppy plants are hardy and easy to cultivate, with few tools or water, and thrive in the less-accessible mountainside fields. In order to survive, farmers again cultivate a different kind of cash crop at the expense of their own previously self-sufficient, if modest, lifestyle.

Modernization in the twenty-first century did not reach far enough to significantly alter the primitive lifestyle in rural areas. Throughout Afghanistan, houses in rural areas do not have electricity, which means that people do not have refrigerators, televisions, and telephones in their homes. People in remote mountainous areas have limited access to the basic amenities of life, such as markets and schools, although villagers can usually obtain occasional consumer items from a market in a nearby town or from nomad traders and merchants. There are no roads connecting remote villages to the district administrative center, and it takes a day or two for people to walk to such centers, and inclement weather can close off all means of travel. There is no medical center in most rural areas, and if someone in the family gets sick they send a person to a store in a nearby town. The person describes the type of illness to the storeowner, who is not a pharmacist or licensed in selling medicine but a self-taught man who dispenses basic remedies, and he will decide how to treat the ailment. There is no postal service in rural areas, and families often send a letter or small items to their relatives in a distant village or town through a person from their own village or town when they plan to visit the city. They take the letter and deliver it to the address themselves, and if they have difficulty finding the person's address or if they are unfamiliar with the city then they ask someone else to do them a favor in delivering the letter or the item to the intended address on their behalf. Poor families adapt themselves to their environment for food, clothes, shelter, and a level of dependency on each other and their community made necessary by circumstances. An individual's welfare is the responsibility of his family, clan, and tribe.

The rural economy means agriculture and animal husbandry. Most men and their grown-up children work on the farm, till the land, fertilize it, sow the seeds, water the field, and do the harvesting. It is a back-breaking task that involves physical labor and compels peasant farmers to extend a helping hand to one another and share their agricultural equipment and animals; only a handful of affluent landowners use agricultural machinery. Poor farmers also engage in other professions such as carpentry, masonry, iron-smithing, and some are part-time specialists, such as shoemakers, butchers, and bricklayers, who work after they complete their daily tasks on the farm, while others travel to near or distant villages to find work. When the farming season ends, farmers take their surplus agricultural produce to the market to be sold and keep the remainder in storage at home to feed their family. Men are also responsible for herding the sheep and cattle and taking some of their dairy products to sell at a nearby market and purchase household items the family needs. There is no transportation system in remote and mountainous areas, and people often use mules and cattle to transport heavy logs, goods, and other such items. Makeshift ferryboats of plastic, wood, or even reeds are commonly used in crossing rivers.

Springs, wells, and rivers are the main source of drinking water, and women and girls make several trips a day from their homes to transport water for drinking, cooking, and washing. Bringing water from a nearby spring or river provides women and girls with the opportunity to socialize with each other and even to flirt with men if they encounter them on their way to springs and rivers or back home. A folk song aptly describes a situation where young men and girls seize rare opportunities to see each other. The song reads:

My beloved
Allowed not to visit me.
My parents permit me not
To leave the house.
I can go out only
When girls go to the spring nearby,
to fetch water.
My beloved you must pass by
So we can catch a glimpse of one another.[1]

These women washing clothes near a spring in Shughnan, Badakhshan, in 2003 were not at all shy about having their photo taken and proudly watched as the camera focused on them. Wet clothes are hung along the stone walls to dry.

While men work on the farm, women in addition to rearing children and cooking food, help men with the lighter task of farming, such as picking walnuts, grapes, melons and watermelons, and collecting brush for use as fuel. Such activities provide women with the opportunity to go out. Women are also responsible for management of the family's food supplies from one harvest season to the next. They could also supplement the family's income by activities such as spinning wool, weaving carpets and rugs, tailoring clothes, and embroidering. Women also make dung patties out of animal waste and paste them onto the wall or leave them on flat rocks or rooftops to dry; these are used as fuel for cooking and heating the house.

The tradition of hospitality is an entrenched cultural trait of all ethnic communities. Guests are enthusiastically welcomed, and the host shows his/her respect by providing them with the best of food and bedding. Well-to-do families have a guestroom furnished with carpets and rugs and use cotton-filled mattresses for sitting and cushions to lean on. The guestroom is decorated with photographs and art works such as embroidered items made by women of the family. The guestroom is usually located at the front of the house, so upon entering the house male guests would not see the women of the family unless the guest is a close relative of the host family. Wives and other female guests are escorted to another room where women of the host family receive and entertain them. People's hospitality toward a guest has been described in these words:

> Hospitality is a basic social value among all social groups in Afghanistan. Muslims in particular regard hospitality to strangers as a religious duty. The offering and acceptance of hospitality also enter host and guest into a reciprocity relations in which the guest, having "eaten the host's bread and salt" (*nan wa namak khurdan*) will, ideally, at some point be able to offer his erstwhile host sustenance or other services in return.[2]

Village mosques may be used to provide shelter to a stranger and also function as a meeting place when male residents discuss issues related to the community. People also conduct meetings outside the compound of their house or under a communal garden when the weather is conducive for such a meeting.

Typical items in a village household include utensils for cooking, such as pots, jugs, cups, teapots, saucers, scooping spoons, a basin for hand washing, and kerosene lamps. Most village houses use wooden and tin-made boxes to hold their clean clothes, jewelry, and other belongings. Wealthy families build rooms with a space on a wall and adjust the manufactured cabinets for keeping precious items such as books and china. Some families use a string-bed with a wooden frame. The mattress for sleeping is rolled up during the daytime. A kitchen with an oven for cooking is used as a dining room as well as a bedroom in winter and the cold season. Families place a small wooden table over the oven and cover it with a large square quilt or blanket. In a dining room with no oven, families use a charcoal brazier filled with hot coals and covered with a thin layer of ashes and place it under the table to keep the heat consistent. After the table is prepared, family members sit around it and pull the large quilt or rug over their bodies to trap the rising heat. Only heads, arms, and shoulders are not covered, and people are free to use the table both as a dining and a working table.

Most village houses have no washroom or toilet facility and only a handful of affluent families can afford such facilities when they build a house. A family's wealth is measured by having fine horses, cattle, and land, and for hosting feasts for various social and religious occasions. Their wealth is also displayed in the finery worn by women of the family, who wear clothes made

Store that sells buckets made from old rubber tires, Kabul, 2003.

of fine and expensive fabrics and jewelry such as golden rings, bracelets, and silver coins sewed on the bibs of their garment and headdress *(chadar)*.

URBAN LIFESTYLES

The *Shahr,* town, is the center of administrative affairs and commercial and business activities. Public life centers around commercial districts, mosques, teahouses, and restaurants. Major bazaar and markets are built along the main road, where one finds all types of workshops established by weavers, dyers, masons, carpenters, and shoemakers and polishers. In most cities, there are small and large establishements such as bookstalls, stationary stores, repair shops, automotive and bicycle repair shops, restaurants, and hotels. Migration of the rural poor to Kabul, the capital of Afghanistan, had increased substantially since the 1960s. Families left rural areas due to hardship of life and difficulty of supporting themselves by working on a small plot of land and their desire that their children receive a modern education in the cities.

One of the major aspects of life in urban areas is the labor movement. Major industrial and manufacturing plants were built in Kabul and a few other cities in the provinces. Blue-collar workers were not allowed to form unions of their own, and some became active members of several political parties. Skyrocketing of consumer items on the one hand and lack of insurance and welfare on the other hand led to growing labor movements in the 1960s. Labor movements were banned since the monarchy was overthrown in 1973. Another aspect of life in urban areas includes political organizations and political movements. Since 1964 a number of secular and religious parties emerged and campaigned for political, social, and economic reforms. Today, Kabul is the center of political parties, particularly the religious parties as well as civic organizations and nongovernmental organizations (NGOs) working to rebuild the country.

The civil war in the 1990s destroyed much of Kabul City. Today, many houses in the undamaged sections of Kabul have rationed electricity, but most families continue to rely on wood and fuel for cooking, heating, and

Blacksmith in Alimardan Street displays rows of axes and shovels for prospective customers, Kabul, 2003.

oil lamps for lighting. Affluent families have furniture manufactured by local carpenters and some have foreign-made furniture. Kabul is a congested city with damaged roads and streets, plenty of cars and taxis, and a lack of free-ways has created traffic jams. The unpleasant aspect of urban life is pollution. The inability of the central government to enforce rules and regulations and provide city services has caused pollution as people leave waste and disposable items on streets and roadsides. Damage to the electricity supply during the civil war caused excessive use of wood and fuel that contributed to air pollu-tion in Kabul.

In major urban areas the street *(kuchah)* constitutes a principal conveyor of news, gossip, and rumors, and individuals residing on the same street iden-tify themselves as *ham-kuchah* or *kuchahgi* and look after one another and guard against strangers with malicious intents. The *kuchah* also serves as play-ground for children, but they are dark at night and in winter they are covered with snow. Unpaved *kuchah* are full of mud when the snow melts or when it rains. Thus, the children move on to the flat roofs of their houses to play. During the civil war in the 1990s, Islamic militias fought for domination of major urban centers such as Kabul and each controlled a segment of the city that transformed the *kuchahs* into battlegrounds. Young boys patrolled the *kuchahs,* some carrying machine guns, and were told by their leaders whom to shoot. Such a situation made it impossible for residents of the city and rival groups to pass in safety.

NOMADIC LIFESTYLE

Nomadic tribes select a camping ground and spend a night or more to rest and graze their flock. When they move to another camping ground, one group leaves ahead of others to scout for a fertile site outside villages and away from the plowed lands belonging to local owners or a community. The rest follow a day later. Each group paints the backs or tails of their animals to distinguish them from the herds of other groups so they can graze their herds together on mountain pasturelands.

Donkeys and camels are used to carry tents and provisions when they move to another location. Women break down the tents, pack them, and load them on the backs of their animals along with small children and other belongings, such as cloth and wooden boxes. Chickens and lambs are tied to the side of the camel. Young boys may walk along the trail and carry some fragile items, such as a kerosene lamp. Women also walk along the trail and carry their infants. A mongrel dog commonly accompanies the nomads and guards both ends of the trail while the group is on the move. The dog is trained to guard the tent against intrusion by strangers without the consent of the master of

Painting of a typical contemporary pastoral scene, showing a grandfather and his grandson as they graze their flock of sheep, by Hesamuddin Ahmadi, Kabul, 2004.

the tent and especially while the group retires for a day or more on the site. It is a common tradition among the nomads to "clip the ears and tails of these dogs for two reasons: to prevent illness and to give them the advantage in a fight—no ripped ears or torn tails for the Afghan nomad dog."[3]

The men's primary responsibility is to guard the tents, protect the family, and keep an eye on the sheep and goats. Women's responsibilities are many and varied, and include assembling and disassembling the tents, cooking food, milking goats and sheep, as well as bearing and rearing their children. Women also are responsible for fetching water for cooking and drinking from a nearby spring or a river, washing clothes, and collecting materials for cooking fuel. If they possess craft skills, they also toil to earn income for the family. Turkmen women are famous for their woven carpets and rugs, saddlebags and pads, and decorative bridal items. They also make quilts, pillows, and mattresses. Nomadic Pushtun women also weave carpets and rugs, make leather bags for carrying water, and purchase other essential items for their living from a local market. Nomadic women do not wear the head-to-toe garment *(chadari)* that women of conservative families must wear in urban areas; the active and heavily manual labor they perform would be seriously hindered by such voluminous clothing. Because they frequently work outdoors and even among men, they are less inhibited in their company, and are not shy to talk to men, even those who are not related to them, and they may even take the initiative, if the opportunity arises, to extend the traditional hospitality to an arriving guest.

A nomad's income derives mostly from exchanging consumer items such as matches, kerosene, tea, sugar, dairy products, jewelry, leather and leather products, rugs, and carpets that local villagers need for wheat grain and other agricultural products. A small group of nomads, known as *Jats* in the southern parts of the country and *Gujar* in northern areas (it is widely believed that they are of Indian origin), frequently travel from one place to another. Most of them are involved in professions such as iron-smithing, fortune-telling, performing dances, and playing music.[4]

COMMUNITIES IN EXILE

Political repression by the pro-Soviet ruling party *Hizb-e-Demokratik-e-Khalq-e-Afghanistan* (the People's Democratic Party of Afghanistan, PDPA) forced many families to leave their homes and seek refuge in Pakistan and Iran a few months after the PDPA seized power through a military coup in April 1978. The exodus of refugees to the neighboring countries increased after the Soviet invasion in December 1979. Families secretly arranged to dispose of their property and make the long, arduous journey across the borders to Peshawar and Quetta, Pakistan, and several cities and towns in Iran. For a family to leave together was risky business, and to minimize the risk, women encouraged men to leave first, find a job, rent a flat, and arrange for the family to join them later. However, in most cases, men had no option but to risk taking their wives and children with them.

Families who already settled in refugee camps or in residential houses in urban and rural areas often assisted their immediate relatives soon after they arrived in Pakistan and Iran. They provided the new arrivals with basic orientation to a new environment, rules and regulations in refugee camps, and the process of refugee registration with responsible government agencies in Pakistan as well as international agencies dealing with refugees. Living in camps with immediate family members and tribes helped refugees maintain their customs, cultures, and ways of life.

Refugees could be classified into upper-class, middle-class, and poor families. Included in the first category were families of the ruling elite, top government officials, religious leaders, and businessmen. Soon after their arrival in

Pakistan, most of them sought refuge to Western Europe and North America. Intellectuals associated with the group played a significant role in politics in exile by publishing papers and journals and organizing meetings and conferences in support of the war of national liberation.

Middle-class families were a small segment of the refugees and brought with them their movable property and financial resources to Pakistan and Iran. They established business in cities such as Peshawar, Quetta; Karachi, Pakistan; and Tehran, Mashhad, and Isfahan in Iran. While male members of the family looked after the family's business, women looked after the children and the household chores. Intellectuals associated with this class played a prominent role in politics, as members and heads of various Islamic parties as well as progressive, liberal, and revolutionary organizations that opposed the Kabul regime and the Soviet occupation of Afghanistan. Conservative Islamic parties supported by the military regime in Pakistan and the clerics in Iran often harassed radical, progressive, nationalist, and liberal intellectuals. A number of such individuals who defied them and opposed their rigid policies of building an Islamic state were assassinated, and many others were forced to seek refuge in Western Europe and North America.

An overwhelming majority of the refugees were skilled and semiskilled laborers and farmers. Those with useful experience and skills were usually able to find some type of employment or worked as servants in the homes of wealthy refugee families or local Pakistanis. Those who lacked any skills usually included widowed women, orphans, and women of childbearing age who were housebound most of their lives in the camps and remained heavily dependent on foreign aid. Families encountered numerous problems in the camps—the tents were suffocating in the hot scorching seasons and did not protect from the freezing temperature in winter. Most refugees experienced severe depression, illness, and posttraumatic stress disorders as a result of their situation, and some used opium and other drugs as their sole means of treatment of their problems. Most children could not attend school because they had to work to help earn money to pay the rent and support the family. Children of refugees who could afford it attended Pakistani schools and schools administered by refugee organizations as well as private schools, but with few or no available Afghanistan-trained educators, they were for the most part educated according to the educational styles and priorities of their hosts.

Lack of employment in Pakistan forced many women into prostitution and beggary. The situation of women begging in the public is characterized by one woman:

I came to Peshawar from Kabul. There are eight people in my family and we all came together. We lost everything in the bombing. Our house was destroyed and everything in it was destroyed or stolen. We were just women and girls in the house. My son and husband were murdered by rockets.... Now we live in Nasir Bagh camp. The girls are very young, 8, 9, and 10. They do not go to school. Usually I come to beg in this spot. Sometimes I go to other places. From early morning until late at night, I get ten, may be twelve Rupees, often young boys will come and hit me. It would be better to die than to keep doing this.[5]

Refugees who settled in Jalozai, Aza Khel, and Akora Khattak camps in the Northwest Frontier Province (NWFP) endured much suffering because of deteriorating living conditions in the camps. The Jalozai camp was known as the "Plastic Camp," where poor families wrapped flimsy plastic sheets around their bodies in a futile attempt to keep warm in freezing temperatures. Many still froze to death. Some families, desperate to survive or to feed their children, would even resort to selling some of them to wealthy men from various Middle Eastern countries who paid high prices, especially for young girls. A poor family might give away their young daughters into marriage to wealthy men, in the misguided hope that their daughters would have a better future outside Pakistan. A woman who married a wealthy man and settled in Dubai described her condition: "My husband sold me here and now I am in a place that every night I am dancing, and I have been raped a lot and the people I am living with, they are taking money from me."[6]

The condition of refugees in Iran was a little bit better than that of refugees in Pakistan. Women were allowed to visit the market and men were hired as laborers on construction projects and many others worked on agricultural farms or were hired as domestic servants. Refugees in Pakistan and Iran were often deprived of their basic human rights and were taken advantage of by the local people, subjected to frequent humiliation and abuse, and received no legal protection by the host governments.

INTERNALLY DISPLACED FAMILIES

A new community type has emerged out of decades of war and disruption in Kabul and in provinces—the internally displaced families. These are, for the most part, people who once had a home in an urban area as well as people who fled their homes in the countryside during the strife with only the possessions they could carry, and later returned to find that everything from their former homes was gone, from their physical dwellings to their social networks and community structure. Included in this category are poor refugees who returned home after several years of living in refugee camps in Pakistan and

Iran and found themselves leaving one miserable and disorganized situation for another one that was even more dangerous and chaotic.

A large number of these people are families with a shattered infrastructure: Women with children who have lost husbands and adult sons, elderly men and women who have lost their children who supported them, young orphans, and single adults. These groups are not usually found in such large numbers in any society, and it is particularly destructive in one that places high emphasis on familial connections and support.

Families settle wherever they can, usually in demolished houses in urban areas where they build makeshift dwellings out of plastic and sticks, covering blown-out walls or gaping roofs. They can also be found in the periphery of town and villages, living in flimsy tents or in caves. These people live a hand-to-mouth existence and rely heavily on donations from humanitarian relief organizations to survive, either because they are unskilled or because the market they used to work in has vanished. These conditions cut across ethnic groups and, because of the numbers involved, will be another factor to consider as community leaders seek to plan economic development for their regions.

This community is left out of many cultural events that were once part of their life. They do not have the means to participate in cultural activities normal communities organize on special occasions such as the two festivals of *Eid* and other festivities, and many lack the family components that are needed. There are no men in most families to carry out the physical work or to even accompany women in public. The elderly are not always mobile and are physically unable to carry out the tasks that their grown-up children would normally do. The orphans have no guidance or anyone to explain to them their own cultural heritage; they will grow up under the influence of whatever community they happened to be in, and continuity to their own history is lost. The amount of aid they need to survive is disproportionately higher than the average refugee families. This is a segment of society less likely to benefit from current methods of assistance, which are superficial.

MEDIA

Radio and television are diversions that provide passive entertainment. Radio remained the sole monopoly of the state since it was established in 1925. The government distributed 30 radios to government officials in Kabul, and by 1928 an estimated one thousand people had radios. There was a temporary halt in the radio programs after conservatives rebelled against King Amanullah, regarding his modernization programs as anti-Islam, forcing him to abdicate the throne and leave the country in 1929. In 1937, the government signed an agreement with the Marconi Company to build a transmitter station in Kabul and a few other cities in the northern and southern parts of the country. In 1940, Radio Kabul was inaugurated and the government provided 500 radio sets for the public at affordable prices. Most radio programs were broadcast in the evening. Since most people did not own a radio, there were loudspeakers installed in the parks and other public gathering places. By the 1970s, the duration of radio broadcasting increased and most people had a radio at home.

In 1978, Japan built a television station in Kabul and it initially broadcasted one-hour daily programs in the evening. The Soviet-backed regime used the television to promote its ideology and recruited young male and female students and professionals to take part in shows and documentaries. It instructed radio and television stations to broadcast in the languages of other ethnic communities, Uzbeki, Turkmeni, Baluchi, Nooristani, and Pashayi, and increased the duration of the broadcasting that started at six in the evening and ended at midnight.[7] By late 1980s, there were about 20 television and 18 radio stations throughout the country. In early 2004, a private television network *Ayina* (Mirror) was established in Shiberghan, providing news and entertainment programs, mainly in Turkmeni and Uzbeki languages, to four northern provinces in close proximity to Shiberghan. In May 2004, the first private television station, Afghan Television Channel, was established in Kabul, and its initial programs included music and films.

Radio and television programs altered dramatically after the Islamic militias seized power in 1992. Most entertainment programs, sports, games, and foreign films were prohibited and Islamic fundamentalists in charge of the broadcasting networks introduced programs that included recitation of the Quran, discussion on Islamic ways of life, and talk shows that encouraged people to abide by Islamic ethics and values. Islamization programs further expanded when the Taliban militia seized Kabul in 1996 and extended their rule in most parts of the country. The Taliban changed the name of Radio Afghanistan to Radio Sharia and they too prohibited programs on music, plays, and other entertainment—all broadcasted news about the Taliban glorified them as heroes of Islam. After the fall of the Taliban in November 2001, two private radio stations, *Kalid* and *Arman,* financed and sponsored by Western countries, were established in Kabul and their programs include local and international news, documentaries, and music. Television sets are available in most teahouses and restaurants in major urban centers, where people listen to news and watch shows and entertainment programs. A handful of affluent families, bureaucratic officials, commanders, and warlords have access to satellite and watch programs in the comfort of their homes.

NEWSPAPERS

In 2003 there were four major government-owned newspapers in Kabul: *Anis* (Companion), *Arman-e-Milli* (National Hope), *Hewad* (Homeland), each with a circulation of about 6,000, and the *Kabul Times* with a circulation between 3,000 to 5,000. Daily, weekly, and monthly papers owned by individuals or political parties in Kabul during that period were estimated to be around 27, each with an estimated circulation ranging from 1,000 to 4,000, while there were about 10 provincial nongovernmental papers. Although most people cannot read and write, newspapers, journals, and magazines are visible mainly in Kabul and in a few major urban provincial centers. There are no newsstands in Kabul, and printed media are available in a few bookstores and customers also can get them from the vendors on the roadside and busy intersections of the Pul-e-Bagh-e-Omumi. With the exception of government offices, people are not in the habit of subscribing to newspapers, journals, periodicals, or magazines. Those who do read them often purchase a copy on their way to work or when they return home in the evening, and they readily share the papers with others. In offices there is usually a single paper that is read over and over by employees as well as the clients. This is one of the factors that explain why media circulation is considerably low in Afghanistan. The papers are also heavily recycled—storeowners often use old papers as bags when customers buy items from their stores.

CULTURE OF LEARNING

Education, either religious or secular, plays an important role in the transformation of people's perspective and way of life. Religious education provided guidance concerning ethics, morality, and terms of interaction with others. During times when Zoroastrian and Buddhism were followed in Afghanistan, religious centers such as monasteries and temples were the main centers of learning. The Buddhist monasteries in Bamiyan drew large numbers of monks and religious teachers to leave India and settle there.

As the Islamic era flourished, the religious schools *(madrasas)* and mosques became traditional centers of learning. The system of education during the heyday of Islamic civilization encouraged debates, discussions, argumentation, and a critical study of subject matters. These vibrant educational institutions produced eminent scholars, jurists, theorists, and scientists who further expanded the horizons of knowledge. Internal conflicts and wars of conquest by imperial powers profoundly reshaped the political and educational systems in the Muslim world that framed these vibrant institutions of learning with new kinds of bureaucratic practices leading to ossification of knowledge and a close-minded system. Present-day *madrasas* in Afghanistan bear little resemblance to their predecessors, and their teachings are now firmly rooted in ritual and recitation rather than innovative thinking and critical discourse.

The *madrasas* did not concern themselves with other fields of knowledge, such as mathematics, geography, or physics. Educational priorities centered around two major issues: the inculcation of proper manners and codes of conduct and the comportment of the students through rigorous discipline, and transmission of religious knowledge through the proper recitation of Quranic verses. The Quran was memorized and recited in Arabic, with no effort made to provide translation or interpret its content or context for students in the local language. Teachers possessed piety but typically lacked a deep educational background or any rigorous training in the field other than a few years of schooling before they were sent out to teach in these schools. Teachers did not receive a regular salary, but they received presents and gifts from the parents of the students.

In *madrasas,* students often began their studies by memorizing the letters of the alphabet and word pronunciation. After students learned how to read a textbook they were called *Ketabkhan,* reader of a book, and then they could proceed to study literary works that provided basic information on Islamic studies and the works of poets and scholars of social distinction. The methods of learning became ossified as the *madrasa* system and did not provide opportunities for students to engage in the critical study of a textbook but often stressed rote memorization of the subject matter. During a test, students are given the questions and instructors simply expect them to write their answers exactly as they had memorized them. *Mullahs* (clerics) in charge of *madrasas* often emphasize the learning of the Arabic language and its grammar, as they believe that grammar is akin to sacred knowledge. Students memorize all the grammatical rules, often without knowing how to apply them in practice. As a result, a student could recite the correct conjugation of Arabic verbs but would not be able to compose a proper sentence in that language.[8] When two students or two *mullahs* of different schools challenged one another to prove one's superiority, it attracted a large crowd of people interested to observe the confrontation between two rival students or *mullahs.* Confrontational debate between two *mullahs* or religious scholars *(mawlawis)* was an event of great significance. Whenever two renowned *mawlawis* would debate,

> each one would come with a large following of his students and donkey-loads of commentary books in Arabic. Arguments against arguments, objections against objections, books against books were produced. The disputation, interrupted by prayers, meals and sleep, was resumed the following day. Strong emotion of anger, exchange of insults and occa-

sionally physical fighting among the rival students were integral parts of the art of disputation. In the end, the opponents would depart without having won a clear-cut victory, promising to come soon for the next round. The expenses for meals and housing of the disputing parties and their numerous followers were paid by the local population, who enjoyed the occasion and were proud of their own *mawlawi*, if he was the strongest, but even if clearly defeated, he was never dismissed. A religious scholar is always a religious scholar even in defeat.[9]

The foundation of modern educational institutions was laid at the beginning of the nineteenth century. King Shir Ali (1863–1879) built a military school in Shirpoor and a civil school in the Bala Hisar. The main objective of these institutions was to imbue a younger generation with utmost loyalty to the state and the king and to train reliable civil service personnel to run the bureaucracy. The educational system followed the British-India and Turkish models. Public education was not a priority, as despotic rulers viewed an enlightened community as a threat to the status quo. For example, King Abd al-Rahman's policy toward public education was characterized as follows:

He did not mind about the ignorance of the nation so long as they remained loyal to their ruler and offered combined opposition to the external foe. He preferred barbarism to intelligence, as the former was more useful in war than the latter.... [He said] knowledge is a noble quality, and it must find its place in noble brains, because dregs of society cannot be allowed to obtain education and commit mischief.[10]

As Afghanistan gradually integrated itself into the modern world, Abd al-Rahman's successor Habibullah (1901–1919) encouraged people to send their children to *madrasa* to learn Islamic sciences. In 1903, he issued an injunction to mosques to round up boys playing on streets in Kabul and provide them with schooling. In a few public schools, religious subjects such as the study of theology remained an integral part of the curriculum in order not to antagonize conservative clerics and religious teachers. In 1907, Habibullah founded the *Dairat al-Talif,* Compilation Department, to write curricula and prepare textbooks, and in 1914, he established *Dar al-Muallimin,* Teacher Training College, to teach students who completed a six-year schooling period.

EDUCATION IN THE POSTINDEPENDENCE ERA

The pace of modern education accelerated after Afghanistan gained its independence from the British in 1919. King Amanullah addressed an audience in Kabul in which he stressed the importance of public education, stating that "we are keenly alive to the value of education. But to bring learning to my people must be a slow process.... We hope to lay our plans well and truly, but not too fast. Religion must march hand in hand with learning else both fall into the ditch."[11]

Education was one of the priorities of the state's policies of development, to the extent that elementary education was made compulsory and remained free of charge. To encourage poor families to send their children to school, the state provided students with textbooks, pencils, and notebooks. Students who attended colleges were provided with stipends and clothes, and those who came from far distances were provided with lodging. In 1921, the state sent a number of male and female students to study abroad. Lack of funds to build more schools for girls caused the state to promote a coeducational system and the Amaniya School, named after Amanullah, admitted a number of females to attend classes along with male students. Families still were reluctant to send their children to school because they did not see an immediate benefit to themselves or their children. To circumvent this problem, the state used a dual strategy based on persuasion and coercion and urged government officials to set an example by sending their children to school and dismissed those who refused to do so.

Conservative clerics and religious leaders viewed public education and state's modernization programs as a threat to their vested interests and began to oppose it. Amanullah's policy of raising taxes to sponsor his development programs generated dismay among the poor and provided clerics and religious leaders with the opportunity to exploit public grievances to advance their own political agenda. Conservative clerics backed by the external forces issued a *fatwa* in which they pronounced Amanullah unfit to rule and called for his overthrow. This factor forced Amanullah to abdicate the throne in January 1929. Opposition forces decried modernization of schools and female students attending classes in these words:

> In the time of Amanullah Khan
> The girls were flirts
> They were going everywhere jumping like Tatar gazelles
> Their legs were shown above their socks
> Paris and London were no match for them
> They had washed their hands of shame, dishonor and holy honor
> And shamed the Nation by their flirting.
> Became ashamed of this act of ignorance of the Afghan king.[12]

Educational programs were disrupted when Habibullah, known as *bacha-e-saqaw*, seized power in January 1929. Soon after, General Mohammad

Nadir seized power, and in October that year schools were reopened, but schools for girls remained closed. After Nadir consolidated his power base, he reopened one of the schools for girls. In order not to antagonize conservative clerics who were against female education, Nadir declared that the primary objective of the school is to train nurses and midwives needed for the female population throughout the country.

Secular education gradually expanded since the 1940s. The *Dairat al-Talim wa Trabiyah* (bureau of education) was founded to supervise the operation of schools and appointed a director who was in charge of provincial schools. The primary school system covered a six-year period and the curriculum included basic courses to prepare students for secondary school. In regions where there was no primary school, a three- or four-year village school was established, headed by one instructor. Students were taught reading and writing, as well as an introduction to religious studies. When village schools were built, most instructors initially were *mullahs* who lacked professional training, but at a later time they were replaced by instructors who had teaching certificates from teachers' training colleges and institutions. Village schools received funding from private as well as state agencies, while the primary, secondary, and vocational schools and institutions of higher education were funded by the state. The state provided textbooks and other educational materials free of charge, as well as lunches to students of secondary schools and lodging to those whose families were not in a position to support their children's higher education.

The number of educational institutions was further expanded in subsequent years with the majority being in Kabul, transforming it into a center of intellectual activity in the country. Kabul University (KU) founded in 1932, became fully operational by 1946, and its major colleges included the school of medicine, law, economics, education, engineering, and pharmacy. A modern campus was built in 1964, which included a number of new colleges. KU also established links with universities in Europe, the United States, and the Soviet Union, and students mainly from upper- and middle-class families were sent for further training and specialization abroad. A number of cadets from the army university as well as army officers were sent to the West, mainly to the Soviet bloc countries for advanced training. In the 1960s and later, the number of institutions of higher education increased. The Polytechnic Institute was founded in Kabul, and a medial college, which later was renamed Nangarhar University, was built in Jalalabad, Nangarhar. In the 1980s and 1990s, universities were built in Bamiyan, Baghlan, Qandahar, Balkh, Herat, and other regions, as well as the building of a number of technical and vocational schools in a number of provinces. Boys and girls did not attend the same school in the beginning, but later they attended the same school at elementary level, separated in secondary schools, and joined again at colleges and universities.

INTELLECTUALS AND THE CULTURE OF DISSENSION

In the 1940s and 1950s, the intellectual strata both in the state and private sectors engaged in activities intended not only to limit the pervasive power of the state but also to make the state accountable to the public. Their struggle eventually paved the road for a new political era, when King Mohammad Zahir promulgated a new constitution in 1964. A number of political parties espousing ideologies ranging from liberalism, nationalism, and socialism to Islam were formed and worked to enlist students in support of their politics. During the constitutional period in 1964–1973, the state failed to provide jobs to students graduating from professional and technical schools. This factor on the one hand and deteriorating standards of living on the other hand contributed to the radicalization of student movement.

A major student protest demonstration occurred in Kabul on the day of *Seyum-e-Aqrab,* October 25, 1965. Students demanded that they be allowed to participate in the parliamentary hearing. To disperse the students, security forces fired on them, which claimed the lives of several students and injured several others. Since then, students organized a series of demonstrations and strikes at the Kabul University campus to protest against the government and its neglect to provide economic opportunities for its people, effectively nulling their own futures when they graduate. Students annually celebrated the day of *seyum-e-Aqrab* until the monarchy was overthrown in 1973. Protest demonstrations of any kind were prohibited both during the Republican period in 1973–1978 and also after a pro-Soviet regime seized power in April 1978.

The main objective of educational programs since 1978 and after the Soviet occupation of Afghanistan in December 1979 was to inculcate students with Soviet-style socialist ideology. To this end, school curricula were revised that included subjects such as socialist ideology and historical and dialectical materialism, and students were sent to the Soviet Union and its bloc countries for orientation and training. Learning the Russian language was encouraged and became part of curriculum in most schools in urban areas. Russian instructors taught classes at Kabul University and other institutions of higher education, and youth organizations and clubs were established to rally younger generations in support of the regime.

LEARNING AND EDUCATION IN EXILE

The war of national liberation in the 1980s led to the closure of most schools in the countryside except a few schools that remained open in the provincial urban areas. The war forced more than 3 million people to settle in Pakistan, about 2.5 million in Iran, and about half a million to leave their hometowns and seek shelters in other provinces within Afghanistan. Refugees had limited access to basic education and health services, but the Internally Displaced Families were the most vulnerable community who often changed residences due to the continuing armed conflict, and did not have access to education, health services, and other necessary services. They remained dependent on the good will of the local people and international organizations for assistance.

Refugees with a background in education established schools to provide much-needed education to their children. International organizations also opened a few schools, including technical schools, to help men and women learn skills and compete in the labor market in Pakistan. The Union of Islamic Parties, comprised of several religious parties, administered *madrasa,* including the *Dawat wa Jihad* University, which was based on the Saudi Arabia system of education. The curriculum of the schools was heavily oriented toward Islamic studies, with a lesser emphasis on science and technology.[13]

Religious education was not limited to educational institutions. Fundamentalist Islamic groups also used mosques to promote their political ideology, with the intention to mobilize people in support of the holy war *(jihad)* and to fight for the establishment of a system of governance that is based on Islamic teachings. Education for girls did not constitute a priority because conservatives and fundamentalists believed that women are only responsible for bearing and rearing children and taking care of household chores. They maintained that girls must refrain from attending classes beyond the fourth grade.[14]

A segment of the refugees in Pakistan also included Isma'ilis from various parts of Afghanistan who settled in the Pakistani cities of Peshawar, Rawalpindi, and Karachi. Isma'ilis were determined that their children will receive a quality education and thorough exposure to a modern world so that they would be better prepared to compete in Afghanistan's job market for positions in the business sector. Karim Aga Khan, the 49th and present Imam of the Isma'ili community, internationally, often reminded his followers of their obligation to prepare themselves and their children for the realities of modern times and of the future. During a visit in Pakistan, he told his followers that when peace is restored in Afghanistan the country will be in a world of meritocracy, free market economy, and pluralism. The Aga Khan emphasized that they must impart a quality education to their children and identify economic sectors with potential growth. He told the gathering, in order to communicate with people outside their own communities, they must learn and speak a language that is "a language of universal communication, a language of science, a language of universal knowledge.... Use that time to prepare for the future."[15]

Based on the Aga Khan's guidance, schools and vocational training centers were established for refugees in Peshawar, Rawalpindi, and Karachi. Curricula for schools emphasized the study of the English language, science, and technology, as well as religious studies and also learning the Urdu language to help refugees assimilate into their new social and cultural environment and find a job. To this end, the Aga Khan Educational Service (AKES) provided funding to cover the cost of running educational and training centers and for recruiting male and female instructors from among the refugees and the local host community. Education and training were made available to boys and girls and men and women on an equal basis.

The Isma'ili leadership also used the prayer houses *(Jamatkhanas)* as centers of public education and awareness. After prayers, professionals conducted programs dealing with issues such as health awareness, community development, clean environment, investment, and methods of improving one's standards of living, so that the people could transcend the grim status quo and begin to embrace modernity.

ISLAMIC MILITIAS AND THE CULTURE OF REPRESSION

In the 1990s, religious fanaticism reached a level of frenzy unparalleled in Afghanistan's history. *Mujahidin* groups fought each other, each attempting to establish its domination. Warring factions murdered men and women of their rival parties when they captured them. They handed down severe punishments to those who violated their rules, amputated the hands of those caught in thievery, and executed those who were found guilty of murder. The Taliban militias came mainly from Pushtun tribal communities; their spiritual leader, Mullah Mohammad Omar, hails from Orazgan and received a rudimentary religious education at a local *madrasa*. To consolidate their rule and deprive people of the means to fight, Taliban militias employed destructive and intimidating tactics, such as setting fire to houses of non-Pushtuns as they captured villages and towns. The Taliban interpreted Islam according to their own narrow understanding of the scriptures and prevailing Pushtun tribal customs and traditions. After establishing their domination, they issued religious edicts and guidelines that had profound negative impacts on lifestyle, traditions, culture, and civil liberties of the citizenry.

The Taliban viewed diversity, pluralism of the faith, customs, and traditions as incompatible with their particular understanding of Islamic teachings. For example, they prohibited playing and listening to music and watching videos, as they considered such actions to detract one's attention from religious activities. Their dogmatic approach to religion and strict adherence to the tradition of the Prophet Muhammad forced men to grow long beards and shave their heads. They coerced people to take time off from their work when it is time for prayers and attend mosques for saying the five daily prayers. Included among their policies was an injunction that barred women from going outdoors in public unless they were accompanied by a close male relative. This made it very difficult for women to attend school or work outside the home. They justified restrictions imposed on women on the grounds that

> It is a matter of pride for all Afghanistan that we have kept our women at home.... The *Sharia* has described everyone's way of conduct. I mean that the *Sharia* allows for a woman to see a male doctor when she becomes ill. The fact of the matter is that no other country has given women the rights we have given them. We have given women the rights that God and his Messenger have instructed, this is to stay in their homes and to gain religious instructions in *hijab* [seclusion].[16]

The Taliban's religious police patrolled the city and used wire cables and batons to beat men and women who violated their rules and regulations or offended their perception of good behavior and codes of conduct. The militias used force and intimidation to manufacture a belief system that would make people submit to their authority without questioning its merit. They detained and executed individuals who did not agree with their strategies of establishing a government based on the Taliban's understanding and interpretation of Islamic teachings and principles. When the international community and human rights groups protested the Taliban's mistreatment of men, women, and children, an official of the Taliban regime defended Taliban's rigid regulations on the grounds that "We do not accept something which somebody imposes on us under the name of human rights which is contradictory to the *Quranic* law. Anybody who talks to us should be within Islam's framework. The holy *Quran* cannot adjust itself to other peoples' requirements. People should adjust themselves to the requirements of the holy *Quran*."[17]

LIFE IN THE POST-TALIBAN ERA: PROSPECTS

The disintegration of the Taliban rogue regime had been an occasion for joyous celebration as well as apprehension at a future of political instability. The U.S.-backed government, headed by Hamid Karzai, remains weak and depends on the United States for military, political, and economic support. Its sphere of influence does not extend beyond the capital, Kabul. Warlords who opportunistically switched sides and allied with the United States in the war against the Taliban and al-Qaeda network continue to maintain their private armies. They threaten individuals and nascent civic organizations working to rebuild a modern civil society and integrate Afghanistan into the modern world.

In spite of harassment by warlords, the people of Afghanistan are determined to rebuild their country and despite their struggles, many express optimism about a better future. Major achievements in the post-Taliban era include the right of women to work outside the home. Although women and girls are allowed to do so, fundamentalist groups continue to oppose women's education and harass them. People also organize picnics, play music and cards, and watch television shows. Relative security in Kabul enabled people who migrated and settled in Europe and North America to return and explore business opportunities. Many such individuals have returned and established businesses that include stores, hotels, and restaurants serving oriental food. Newly established restaurants include Thai, Indian, Turkish, Iranian, and Chinese restaurants in Kabul.

The prospect for Afghanistan to emerge from the ruins of war and integrate itself into the lives of the twenty-first century largely depends on the willingness of the people to reconcile their differences and transcend their narrow tribal and regional interests. It is only after achieving this objective that they would be able to establish a durable system of governance that ensures political, social, and economic equality. Many believe that pluralism and diversity must be viewed as a basis of strength, not as a weakness, in the rebuilding of a new society where people of various backgrounds live in harmony and peace and work for the good of the entire community.

NOTES

1. Common folk songs among the Hazara community; English translations by the author.

2. Margaret A. Mills, *Rhetorics and Politics in Afghan Traditional Storytelling* (Philadelphia: University of Pennsylvania Press, 1991), p. 268.

3. Louis Dupree, *Afghanistan* (Karachi, Pakistan: Oxford University Press, 2002), p. 177.

4. Dupree, *Afghanistan,* p. 180.

5. Deborah Ellis, *Women of the Afghan War* (Westport, CT: Praeger Publishers, 2000), p. 170.

6. Ellis, *Women of the Afghan War,* p. 145.

7. For details see, Shahjahan Sayed and Inam-ur-Rahman, "Radio Kabul: A Political History and Development," *Central Asian Journal* no. 49 (Winter 2001): 135–153.

8. Sayed Bahmouddin Majrooh, "Education in Afghanistan, Past and Present: A Problem for the Future." In *The Sovietization of Afghanistan,* ed. S. B. Majrooh and S. M. Y. Elmi (Peshawar, Pakistan: Afghan Information Center, 1987), pp. 129–130.

9. Majrooh, "Education in Afghanistan, Past and Present," pp. 129–130.

10. "Political Department, Afghanistan, 1893, nos. 511–539" in *Education in the Doldrums: Afghan Tragedy*, ed. S. B. Ekanayake (Islamabad, Pakistan: Al-Noor Publishers and Printers, 2000), p. 14.

11. Lowell Thomas, *Beyond Khyber Pass: Into Forbidden Afghanistan* (New York: The Century Co., 1925), p. 212.

12. Cited in S. B. Ekanayake, *Education in the Doldrums: Afghan Tragedy* (Islamabad, Pakistan: Al-Noor Publishers and Printers, 2000), p. 97.

13. Jamil al-Rahman Kamgar, *Tarikh-e-Maarif-e-Afghanistan az 1126–1371* [History of education in Afghanistan: 1747–1992] (Peshawar, Pakistan: Maiwand Publication Center, 1367/1997), pp. 108–109.

14. Kamgar, *Tarikh-e-Maarif-e-Afghanistan az 1126–1371*, p. 125.

15. Text of the Aga Khan Speech, 13 November 1994, Islamabad, Pakistan.

16. Peter Marsden, *The Taliban: War, Religion, and the New Order in Afghanistan* (New York: Zed Books, 1998), p. 98.

17. Amnesty International, *Women in Afghanistan: Pawns in Men's Power Struggles* (London, England: Amnesty International Secretariat, November 1999), p. 6.

Glossary

Ahl al-Ketab   People of the book

Alaqadar   Estate or landowner, subdistrict officer in a province

Alaqadari   Subdistrict

Allah Akbar   God is Great

Ambaq   Cowives

Amir   Commander, leader

Anjuman   Association

Arbab   Chief, landlord, master, also known as *malik* or *qaryadar*

Ashura   The tenth day of the month of Muharram

Ayatollah   The highest rank in the Shia clerical system of leadership

Azadi   Freedom

Bacha   Boy, child

Bahar   Spring season

Baig   Lord, chief of a community

Bait al-mal   Treasury, public property, or fund

Barak   Woolen cloth

Chadar   Veil, mantle, or shroud wore by women

Dawa   Invitation

Deh-Khuda   Tribal chief

Diwan   Court

Dubaiti   Couplet in poetry

Enqilab   Revolution

Enqilabi Revolutionary

Fard Couplet in poetry, a person

Farman Decree

Fatwa Religious decree, edict

Ghazal Lyric poetry, drinking song, amorous talk

Ghazi Warrior hero against infidels

Geleem Rug

Hadith Traditions of Prophet Muhammad

Hajji One who performs a pilgrimage to Mecca, Saudi Arabia

Halaal Ritual for slaughtering of animals according to Islamic law

Hamun Desert, plain

Harakat Movement

Hawala Money order

Hazaragi A Persian dialect spoken among the Hazaras

Hijab Seclusion

Hizb Party

Hizbullah Party of God

Ijma Reunion, gathering, assembly

Ikhwan al-Muslimin Islamic brotherhood

Ilm Knowledge

Imam Religious leader

Isma'ili A Shia community whose spiritual leader is Karim Aga Khan IV, the 49th and present Imam of the community internationally

Ithna Ashari The Shia community whose 12th Imam Mahdi disappeared around 873 A.D.

Itihad-e-Milli National Unity

Jabha Front

Jamatkhana A congregational house where Isma'ilis gather to say their prayers

Jamiat Multitude, society

Jerib Unit of measurement about 0.2 hectares

Jihad Holy war

Jizya Per capita tax

Joi A type of water provision system consisting of networks of wells and springs

Kafir Unbeliever, infidel

Kafiristan Land of the Kafirs

Kalima Word, logos, speech, discourse

Kamadia Assistant treasurer within the leadership of Isma'ili community

Kariz A type of water provision system consisting of underground water channels and a series of wells that lead water from an underground source to outlying areas; also known as *qanat*

Khahar Khandah Adopted sister, term for a woman's girlfriend

Khalifa Caliph, vicar, successor, title of religious leaders and professional men

Khalq Mass, people

Khan Title of nobility

Khanaqah Convent, monastery

Kharaj Tax, tribute, toll, poll tax

Kochi Nomads

Kuchahgi Residents of the same alley or street

Loya Jirgah Grand assembly of tribal chiefs or tribal elders

Madrasa Religious school

Mahr Marriage portion settled upon the wife

Malik Chief, landlord, master also known as *arbab* or *qaryadar*

Masawat Equality

Masjid Mosque

Mawlawi A learned man, one of the orders of tariqah founded by Rumi

Memar Architect

Millat Nation

Mir Title of nobility, tribal chief

Muezzin The crier who calls worshippers to prayers during the five daily prayers

Muhtasib Police officer, religious police

Mukhi Treasurer in the Isma'ili system of religious hierarchy

Mulk-e-Ama Public landownership, land collectively controlled by families in a clan

Mulk-e-Khalisa Joint land ownership between blood relatives

Mulk-e-Shakhsi Private landownership

Mulk-e-Waqfa Land ownership by religious institutions

Mullah Cleric, religious leader

Musulman One who believes in Islam

Nahzat Resurgence

Nakhta Mourning songs sung by women

Namaz Prayer

Nasr Victory

Naw Rooz   First day of a year

Pakhsa   A building style that employs compressed mud for building walls

Parcham   Banner

Pardah-e-bekarat   Virginity

Pasdar   Guardian

Pir   Religious leader

Purghu   System by which farmers share their respective oxen in order to plow their land or perform other activities requiring draft animals

Qalah   Fortress, castle-like structure distinguished by thick walls, a single fortified entrance and defensive towers

Qalee   Carpet

Qarya   Village

Qaryadar   Chief, landlord, master, also known as *malik* or *arbab*

Qiyas   Analogy, comparison, inference, reasoning

Rubayi   Quatrains composed of two or four hemistiches, the first, third, and fourth rhyme together; each hemistich is of the same measure

Ruybar   Liaison that arranges marriages

Sarai   Inn

Sar-bayland   Distinguished, eminent, honorable

Sardar   A title for nobility

Sazman   Organization

Shabnamah   Night letters

Shahnamah   Book of kings

Sharia   Religious law of Islam

Shayatin   Devils

Shula   A flame, a blaze

Shura   Council

Sigha   Temporary marriage

Sufi   A mystic, a devotee, a pious man

Sunna   Custom, tradition of Islam

Tab-Khaneh   A type of heating system where a single fire in one room heats other rooms by means of a network of channels under the floor

Takyakhana   Shrine to Imam Hussein

Talaq   Divorce

Tanoor   A clay oven used for baking *nan*

Taqiyya   Dissimulation of one's faith in a hostile environment

Tariqah Path

Ulama Religious scholars

Ummah Community of believers

Ustad Teacher, master

Wali Governor

Waqf To endow, to dedicate

Watan Homeland

Wilayat Province

Wuluswal Pushtu word meaning a district officer

Wuluswali Pushtu word referring to a district in a province

Zakat Islamic income tax

Zikr Meditation

Ziyaratgah Refers to a site that is the tomb of a respected religious figure

Bibliography

Adamec, Ludwig W. *Dictionary of Afghan Wars, Revolutions, and Insurgencies.* Lanham, MD: Scarecrow Press, 1996.

———. *Historical Dictionary of Afghanistan,* 2nd ed. Lanham, MD: Scarecrow Press, 1997.

Afghanistan: A Country Study. Baton Rouge, LA: Claitor's Publication Division, 2001.

Afghanistan, The Forgotten War: Human Rights Abuses and Violations of the Laws of War Since the Soviet Withdrawal, An Asia Watch Report. New York: Asia Watch, 1991.

Afghanistan. Kabul: Aryana Dayirat al-Maarif [Aryana Encyclopedia], October 1955.

Afghanistan, Vizarat-i Plan. *An English Translation of The Third Five Year Economic and Social Plan of Afghanistan, 1967–1971.* Kabul, Afghanistan: s.n., 1967.

Aga Khan IV. "Speech Delivered at the Development Symposium Held at the World Bank," Washington, D.C., 10 November, 1999.

Ahang, Mohammad Kazem. *Sayr-e Journalism dar Afghanistan* [Chronology of Journalism in Afghanistan]. Peshawar, Pakistan: Maiwand Publication Centre, 1379/1999.

Ahmad, Jamal-ud-Din and Muhammad Abdul Aziz, with a Foreword by Muhammad Iqbal. *Afghanistan: A Brief Survey.* New York: Longmans, Green, 1936.

Akhramovich, R.T. (Roman Timofeevich). *Outline History of Afghanistan After the Second World War.* Moscow, Russia: Nauka Publishing House, Central Department of Oriental Literature, 1966.

Ali, Ahmed, tr. *Al-Quran* [A commentary translation]. Princeton, NJ: Princeton University Press, 1984.

Ali, Mohammed. *Manners & Customs of the Afghans.* Lahore, Pakistan: Punjab Educational Press, 1958.

Alidina, Sherali, and Kassim Ali, compiled and trans. *Precious Pearls: Collected Speeches (Farman) of Sultan Mohammad Shah, Aga Khan III*. Karachi, Pakistan: Isma'ili Association, 1961.

Allen, Terry. *Timurid Herat*. Wiesbaden, Germany: Reichert, 1983.

Amin, Hamidullah, and Gordon B. Schilz. *A Geography of Afghanistan*. Omaha, Nebraska: Center for Afghanistan Studies, 1976.

Amnesty International. *Afghanistan: International Responsibility for Human Rights Disaster*. New York: Amnesty International, 1995.

———. *Afghanistan: The Legacy of Human Suffering in a Forgotten War: Compilation Document*. New York: Amnesty International, 1999.

———. *Women in Afghanistan: Pawns in Men's Power Struggles*. London, England: Amnesty International Secretariat, November 1999.

Anwar, Raja. *The Tragedy of Afghanistan: A First Hand Account*, tr. Khalid Hasan. London, England: Verso, 1988.

The Archaeology of Afghanistan from Earliest Times to the Timurid Period. New York: Academic Press, 1978.

Arnold, Anthony. *Afghanistan's Two-party Communism: Parcham and Khalq*. Stanford, CA: Hoover Institution Press, Stanford University, 1983.

Asrari and Amanov. *Adabiyat-e-Shafahi-e-Mardum-e-Tajik* [Oral Literature of the Tajiks], tr. Abdul Qayum Qawim and Mohammad Afzal Banuwal. Kabul, Afghanistan: Publications of Cultural Council of Kabul University, 1364/1985.

Azoy, G. Whitney. *Buzkashi: Game and Power in Afghanistan*. Philadelphia: University of Pennsylvania Press, 1982.

Baily, John. *Music of Afghanistan: Professional Musicians in the City of Herat*. New York: Cambridge University Press, 1988.

Banuwal, Mohammad Afzal. *Namonaha-e-az Farhang-e-Shafahi-e-Mardum-e-Andarab* [Examples of Oral Cultures of the People of Anadrab]. Kabul, Afghanistan: Kabul University, Publications of Cultural Council, 1363/1984.

Barfield, Thomas J. (Thomas Jefferson). *The Central Asian Arabs of Afghanistan: Pastoral Nomadism in Transition*. Austin: University of Texas Press, 1981.

Baygan, Khayr Mohammad. *Dastanha-e-chand az Tarikh-e Siyasi Afghanistan* [A few stories from the political history of Afghanistan]. Peshwar, Pakistan: Maiwand Publication Centre, 1999.

Bellew, H. W. (Henry Walter). *Afghanistan and the Afghans: Being a Brief Review of the History of the Country and Account of its People, with a Special Reference to the Present Crisis and War with the Amir Sher Ali Khan*. Lahore, Pakistan: Sang-e-Meel Publications, 1979.

———. *An Inquiry into the Ethnography of Afghanistan*. Karachi, Pakistan: Indus Publications, 1977.

———. *The Races of Afghanistan: Being a Brief Account of the Principal Nations Inhabiting that Country*. Lahore, Pakistan: Sang-e-Meel Publications, 1999.

Biddulph, J. (John). *Tribes of the Hindoo Koosh*. Karachi, Pakistan: Indus Publications, 1977.

Blanc, Jean-Charles. *Afghan Trucks.* New York: Stonehill, 1976.

Bonner, Arthur. *Among the Afghans.* Durham, NC: Duke University Press, 1987.

Bosworth, Clifford Edmund. *The Ghaznavids; their Empire in Afghanistan and Eastern Iran, 994–1040.* Edinburgh, Scotland: Edinburgh University Press, 1963.

————. *The History of the Saffarids of Sistan and the Maliks of Nimruz: 247/861 to 949/1542–1543.* Costa Mesa, CA: Mazda Publishers in association with Bibliotheca Persica, 1994.

————. *The Later Ghaznavids: Splendour and Decay: The Dynasty in Afghanistan and Northern India, 1040–1186.* New York: Columbia University Press, 1977.

Bowersox, Gary W. *Gemstones of Afghanistan.* Tucson, AZ: Geoscience Press, 1995.

Canfield, Robert L. *Faction and Conversion in a Plural Society: Religious Alignment in the Hindu Khush.* Ann Arbor: University of Michigan Press, 1973.

Centlivres-Demont, Micheline. *Popular Art in Afghanistan: Paintings on Trucks, Mosques, and Tea-houses.* Graz, Austria: Akadem. Druck- u. Verlagsanst, 1976.

Chohan, Amar Singh. *A History of Kafferistan: Socio-economic and Political Conditions of the Kaffers.* New Delhi, India: Atlantic Publishers, 1989.

Clark, Hartley. *Bokhara. Turkoman and Afghan Rugs.* London, England: John Lane, 1922.

Clark, Richard J. and others. *Report on a Collection of Amphibians and Reptiles from Afghanistan.* San Francisco: California Academy of Sciences, 1969.

Daftary, Farhad. *The Isma'ilis: Their History and Doctrines.* Cambridge, MA: Cambridge University Press, 1990.

Dupaigne, Bernard and Francoise Cousin. *Afghan Embroidery.* Lahore, Pakistan: Ferozsons, 1993.

Dupree, Louis. *Afghanistan.* Karachi, Pakistan: Oxford University Press, 2002.

————. "It Wasn't Woodstock, But the First International Rock Festival in Kabul." *The American Universities Field Staff, AUFS* 20, no. 2 (May 1976): 1–11.

————. "A Note on Afghanistan: 1971," *AUFS Reports* 15, no. 2 (July 1971): 1–35.

————. "The Role of Folklore in Modern Afghanistan." *American Universities Field Staff, AUFS* no. 48 (1978): 1–7.

————. "Saint Cults in Afghanistan." *American Universities Field Staff, AUFS* 20, no. 1 (May 1976): 1–26.

Dupree, Louis, and Linette Albert, and foreword by Phillips Talbot. *Afghanistan in the 1970s.* New York: Praeger, 1974.

Edelberg, Lennart. *Nuristani Buildings.* Aarhus, Denmark: Jysk arkologisk selskab, 1984.

Ekanayake, S. B. *Education in the Doldrums: Afghan Tragedy.* Islamabad, Pakistan: Al-Noor Publishers and Printers, 2000.

Ellis, Deborah. *Women of the Afghan War.* Westport, CT: Praeger Publishes, 2000.

Emadi, Hafizullah. *Afghanistan's Gordian Knot: An Analysis of National Conflict and Strategies for Peace.* Honolulu: East-West Center, 1990.

————. *China's Foreign Policy Toward the Middle East.* Karachi, Pakistan: Royal Book Company, 1997.

————. "Exporting Iran's Revolution: The Radicalization of the Shiite Movement in Afghanistan." *Middle Eastern Studies* 31, no. 1 (January 1995): 1–12.

————. "The Hazaras and Their Role in the Process of Political Transformation in Afghanistan." *Central Asian Survey* 16, no. 3 (1997): 363–387.

————. "Kabul." *Encyclopedia of Urban Cultures: Cities and Cultures Around the World*, vol. 2. Danburry, CT: Grolier, 2002, pp. 437–445.

————. "Nation-Building in Afghanistan." *Contemporary Review* 283, no. 1652 (September 2003): 148–155.

————. *Politics of Development and Women in Afghanistan.* New York: Paragon House Publishers, 1993; 2nd ed., Karachi, Pakistan: Royal Book Company, 2002.

————. *Politics of the Dispossessed: Superpowers and Development in the Middle East.* Westport, CT: Praeger Publishers, 2001.

————. "Radical Islam, Jihad, and Civil War in Afghanistan." *Internationales Asienforum* 30, nos. 1–2 (1999): 5–26.

————. "Radical Political Movements in Afghanistan and their Politics of Peoples' Empowerment and Liberation." *Central Asian Survey* 20, no. 4 (2001): 427–450.

————. *Repression, Resistance, and Women in Afghanistan.* Westport, CT: Praeger Publishers, 2002.

————. *State, Revolution, and Superpowers in Afghanistan.* New York: Praeger Publishers, 1990; 2nd ed. Karachi, Pakistan: Royal Book Company, 1997.

————. "Struggle for Recognition: Hazara Isma'ili Women and their Role in the Public Arena in Afghanistan." *Asian Journal of Women's Studies*, 8, no. 2 (2002):76–103.

Errington, Elizabeth, Joe Cribb, and Maggie Claringbul, eds. *The Crossroads of Asia: Transformation in Image and Symbol in the Art of Ancient Afghanistan and Pakistan.* Cambridge, England: Ancient India and Iran Trust, 1992.

Ewans, Martin. *Afghanistan: A Short History of Its People and Politics.* New York: HarperCollins, 2002.

Farhang, Mir Mohammad Siddiq. *Afghanistan dar panj Qarn-e-Akhir* [Afghanistan in the last five centuries], vols. 1–3. Peshawar, Pakistan: Author, 1373/1994.

Fayzzad, Mohammad Alam. *Jirgaha-e-Bozurg-e-Milli Afghanistan, Loya Jirgahs, wa Jirgaha-e-Namnihad wa Tahti Tasalut-e-Kamunistha wa Rus-ha* [Grand National Assemblies of Afghanistan, Loya Jirgahs, and So-Called Jirgahs Held Under Communists and Russians]. Islamabad, Pakistan: Author, 1368/1989.

Ferrier, Joseph Pierre. *Caravan Journeys and Wanderings in Persia, Afghanistan, Turkistan, and Beloochistan, with Historical Notices of the Countries Lying Between Russia and India.* New York: Oxford University Press, 1976.

Fletcher, Banister. *A History of Architecture*, 18th ed. New York: Charles Scribner's Sons, 1975.

Fraser-Tytler, William Kerr. *Afghanistan: A Study of Political Developments in Central and Southern Asia.* New York: Oxford University Press, 1967.

Frederiksen, Birthe. *Caravans and Trade in Afghanistan: The Changing Life of the Nomadic Hazarbuz.* New York: Thames and Hudson, 1995.

Fry, Maxwell J. *The Afghan Economy: Money, Finance, and the Critical Constraints to Economic Development.* Leiden: Brill, 1974.

Gankovsky, Yuri V., et al. *A History of Afghanistan,* tr. Vitaly Baskakov. Moscow, Russia: Progress Publishers, 1985.

Gaulier, Simone. *Buddhism in Afghanistan and Central Asia.* Leiden: Brill, 1976.

Gharwal, Asad. *Award-Winning, Low-Fat Afghani Cooking.* Minneapolis, MN: Chromined Publishing, 1995.

Ghubar, Mir Ghulam Mohammad. *Afghanistan dar Masir-e-Tarikh* [Afghanistan in the path of history]. Tehran, Iran: Entisharat-e Jamhoori, 1374/1995.

———. *Afghanistan dar Masir-e-Tarikh* [Afghanistan in the path of history], vol. 2. Herndon, VA: Hashmat Khalil Ghubar, 1999.

Girardet, Edward. *Afghanistan: The Soviet War.* New York: St. Martin's Press, 1985.

Gohari, M. J. *The Taliban: Ascent to Power.* Karachi, Pakistan: Oxford University Press, 2001.

Goodwin, Jan. *Caught in the Crossfire.* New York: E. P. Dutton, 1987.

Goswami, Jaya. *Cultural History of Ancient India: A Socio-Economic and Religio-Cultural Survey of Kapisa and Gandhara.* Delhi, India: Agam Kala Prakashan, 1979.

Goya, Sarwar. "The Green Dome or the Mausoleum of the Timurid Princess." *Afghanistan* 1, no. 1 (January–March 1946): 16–19.

Grassmuck, George, Ludwig W. Adamec, and Frances H. Irwin, eds. *Afghanistan: Some New Approaches.* Ann Arbor: Center for Near Eastern and North African Studies, University of Michigan, 1969.

Gregorian, Vartan. *The Emergence of Modern Afghanistan: Politics of Reform and Modernization, 1880–1946.* Stanford, CA: Stanford University Press, 1969.

Griffiths, John Charles. *Afghanistan: Key to a Continent.* Boulder, CO: Westview Press, 1981.

Grimes, Barbara F., ed. *Ethnologue: Languages of the World.* Dallas: Summer Institute of Linguistics, 1992.

Grube, Ernst J. *The Classical Style in Islamic Painting: The Early School of Herat and its Impact on Islamic Painting of the Later Fifteenth, the Sixteenth, and Seventeenth Centuries; Some Examples in American Collections.* Venice, Italy: Edizioni Oriens, 1968.

Guillaume, Olivier, ed. *Greco-Bactrian and Indian Coins from Afghanistan.* New York: Oxford University Press, 1991.

Habibullah, Amir. *My Life: From Brigand to King. Autobiography of Amir Habibullah.* London, England: Octagon Press, 1990.

Hallet, Stanley Ira and Rafi Samizay. *Traditional Architecture of Afghanistan.* New York: Garland, 1980.

Hamidi, Hakim. *A Catalog of Modern Coins of Afghanistan.* Kabul, Afghanistan: Ministry of Finance, 1967.

Hanegbi, Zohar. *Afghanistan: The Synagogue and the Jewish Home.* Jerusalem, Israel: Centre for Jewish Art, Hebrew University, 1991.

Hassinger, Jerry D. "A Survey of the Mammals of Afghanistan: Resulting from the 1965 Street Expedition, Excluding Bats." *Fieldiana: Zoology* 60 (6 April 1973).

Helms, S. W. (Svend W.). *Excavations at Old Kandahar in Afghanistan, 1976–1978: Conducted on Behalf of the Society for South Asian Studies (Society for Afghan Studies): Stratigraphy, Pottery, and other Finds.* Oxford, England: Archaeopress, 1997.

Hisari, Sultan Husain. *Samandehi Mimari-e Maskan-e-Manatiqi Markazi Afghanistan, Hazarajat* [Ordering Dwelling Architecture of Central Afghanistan, Hazarajat]. Tehran, Iran: Publications of Shahid Behishti University, 1376/1997.

Hobbs, Frank. *Afghanistan: A Demographic Profile.* Washington, D.C.: Center for International Research, Bureau of the Census, U.S. Department of Commerce, 1988.

Huldt, Bo. *The Tragedy of Afghanistan: The Social, Cultural, and Political Impact of the Soviet Invasion.* New York: Croom Helm, 1988.

Hunzai, Faquir M., tr. *Shimmering Light: An Anthology of Isma'ili Poetry.* London, England: I.B. Tauris, 1996.

Husaini, Nimat. *Sima-ha wa Awa-ha* [Pictures and Sounds], vol. 1. Kabul, Afghanistan: Government Press, 1367/1988.

Hyman, Anthony. *Afghanistan under Soviet Domination, 1964–1983.* New York: St. Martin's Press, 1984, 1982.

Insect Fauna of Afghanistan and Hindukush. [Kyoto], Japan: The Committee of the Kyoto University Scientific Expedition to the Karakoram and Hindukush, Kyoto University, 1963.

International Labor Organization. *Yearbook of Labour Statistics.* Geneva, Switzerland: ILO, 1982.

International Seminar on Bamiyan: Challenge to World Heritage. New Delhi, India: Bhavana Books & Prints, 2002.

Ismailpur, M. "Tiyater dar Afghanistan [Theater in Afghanistan]," *Dur-e-Dari* nos. 9–10 (Spring and Summer, 1378/1999): 91–94.

Jobel, Mohammad Haidar. *Tarikh-e-Adabiyat-e-Afghanistan* [History of Literature in Afghanistan]. Kabul, Afghanistan: Maiwand Publication Center, 1382/2003.

Jones, Schuyler. *Men of Influence in Nuristan: A Study of Social Control and Dispute Settlement in Waigal Valley, Afghanistan.* New York: Seminar Press, 1974.

The Kabul Times Annual. Kabul: Kabul Times Publishing Agency, 1967.

Kamali, M. H. *Law in Afghanistan: A Study of the Constitutions, Matrimonial Law, and the Judiciary.* Leiden: E. J. Brill, 1985.

Kamgar, Jamil al-Rahman. *Tarikh-e-Maarif-e-Afghanistan az 1126–1371* [History of Education in Afghanistan from 1747–1992]. Peshawar, Pakistan: Maiwand Publication Center, 1376/1997.

Kaplan, Robert D. *Soldiers of God: With the Mujahidin in Afghanistan.* Boston: Houghton Mifflin, 1990.

Katib, Faiz Mohammad. *Nijad Namah-e-Afghan* [Ethnography of the Afghans]. Peshawar, Pakistan: Al-Azhar Ketabkhanah, 2000.

———. *Seraj al-Tawarikh* [Torch of History], vols. 1–2. Kabul, Afghanistan: Ministry of Education, 1331/1952.

Kazimee, Bashir Ahmad. *Urban/rural Dwelling Environments: Kabul, Afghanistan, Case Studies, Proposed Model.* Cambridge: Massachusetts Institute of Technology, 1977.

Khan, Abd al-Rahman. *The Life of Abdur Rahman, Amir of Afghanistan.* Karachi, Pakistan: Oxford University Press, 1980.

Khan, Azmat Hayat. *The Durand Line: Its Geo-Strategic Importance.* Peshawar, Pakistan: Area Study Centre, University of Peshawar, Hanns Seidel Foundation, 2000.

Khan, Muhammad Hayat. *Afghanistan and its Inhabitants.* Lahore, Pakistan: Sang-e-Meel Publications, 1981.

Khasta, Khal Mohammad. *Maasirin Sukhanwar* [Contemporary Writers]. Kabul, Afghanistan: Government Press, 1339/1960.

————. *Yadi az Raftagan: Mushtamil bar biyugrafi edda-e- az Shuara-e-Kishwar* [Remembering the passed away figures: Including biography of a number of the country's poets]. Kabul, Afghanistan: Ministry of Press and Information, Government Press, 1344/1965.

Khusraw, Nasir. *Diwan-e-Ashar-e Hakim Nasir Khusraw Qubadiyani Ba Zamima-e-Roshnayinama, Saadatnama, Muqtaat wa adabiyat-e Mutafariqa az Roye Nuskha-e Tashih shuda-e Marhoom Taqizada Hamra-e Sharh-e-Hal wa Tahlili Tarikhi wa Eijtima-e Dawran-e-Ao.* [Collection of Nasir Khusraw Qubadiyani's Poetry including his works, Roshnayinama, Saadatnama, short poems and miscellaneous articles produced from the printed copy edited by the late Taqizada with his biography and socio-historical analysis of his time]. Tehran, Iran: Nashr-e-Chakama, 1361/1982.

Kitamura, Shiro. *Flora of Afghanistan.* Kyoto, Japan: Committee of the Kyoto University Scientific Expedition to the Karakoram and Hindukush, Kyoto University, 1960.

Kushkaki, Sabahuddin. *Daha-e-Qanun-e-Asasi: Ghaflat Zadagi-e-Afghanha wa Fursat Talabi-e-Rusha* [The decade of the constitution: Afghans ignorance and Russian opportunism]. Peshawar, Pakistan: Shura-e-Saqafati Jihad-e-Afghanistan, 1365/1986.

Laber, Jeri. *Tears, Blood, and Cries: Human Rights in Afghanistan Since the Invasion, 1979–1984.* New York: U.S. Helsinki Watch Committee, 1984.

Lali, Ali Dad. *Sayri dar Hazarajat: Tahlil-e Jamia Shenasi-e Mazhabi, Siyasi, Ejtimaei, Farhangi, wa Akhlaqi Jamia-e Tashayu dar Afghanistan* [An excursion to Hazarajat: Sociological analysis of religion, politics, society, culture, and ethics of the Shia community in Afghanistan]. Qum, Iran: Ehsani, 1372/1993.

Lee, Jonathan L. *The Ancient Supremacy: Bukhara, Afghanistan, and the Battle for Balkh, 1731–1901.* New York: E. J. Brill, 1996.

Leviton, Alan E. "Report on a Collection of Reptiles from Afghanistan," In *Proceedings of the California Academy of Sciences*, 4th ser., vol. 29, no. 12. San Francisco: Published by the academy, 1959, pp. 445-463.

Lindisfarne, Nancy. "Women Organized in Groups: Expanding the Terms of the

Debate," in *Organizing Women: Formal and Informal Women's Groups in the Middle East*, ed. Dawn Chatty and Annika Rabo. Oxford, England: Berg, 1997, pp. 211–238.

Lindsey, Linda L. *The Health Status of Afghan Refugees: Focus on Women*. East Lansing, Michigan State University, Office of Women in International Development, 1990.

Madadi, Wahab. "Sabkha-e-musiqi-e-mahali Afghani." [Local Afghani Music styles], *Farhang-e-Mardom* 3, no. 2 (Dalw-Hut 1359/1980): 76–82.

Majmua-e-az foklor-e-amiyanah-e-zaban-e-Dari [A collection of the Dari Language Folklore]. Kabul, Afghanistan: Nashrat-e-Ketabkhanah-e-Kiyumars, n.d.

Majrooh, Sayed Bahaouddin, and Sayed Mohammad Yusuf Elmi. *The Sovietization of Afghanistan*. Peshawar, Pakistan: Afghan Information Center, 1986.

Marsden, Peter. *The Taliban: War, Religion, and the New Order in Afghanistan*. New York: Zed Books, 1998.

Marwat, Fazal-ur-Rahim Khan. *The Evolution and Growth of Communism in Afghanistan, 1917–1979: An Appraisal*. Karachi, Pakistan: Royal Book Co., 1997.

Masson, Charles. *Narrative of Various Journeys in Balochistan, Afghanistan, and the Panjab*. New York: Oxford University Press, 1974–1977.

Matinuddin, Kamal. *The Taliban Phenomenon: Afghanistan 1994–1997*. Karachi, Pakistan: Oxford University Press, 1999.

McChesney, R. D. *Waqf in Central Asia: Four Hundred Years in the History of a Muslim Shrine, 1480–1889*. Princeton, NJ: Princeton University Press, 1991.

Mills, Margaret A. "Off the Dust and the Wind: Arranged Marriages in Afghanistan," in *Everyday Life in the Muslim Middle East*, ed. Donna Lee Bowen and Evelyn A. Early. Bloomington: Indiana University Press, 1993, pp. 47–56.

———. *Rhetorics and Politics in Afghan Traditional Storytelling*. Philadelphia: University of Pennsylvania Press, 1991.

Muhammad, Fayz. *Kabul Under Siege: Fayz Muhammad's Account of the 1929 Uprising*. Translated, abridged, reworked and annotated by R. D. McChesney. Princeton, NJ: Markus Wiener Publishers, 1999.

Naderi, Nooruddin Rawnaq. *Armaghan-e-Zendan*. Handwritten collection of Naderi's poems by Ewaz Akif. Karachi, Pakistan, 2000.

Naghat. "Shiwaha wa dawraha-e nasr-e Farsi." [Styles and periods of Persian prose writing]. *Adab* 10, no. 4 (1341/1962): 7–18.

Najimi, Abdul Wasay. *Herat, the Islamic City: A Study in Urban Conservation*. London, England: Curzon, 1988.

Narain, R. B. *Buddhist Remains in Afghanistan*. Varanasi, India: Kala Prakashan, 1991.

Negargar, M. I. "Afghan Folk Literature after Soviet Invasion." *Writers Union of Free Afghanistan, WUFA* 2, no. 2 (April–June 1987): 78–91.

"New Mobile Network Launched." *The Kabul Times* 37, no. 28, Sunday, 29 June 2003, p. 1.

Nojumi, Neamatollah. *The Rise of the Taliban in Afghanistan: Mass Mobilization, Civil War, and the Future of the Region*. New York: Palgrave, 2002.

Nyrop, Richard F., and Donald M. Seekins. *Afghanistan: A Country Study.* Washington, D.C.: Foreign Area Studies, the American University, 1986.

Oudenhoven, Nico Van. "Common Afghan Street Games and Child Development." *Afghanistan Journal* JG. 7, Heft 4 (1980): 126–138.

Paine, Sheila. *The Afghan Amulet: Travels from the Hindu Kush to Razgrad.* New York: St. Martin's Press, 1994.

Pajohish, Mohammad Ehsan. *Nazari ba Tarikh-e Qizilbash-ha dar Afghanistan* [A glance at the history of the Qizilbash in Afghanistan]. Peshawar, Pakistan: Ketabkhanah-e-Shams, 1379/2000.

Partap, Uma. *Bee Flora of the Hindu Kush-Himalayas: Inventory and Management.* Kathmandu, Nepal: International Centre for Integrated Mountain Development, 1997.

Pathak, P. V. *The Afghan Connection: Indo-Afghan Relations in the Pre-Buddhist Era: Archaeological and Ethno-Archaeological Review of the Socio-cultural Ties of Afghanistan With the Mainland India.* Raigad, India: Prajna Prakashan, 1999.

Poladi, Hassan. *The Hazaras.* Stockton, CA: Mughal, 1989.

Pope, Arthur Upham. *Persian Architecture: The Triumph of Form and Color.* New York: G. Braziller, 1965.

Poullada, Leon B. *Reform and Rebellion in Afghanistan, 1919–1929: King Amanullah's Failure to Modernize a Tribal Society.* Ithaca, NY: Cornell University Press, 1973.

Qawim, Abdul Qayum. *Namonaha-e-az Adabiyat-e-Shafahi-e-Mardum-e-Takhar* [Examples of Oral Literature of the People of Takhar]. Kabul, Afghanistan: Kabul University, Scientific Research Projects of Kabul University, 1364/1985.

Rahim, Sardar Mohammad. *Barg-ha-e az Tarikh-e-Maasir-e-Watan-e-Ma* [Pages from the contemporary history of our country], tr. and comp. Ghulam Sakhi Ghayrat. Peshawar, Pakistan: Fazl Publishing Centre, 1987.

Raji, Abdul Shukoor. "*Traditional Dwellings: Domestic Heating Systems of Afghanistan.*" Master's Thesis, University of Newcastle Upon Tyne, 1986.

Raverty, H. G. (Henry George). *Ghaznin and its Environs: Geographical, Ethnographical and Historical: An Account Extracted from the Writings of the Little Known Afghan and Tajik Historians, Geographers, and Genealogists.* Lahore, Pakistan: Sang-e-Meel Publications, 1995.

RAWA, Revolutionary Association of the Women of Afghanistan. *Barnama, Wazayif wa Asasnamah-e-Jamiat-e-Enqilabi-e-Zanan-e-Afghanistan* [Policy, Responsibility, and Platforms of the Revolutionary Association of the Women of Afghanistan, RAWA], *Tabistan* 1359 [Summer 1980], n.p.

Riyazi, Hashmatullah. *Gulha-e az Gulistan-e Shair-e Farsi: Az Rabia ta Parwin* [Flowers from the Persian garden of poetry: from Rabia to Parwin], vol. 1. Tehran, Iran: Nashr-e Pardis, 1380/2001.

———. *Gulha-e az Gulistan-e Shair-e Farsi: Az Nima ta Kunun* [Flowers from the Persian garden of poetry: from Nima to present], vol. 2. Tehran, Iran: Nashr-e Pardis, 1380/2001.

Robertson, George Scott. *The Kafirs of the Hindu-Kush.* London, England, Lawrence & Bullen, Ltd., 1896.

Robinson, J. A., Captain. *Notes on Nomad Tribes of Eastern Afghanistan.* Quetta, Pakistan: Nisa Traders: Sole Distributors, Gosha-e-Adab, 1978.

Saberi, Helen, with the assistance of Najiba Zaka and Shaima Breshna; illustrations by Abdullah Breshna. *Afghan Food and Cookery: Noshe Djan.* New York: Hippocrene Books, 2000.

Sadi, Muslihuddin. *Sharh-i Bustan,* ed. Muhammad Khazaili. Tehran, Iran: Sazman-i Intisharat-i Javidan, 1362/1983.

Safa, Abdul Ghafoor and Mohammad Yunus Sakayi. *The Tomb of Hazrat-e-Ali: Historical Background and Recent Events.* Peshawar, Pakistan: Society for the Preservation of Afghanistan's Cultural Heritage, 1999.

Sahar, David. "The Art of Gudiparan bazi." http://www.afghana.com/Entertain ment/Gudiparanbazi.htm.

Sakata, Hiromi Lorraine. *Music in the Mind: The Concepts of Music and Musician in Afghanistan.* Kent, OH: Kent State University Press, 1983.

Sarianidi, V. I. (Viktor Ivanovich). *The Golden Hoard of Bactria: From the Tillya-tepe Excavations in Northern Afghanistan.* New York: Abrams, 1985.

Sayed, Shahjahan and Inam-ur-Rahman. "Radio Kabul: A Political History and Development." *Central Asian Journal* no. 49 (Winter 2001): 135–153.

Schurmann, Franz. *The Mongols of Afghanistan: An Ethnography of the Moghols and Related Peoples of Afghanistan.* 's-Gravenhage, Netherlands: Mouton, 1962.

Seherr-Thoss, Sonia P. *Design and Color in Islamic Architecture; Afghanistan, Iran, Turkey.* Washington, D.C.: Smithsonian Institution Press, 1968.

Sen Gupta, Nilima. *Cultural History of Kapisa and Gandhara.* Delhi, India: Sundeep, 1984.

Shahrani, Enayatullah. "The History of Fine Arts in Afghanistan." *Afghanistan* 26, no. 3 (December 1973): 17–22.

Shahrani, M. Nazif Mohib. *The Kirghiz and Wakhi of Afghanistan: Adaptation to Closed Frontiers.* Seattle: University of Washington Press, 1979.

Shahristani, Shah Ali Akbar. *Namonaha-e-az Farhang-e-Shafahi-e-Hazaragi* [Examples from Hazara Oral Cultures]. Kabul, Afghanistan: Kabul University, Publications of Cultural Council, 1363/1984.

Sharq, Mohammad Hasan. *Karbas Push-ha-e-Berahnapa: Khatirati Mohammad Hasan Sharq az 1310–1370* [Shabby clothed and bare-feet people: Memoirs of Mohammad Hasan Sharq from 1931–1991]. Peshawar, Pakistan: Saba Ketabkhanah, n.d.

Sitholey, Rajendra Varma. *Jurassic Plants from Afghan-Turkestan.* Calcutta, India: Geological Survey of India, 1940.

Slobin, Mark. *Music in the Culture of Northern Afghanistan.* Tucson: Wenner-Gren Foundation for Anthropological Research, University of Arizona Press, 1976.

Smith, Harvey H., Donald W. Bernier, Frederica M. Bunge, Frances Chadwick Rintz, Rinn-Sup Shinn, and Suzanne Teleki. *Area Handbook for Afghanistan,* 4th ed. Washington, D.C.: U.S. Government Printing Office, 1973.

Stark, Freya. *The Minaret of Djam: An Excursion in Afghanistan*. London, England: J. Murray, 1970.

St. John, Katherine. *Afghan Dance: A Cultural and Historical Study of Women's Dance from Herat, Afghanistan 1970–1980*. Salt Lake City, UT: Eastern Arts, 1993.

Stucki, Anneliese. "Horses and Women: Some Thoughts on the Life Cycle of Ersari Turkmen Women." *Afghanistan Journal* 5, no. 4 (1978): 140–149.

Szabo, Albertand, Thomas J. Barfield, and foreword by Eduard F. Sekler. *Afghanistan: An Atlas of Indigenous Domestic Architecture*. Austin: University of Texas Press, 1991.

Taniwal, Hakim K. "The Impact of Pashtunwali on Afghan Jihad." *Writers Union of Free Afghanistan, WUFA* 2, no. 1 (January–March 1987): 1–24.

Tapper, Nancy. *Bartered Brides: Politics, Gender, and Marriage in an Afghan Tribal Society*. New York: Cambridge University Press, 1991.

Tarzi, Mahmud. *Reminiscences: A Short History of an Era, 1869–1881*. New York: The Afghanistan Forum, 1998.

Thomas, Lowell. *Beyond Khyber Pass*. New York: The Century Co., 1925.

Tradition and Dynamism Among Afghan Refugees: Report of an ILO Mission to Pakistan (November 1982) on Income-generating Activities for Afghan Refugees. Geneva, Switzerland: International Labor Office, UN High Commissioner for Refugees, 1983.

United Nations. Economic and Social Commission for Asia and the Pacific, *Atlas of Mineral Resources of the ESCAP Region. Vol. 11, Geology and Mineral Resources of Afghanistan*. New York: United Nations, 1995.United States, Central Intelligence Agency, CIA. *The World Factbook*. Washington, D.C.: CIA, 2002.

Upasaka, Si Esa. *History of Buddhism in Afghanistan*. Sarnath, Varanasi, India: Central Institute of Higher Tibetan Studies, 1990.

Urban, Mark. *War in Afghanistan*. Basingstoke: Macmillan, 1990.

Varma, K. M. (Kalidindi Mohana). *Technique of Gandharan and Indo-Afghan Stucco Images: Including Images of Gypsum Compound*. Santiniketan, India: Proddu, 1987.

Vollmann, William T. *An Afghanistan Picture Show, or How I Saved the World*. New York: Farrar, Straus and Giroux, 1992.

Waller, John H. *Beyond the Khyber Pass: The Road to British Disaster in the First Afghan War*. New York: Random House, 1990.

Wilber, Donald Newton, Elizabeth E. Bacon and Others. *Afghanistan: Its People, Its Society, Its Culture*. New Haven, CT: HRAF Press, 1962.

Wilson, H. H. *Ariana Antiqua; a Descriptive Account of the Antiquities and Coins of Afghanistan*. Delhi, India: Oriental Publishers, 1971.

"Women Radio Initiative in Mazar." *The Kabul Times* 37, no. 20, Sunday, 1 June 2003, p. 3.

Yaldram, Mohammad Salih Rasikh. *Tarikh wa Farhang-e-Turkman-ha* [History and culture of the Turkmens]. Kabul, Afghanistan: Anjuman-e-Farhangi Makhdum Quli Feraghi, 1381/2002.

Ziray, Salih Mohammad. *Manasibat-e-fiyudali dar kishwar wa Islahat-e-demokratik-*

e-Arzi [Feudal relations and democratic land reform in Afghanistan]. Kabul, Afghanistan: Ministry of Information and Culture, Government Press, 1357/ 1978.

Zulfacar, Maliha. *Afghan Immigrants in the USA and Germany: A Comparative Analysis of the Use of Ethnic Social Capital.* Munster, Germany: Lit Verlag, 1998.

Resource Guide

Adamec, Ludwig W. *Dictionary of Afghan Wars, Revolutions, and Insurgencies.* Lanham, MD: Scarecrow Press, 1996.

———. *Historical Dictionary of Afghanistan,* 2nd ed. Lanham, MD: Scarecrow Press, 1997.

Afghanistan: A Country Study. Baton Rouge, LA: Claitor's Publication Division, 2001.

Amin, Hamidullah, and Gordon B. Schilz. *A Geography of Afghanistan.* Omaha, Nebraska: Center for Afghanistan Studies, 1976.

Azoy, G. Whitney. *Buzkashi: Game and Power in Afghanistan.* Philadelphia: University of Pennsylvania Press, 1982.

Bonner, Arthur. *Among the Afghans.* Durham, NC: Duke University Press, 1987.

Dupaigne, Bernard and Francoise Cousin. *Afghan Embroidery.* Lahore, Pakistan: Ferozsons, 1993.

Dupree, Louis. *Afghanistan.* Karachi: Oxford University Press, 2002.

Ellis, Deborah. *Women of the Afghan War.* Westport, CT: Praeger Publishers, 2000.

Emadi, Hafizullah. "Kabul." *Encyclopedia of Urban Cultures: Cities and Cultures Around the World,* vol. 2 Danburry, CT: Grolier, 2002, pp. 437–445.

———. *Repression, Resistance, and Women in Afghanistan.* Westport, CT: Praeger Publishers, 2002.

Ewans, Martin. *Afghanistan: A Short History of its People and Politics.* New York: HarperCollins, 2002.

Gohari, M.J. *The Taliban: Ascent to Power.* Karachi, Pakistan: Oxford University Press, 2001.

Goodwin, Jan. *Caught in the Crossfire.* New York: E.P. Dutton, 1987.

Habibullah, Amir. *My Life: From Brigand to King. Autobiography of Amir Habibullah.* London: Octagon Press, 1990.

Hallet, Stanley Ira, and Rafi Samizay. *Traditional Architecture of Afghanistan.* New York: Garland, 1980.

Huldt, Bo. *The Tragedy of Afghanistan: The Social, Cultural, and Political Impact of the Soviet Invasion.* New York: Croom Helm, 1988.

Kamali, M.H. *Law in Afghanistan: A Study of the Constitutions, Matrimonial Law, and the Judiciary.* Leiden: E.J. Brill, 1985.

Nojumi, Neamatollah. *The Rise of the Taliban in Afghanistan: Mass Mobilization, Civil War, and the Future of the Region.* New York: Palgrave, 2002.

Paine, Sheila. *The Afghan Amulet: Travels from the Hindu Kush to Razgrad.* New York: St. Martin's Press, 1994.

Poladi, Hassan. *The Hazaras.* Stockton, CA: Mughal, 1989.

Saberi, Helen, with the assistance of Najiba Zaka and Shaima Breshna. *Afghan Food and Cookery: Noshe Djan.* New York: Hippocrene Books, 2000.

Sakata, Hiromi Lorraine. *Music in the Mind: The Concepts of Music and Musician in Afghanistan.* Kent, OH: Kent State University Press, 1983.

Slobin, Mark. *Music in the Culture of Northern Afghanistan.* Tucson: Wenner-Gren Foundation for Anthropological Research, University of Arizona Press, 1976.

Szabo, Albert, Thomas J. Barfield, and foreword by Eduard F. Sekler. *Afghanistan: An Atlas of Indigenous Domestic Architecture.* Austin: University of Texas Press, 1991.

Tapper, Nancy. *Bartered Brides: Politics, Gender, and Marriage in an Afghan Tribal Society.* New York: Cambridge University Press, 1991.

Web sites

Afghan Online Press Web site. A source for news, archives, polls, a discussion forum, and more: http://www.aopnews.com/

Afghan Women's Mission Web site: http://afghanwomensmission.org/index.php

RAWA Web site. The Revolutionary Association of the Women of Afghanistan was established in Kabul, Afghanistan, in 1977: http://rawa.fancymarketing.net/rawa.html

Index

Abortion, 179; *See also* Families; Fertility

Achmaemenid Empire, 26

Administrative divisions, 7, 8, 123

Afghan hound, 5–6

Afghani, Sayed Jamal al-Din, 65

Afghanistan Interim Government (AIG), 47–48. *See also* Masoud, Ahmad Shah; Mojaddadi, Sebghatullah; Rabbani, Burhanuddin

Afghan *Millat* (Afghan Social Democratic Party), 38. *See also* Political organizations

Aga Khan III, 60, 76, on women's education, 182

Aga Khan IV, 60, 76–78, 153–54; on women's education, 182–83

Aga Khan Development Network (AKDN), 75–78; development projects, 77–78; and education, 215–16. *See also* Isma'ilis

Agriculture, 12, 16–21, 196–97; irrigation in, 19–20, 125–26; opium cultivation, 17–18; *purghu* (shared oxen system), 20–21; tenant farming, 19. *See also* Economy; Water supply and Distribution

AIG (Afghanistan Interim Government), 47–48

Aimaq, 10. *See also* Ethnic and religious groups

AKDN (Aga Khan Development Network), 75–78, 215–16

Ali, Shir (king), 30–31; and education 211; relations with Britain, 104

Amanullah (king), 23–24, 31–33, 38, 55; educational reforms, 211–12; exile, 24; foreign policy, 32; and media 207; rebellions against, 32–33; social reforms regarding women, 32, 183

Ambaq (cowife) 167. *See also* Marriage; Polygamy

Amin, Hafizullah (president), 43–45

Anglo-Afghan wars, 30–31

Anglo-Russian Treaty, 31

Animal husbandry, 12, 21, 197; and Zoroastrianism, 54. *See also* Economy

Animals, 5–6; animal fights, 158; tazi, Afghan hound, 5–6

Anjuman-e-Adabi-e-Kabul (Kabul Literary Association), 93

Anjuman-e-Pushtu (Pushtu Society), 93

Ansari, Abdullah, 61, 83

Anti-state activities: labor movements, 201; rebellions, 32–35, 43, 69–70; student demonstration, 214. *See also* Assassinations

April 1978 coup, 42–43; role of intelligentsia, 24. *See also* Democratic Republic of Afghanistan

Arabs, 10–11; political power, 55–56, 82–83. *See also* Ethnic and religious groups

Architecture: building materials, 112, 119; building techniques, 119–22; caravanserais, 116–17; defense aspects 126–27; domestic architecture, 118–27; foreign influences, 112, 132; religious architecture, 111–13, 116; structural ornamentation, 117–18; traditional influences, 118–19; urban architecture, 123–25; village settlement patterns, 125–28; windmills, 125. *See also* Arts; Housing; *Memar,* the architect

Arranged marriage. *See* Marriage

Arts: Ali, Shir (king), and Punjabi music, 104; cinema, 108; constraints on, by the Taliban, 99–101, 108; dance, 103, 107–8; Gandhara Buddha statues in Bamiyan, 99, 112; Kabul Society of Fine Arts, 100; music, 103–7; *Nakhsh* (illuminations), 99; performing arts 101–3; visual arts, 99–100. *See also* Architecture

Asasiyun, 59. *See also* Isma'ilis

Assassinations: Ahmad Shah Masoud, 49; of heads of state: Hafizullah Amin, 45; Mohammad Daoud, 42; Mohammad Nadir, 35, 67; Noor Mohammad Taraki, 44. *See also* Anti-state activities; Najibullah

Aviation industry, 14

Avicenna (Abu Ali Sina), 87

Babur, Zahir al-Din Muhammad (king), 28

Bakhtari, Wasif, 96

Balkhi, Rabia, 86

Baluchis, 11. *See also* Ethnic and religious groups

Bamiyan province, 112; as center of Buddhism, 54; and Hazaras, 75; *Shahr-e-Ghulghulah,* City of Screams massacre (1221), 28

Banks and banking, 15. *See also* Commerce

Barter system, 15. *See also* Commerce

Bazar (bazaar), 135. *See also* Lifestyle, urban

Billah, al-Mustansir, *Imam,* 59

Bin Laden, Osama, 49

Bonn Conference (2001), 50

Brahois, 11. *See also* Ethnic and religious groups

Brezhnev, Leonid, 41

Britain: Anglo-Russian Treaty (1895), 31; colonialism, 30–31, 64–65; Gandumak Treaty (1879), 30; Rawalpindi Treaty (1919), 31; relations with Afghanistan, 30, 32, 104

Buddhism, 54; Gandhara Buddha statues in Bamiyan, 99, 112; influence on architecture, 112

Burqa (*chadari*), 148–50, 170–71. *See also* Clothing

Buzkashi (sport), 158–61

Calendar, Muslim: lunar, 152; solar 154. *See also* Festivals and feasts; Holidays

Caravanserais, 116–17. *See also* Architecture

Chadar (veil), 148; political aspects, 149–50, 170–71. *See also* Clothing

Chadari (burqa), 148–50, 170–71. *See also* Clothing

Chai (tea), 141–42. *See also* Cookery

Chai khanah (teahouse), 135. *See also* Lifestyle, urban

Chapandaz (rider in *buzkashi*), 160–61. *See also* Sports and games

Children. *See* Families

Children's games, 156–57. *See also* Sports and games

Christians, Christianity, 12, 62–63

Circumcision, 178

City planning, 123–25. *See also* Lifestyle, urban

Civil war: damage from, 14–15, 23, 132, 152, 201–2, 214–15; impact on education; 214–15; impact on family structure, 207–8; tribal and regional conflict as cause, 73–74; United States intervention in, 49–50

Class, social, 21–26; dispossessed (lowest social class), 25–26; elites, 21–22; entrepreneurs, 25; intelligentsia, 24; landowners, 22; *Mullahs* (religious leaders), 23–24; nomads and seminomads, 22–23; peasantry, 22; refugees, 25–26; workers, 25

Clergy. *See Mullahs*

Climate, 4

Clothing: headgear and turbans, 147–49; men's clothing, 145–46, Sikhs' traditional clothing, 151; women's clothing, 148–51

Colonialism, 30–33, 64–65

Commerce, 15–16

Communications, 14–15, 77

Competitive nature, in games, 156–61

Constitutional period (Constitutional decade) (1964–1973), 38–40; and literature, 95

Constitutions: (1923), and equality, 31–32; (1931), and civil rights, 35; (1964), and education, 40, 214; (1964), and freedom of the press,

38; (1964), and women's movement, 183; (2004), 50

Cookery, 136–45; *chai* (tea) 141–42; cooking utensils, 139; as expression of hospitality, 137–38; *halaal* (rites of slaughter), 139; Islamic influence, 139, 141; meals, 138, 141; *nan*, 142–43; spices, 139–40

Costumes, traditional. *See* Clothing

Cyrus II (Achmaemenid king), 26

Dance, 103, 107–8

Daoud, Mohammad (prime minister, 1953–1963, president, 1973–1978), 36–37, 40–42; assassination, 42; engineers coup, 40, establishes *Club-e-Milli* (National Club), 36; foreign policy, 41. *See also* Republican Order (1973–1978)

Decree no. 6 (loans and mortgages), 43

Decree no. 8 (land reform), 43

Democratic Republic of Afghanistan (Kabul regime), 42–46, 68–70

Deoband School of Theology (India), 65

Dispossessed (lowest social class). *See* Social class

Divorce, 179–80; custody of children, 179. *See also* Marriage

Dowry. *See* Engagement; Marriage

Durand Line, and Afghanistan-Pakistan relations, 31, 37

Durani, Ahmad Shah (Abdali) (king), 29–30; Durani dynasty, 30

Economy, 12–21, 197; cultural influences, 18–19. *See also* Agriculture; Animal husbandry; Commerce; Handicrafts; Industries; Trade

Education, 181–82, 209, 213–14; education of women, 181; and Quran, 210–11; religious influences, 65–66, 209–15; secular, 213–14; under Soviet rule, 45

Eid festivals, 151–53. *See also* Calendar, Muslim; Festivals and feasts; Holidays

Elites, 21–22, 64. *See also* Social class

Embroidery, 190–92. *See also* Handicrafts

Energy, 13–14

Engagement, 172–73. *See also* Marriage

Entrepreneurs, 25. *See also* Social class

Eternal Flame, 67. *See also* Political organizations, revolutionary

Ethnic and religious groups, 7–12; conflicts exploited by the Taliban, 49 (*see also* Civil war); ethnic minorities, 9–12

Families: childrearing, 177–79; dominance of males in, 168; economic role, 18–19; extended, 166; fertility, 178–79; impact of war, 207; role of women, 168–71; structure, 165–69, 199; tribal identity 166–67. *See also* Marriage; Women

Farming, 19–21, 196. *See also* Agriculture

Farsiwan, 11. *See also* Ethnic and religious groups

Fertility, 178–79

Festivals and feasts, 151–55; controls on, by the Taliban, 155. *See also* Calendar, Muslim; Holidays

Firdawsi, Abdul Qasim, 86

Folksongs, 85. *See also* Poetry

Food and drink. *See* Cookery

Foreign relations: with Britain, 30, 32, 104; with Iran, 41; with Pakistan, 31, 37, 48; with Russia, 30–31; with Soviet Union, 32, 36–37, 41, 44–46; with United States, 48–50

Games, traditional, 156–57. *See also* Sports and games

Gandhara Buddha statues, Bamiyan, 99, 112; *See also* Arts; Buddhism

Gandumak Treaty (1879), 30

Geneva Accord, 46

Genghis Khan (Mongol leader), 28, 88

Geography and landscape, 1–4; animals, 5–6; climate, 4–6; mineral resources, 6; plant life, 4–5

Ghaznawid era, 27–28; and literature, 86–87

Ghilzai, 29. *See also* Ethnic and religious groups

Ghorid rule, 28

Gilani, Sayed Ahmad, 72; on women's education, 182

Grand Assembly, (1928), 32; (1930), 35; (1964), 38, (2002), 50, (2004), 50

Gudiparanbazi (kite flying), 161–62. *See also* Sports and games

Guild system, 115–16

Habibullah (king), 31, 33–34; and education, 211–12; and religion, 66–67

Hadith (Traditions of Prophet Muhammad), 56

Halaal (rites of slaughter), 139. *See also* Cookery

Hanafi School of Islamic Jurisprudence (basis of civil and criminal laws), 57, 66. *See also* Sunni schools of jurisprudence

Hanbali school of jurisprudence, 57. *See also* Sunni schools of jurisprudence

Handicrafts, 188–92, 203; embroidery, 190–92; weaving, 188–90. *See also* Economy

Harakat-e-Islami (Islamic Movement), 72, 74. *See also* Political organizations, Shia

Hashim, Mohammad (prime minister), 35

Hawala (currency transaction system), 15–16. *See also* Commerce

Hazaras, 9, 32, 41, 70, 72; established *Shura-e-Itifaq* (Solidarity Council), 70; Massacre in Kabul (1995), 47–48; as oppressed minority, 9; Taliban offensive in Balkh Province (1998), 75; ties to Iran, 48; uprising in Chindawal ghetto, Kabul (1979), 69. *See also* Ethnic and religious groups

Health, 178–79

Heating systems, 127–28. *See also* Architecture

Helmand Treaty, 39

Hijab (seclusion), 66, 169–71. *See also* Women

Hindus, 11–12, 62; Hindu festivals, 155; and Vedic literature, 81–82. *See also* Ethnic and religious groups

History: ancient, 26–28; Anglo-Afghan wars, 30–31; colonial intervention, 30–31; Constitutional Period (1964–1973), 38–39; Durani rule, 29–30; Islamic rule, 47–49; postindependence, 31–37; pro-Soviet regimes, 42–46; Republican Order (1973–1978), 39–42; Soviet occupation (1979–1989), 45–46; the Taliban, 48–49; United States intervention, 49–50

Hizb-e-Demokratik-e Khalq-e-Afghanistan (Peoples Democratic Party of Afghanistan, PDPA), 41–44, 68, 95, 204; renamed *Hizb-e-Watan* (Homeland Party), 36, 46; split into factions: *Parcham* (banner) and *Khalq* (masses), 38; women members, 184–85. *See also* Political organizations, pro-Soviet

Hizb-e-Islami (Islamic Party), 47–48, 72, 187. *See also* Political organizations, Sunni

Hizb-e-Wahdat (Unity Party), 72, 74. *See also* Political organizations, Shia

Holidays, 153–55; *Eid* festivals, 151–53; *Jashn* (Independence Day), 155; *Milad al-Nabi*, 153; *milah-e-vaisakhi*, 155; *Muharram*, 153; *Naw Rooz*, 154–55. *See also* Calendar, Muslim; Festivals and feasts

Homosexuality, 181

Hospitality, 126, 136–38, 198–99

Housing: building materials, 119, 122; building techniques, 119–22; mud houses, 113–14, 120–26; portable housing, 128–32; stone houses, 122; wood-frame houses, 122, 126. *See also* Architecture

Hulegu (Mongol ruler), 60

Hussein, Imam (grandson of Prophet Muhammad), 57–58, 75

Huts, 130–32. *See also* Housing

Ijma (consensus of the community), 56. *See also* *Sharia* (system of Islamic law)

Ikhwan al-Muslimin (Islamic Brotherhood), 38, 43, 45, 67, 185. *See also* Political organizations, Sunni

Industries, 12–14; aviation, 14; communications, 14–15; energy resources, 13; oil and gas, 13–14; transportation, 14

Intelligentsia, 24, 64, 90–91, 94–95, 214. *See also* Social class

Iran: Helmand Treaty (1973), 39; support of Shia opposition groups, 48, 69–70, 72; treatment of refugees, 206

Irrigation systems, 19–20, 125–26. *See also* Water supply and distribution

Islam: Arab roots, 55–56; conversions, 55–56; contributions to the arts and literature, 82, 104; Deoband School of Theology (India), 65; education in, 73, 74; fundamental-

ism (*see* Islamic fundamentalism);
growth of, 27, 54–56, 65, 75–78;
Muslim calendar, 152, 154; and
nationalism, 64–65; postindependence period, 65–68; Shia and
Sunni schools of jurisprudence, 57–
58; Shia-Sunni split in, 56; Sufis,
60–62. *See also Jihad*; Muhammad,
The Prophet; *Mullahs*; Muslims
Islamic Brotherhood, 38, 43, 45, 67,
185. *See also* Political organizations,
Sunni
Islamic Emirate of Afghanistan. *See*
Taliban
Islamic fundamentalism, 47–49, 63,
67–68, 70, 71; religious education
in Pakistan and Iran, 73, 74; resis-
tance literature, 98; and women,
187. *See also Jihad*; Taliban
Islamic Movement, 72, 74. *See also*
Political organizations, Shia
Islamic Party, 47–48, 72, 187. *See also*
Political organizations, Sunni
Islamic Society, 67, 70, 72, 84. *See also*
Political organizations, Sunni
Isma'ilis, 58–60, 72–73, 182; Aga
Khan Development Network, 75–
78; *asasiyun* and assassin mythol-
ogy, 59; and education, 215–16;
Isma'ili festivals, 153–54; Isma'ili
rule, 58–60; split into Mustalians
and Nizaris, 59; support of secular
political movements, 73; *taqiyya*,
60; under Sunni rule, 60. *See also*
Aga Khan
Ithna Ashari (Twelvers), 58. *See also*
Muslims, Shia

Jamatkhana (prayer houses), 215–16
Jamiat al-Ulama-e-Islami (Society of
Islamic Scholars), 67, 75
*Jamiat-e-Enqilabi-e-Zanan-e-Afghani-
stan* (Revolutionary Association of
Women of Afghanistan, RAWA),
185–88. *See also* Meena; Political
organizations, revolutionary
Jamiat-e-Islami (Islamic Society), 67,
70, 72, 84. *See also* Political organizations, Sunni
Jews, 12, 62. *See also* Ethnic and religious groups
Jihad (holy war), 69, 71, 73, 98; as an
agent of change, 64; *jihad* culture,
73; and religious education in Pakistan and Iran, 73, 74; and *ummah*
(community of believers), 64. *See
also* Islamic fundamentalism; *Mujahidin*
Joi (water channel), 19–20, 125–26.
See also Water supply and distribution

Kabul (capital), 7; architecture, 123–
24; education, 213
Kabul regime (Democratic Republic
of Afghanistan), 42–46, 68–71
Kabul Society of Fine Arts, 100
Kalakani, Abdul Majid (Majid Agha),
45, 96
Kanishka (king), 27, 54
Kariz (underground canal), 19–20,
125–26. *See also* Water supply and
distribution
Karmal, Babrak (president), 39, 42,
45–46, 70–71
Karzai, Hamid (interim president
2002, president 2004), 188, 217–
18; Bonn Conference (2001), 50;
convenes *Loya Jirgah* (2002, 2004),
50; elected president, 49–50
Khaliq, Abdul, 35
Khalq (masses), 38, 41–44, 46. *See
also Hizb-e-Demokratik-e Khalq-e-
Afghanistan* (Peoples Democratic
Party of Afghanistan, PDPA); *Parcham* (Banner); Political organizations, pro-Soviet
Khattak, Khushhal, 88–89

Khurasani, Abu Muslim, 27, 56
Khusraw, Nasir, 87–88
Kite flying, 161–62. *See also* Sports and games
Kuchah (street), 200, 202. *See also* Lifestyle, urban
Kushanid dynasty, 27, 54

Labor movements, 201. *See also* Anti-state activities
Landay (folksongs), 85. *See also* Poetry
Landowners, 22. *See also* Agriculture; Landownership; Social class
Landownership, 18
Land reform (Decree no. 8), 43
Language: Persian (Dari), 7; Pushtu, 7
Lifestyle: nomadic, 202–4; post-Taliban, 217–18; refugee, 204–6; rural, 196–200 (*see also* Village settlement patterns); Urban, 124, 135, 200–202 (*see also* City planning)
Literature: anti-colonial literature, 89–90; anti-Soviet literature, 97–98; Arab influence, 83; during Ghaznawid era, 86–87; and intellectuals 90–91; modern literature, 96–97; Muslim contributions to, 82, 98; Persian literature, 86–89, 92–93; poetry, 83–85, 91–92; post-WWII, 93–97; prose, 85; Pushtu literature, 92; under Soviet rule, 97–98; Vedic literature, 81–82
Loans and mortgages (Decree no. 6), 43
Loya Jirgah (Grand Assembly), (1928), 32; (1930), 35; (1964), 38, (2002), 50, (2004), 50. *See also* Milli Jirgah
Lunar calendar, 152. *See also* Calendar, Muslim; Festivals and feasts; holidays

Madrasa (religious school), 65–66, 209–10; in Pakistan, 73. *See also* Education; Islam
Mahdi, Muhammad, *Imam,* 58

Mahmood (King), 62
Mahmood, Shah (prime minister), 29–30, 35–36
Mahr, 175. *See also* Marriage
Maiwandwal, Mohammad Hashim (prime minister), 39
Maliki School of jurisprudence, 57. *See also* Sunni schools of jurisprudence
Marriage, 166–68; arranged, 172; dowry, 174; importance of virginity, 172, 176–77; laws governing, for women's protection, 183; marriage age 174; matchmaking, 173; parceled marriage, 173; wedding ceremony, 175–76; wedding expenses, 174–75. *See also* Divorce; Engagement; Families
Masoud, Ahmad Shah (interim defense minister), 47–48; Assassinated, 49
Mawlawis, 210–11. *See also* Quran
Meals, 138, 141. *See also* Cookery
Media, 207–8; constraints on, under Taliban, 208; newspapers, 36, 45, 92, 209
Meena (founder of RAWA), 187. *See also* Jamiat-e-Enqilabi-e-Zanan-e-Afghanistan (Revolutionary Association of Women of Afghanistan, RAWA)
Memar, the architect, 114–15
Mens' clothing, 145–47
Milad al-Nabi (birthday of Prophet Muhammad), 153
Milah-e-vaisakhi (*vaisakhi* picnic), 155. *See also* Festivals and feasts
Milli Jirgah, 41. *See also* Loya Jirgah (Grand Assembly)
Minaret, 112–13. *See also* Architecture
Mineral resources, 6
Modernization programs, 36–37, 43, 183–84; and women's movement, 183

Moghul rule, 28
Mohammad, Dost (king), 30
Mohammadzai dynasty, 30–31, 34–37
Mojaddadi, Sebghatullah (interim president), 47, 68, 72, 74; on women's education, 182
Mongol rule, 28
Mongols, 11. *See also* Ethnic and religious groups
Monuments, 111–13. *See also* Architecture
Mosques, 116; in villages, 199. *See also* Architecture
Muassisah-e-Khayriyah-e-Zanan (Women's Welfare Association, WWA), 184. *See also* Political organizations
Muhammad, The Prophet, 54–57; *hadith* (traditions of Prophet Muhammad), 56
Muharram, 57–58, 153. *See also Takyakhana* (shrine to Imam Hussein)
Al-Muizz, *Imam*, 58
Mujahidin, 216. *See also Jihad*; Northern Alliance; Taliban; Warlords
Mullahs (religious leaders), 23–24, 57, 70, 75–76; opposition to women's education, 181, 210. *See also* Social class
Music, 103–7; popularized by radio broadcasts, 105
Musical instruments, 104–6
Muslims: calendar of, 152, 154; Isma'ilis, 58–60, 72–73, 182, 215–16; *Ithna Ashari* (Twelvers), 58; and nationalism, 64–65; religion of (*see* Islam); Shias, 57–58, 69–70, 72; Sufis, 60–62; Sunnis, 56–57

Nadir, Mohammad (king), 33–35, 66; assassination, 67; pro-British policies, 35
Najibullah (president), 46
Nakhsh (illuminations), 99. *See also* Arts

Nakhta (folksongs), 85. *See also* Poetry
Names, personal, 166–67; choosing a name for newborn baby, 177. *See also* Families
Nan (bread), 142–43. *See also* Cookery
National Agency for Campaign against Illiteracy, 43
National Geographic magazine cover, 170–71. *See also* Women
Naw Rooz (New Year festival), 154; banned by Taliban, 155; link to Zoroastrianism, 54
Newspapers, 36, 45, 92, 209; and freedom of the press, 38. *See also* Media
Nomads and seminomads, 22–23; housing 113, 128–32; impact of civil war on, 23, 132. *See also* Social class
Non-Muslims, 62–63; discrimination by Taliban, 62
Nooristan, 10, 126, 146–47; resists spread of Islam, 55
Northern Alliance, 48–49; ties to Iran, 48

Oil and gas, 13–14
Omar, Mohammad, *Mullah* (*Amir al-Mominin*, "commander of the faithful"), 75, 216. *See also* Taliban
Operation Enduring Freedom (military operation), 49–50
Opium, 17–18, 196. *See also* Agriculture
Opyani, Ghulam Qadir, 65

Pakhsa (building technique), 119–22. *See also* Architecture; Housing
Pakistan: and Durand Line (1893), 31; relations with Afghanistan, 31, 37, 73; support of Islamic fundamentalists, 70; treatment of refugees, 206
Parcham (Banner), 38, 41–44. *See*

also *Hizb-e-Demokratik-e Khalq-e-Afghanistan* (Peoples Democratic Party of Afghanistan, PDPA); *Khalq* (masses); Political organizations, pro-Soviet

Pashayis, 11. *See also* Ethnic and religious groups

Patriarchal system. *See* Families

PDPA (Peoples Democratic Party of Afghanistan). *See Hizb-e-Demokratik-e Khalq-e-Afghanistan. See also* Political organizations, pro-Soviet

Peasantry, 22. *See also* Social class

Peoples Democratic Party of Afghanistan, PDPA. *See Hizb-e-Demokratik-e Khalq-e-Afghanistan*

People's Liberation Organization, 38, 43, 45. *See also* Political organizations, revolutionary

Persian language (Dari), 7, 56, 83; chosen language for dissemination of Islamic teachings, 56

Persian literature, 85–89; Ghaznawid era, 86–87; in Ghazni, 86; postindependence period, 92–93

Persian poetry, 84

Pir (religious leader), 55, 60, 77

Plant life, 4–5

Pluralism, 54. *See also* Religion

Poetry, 83–84, 92; epic, 91; modern, 83–84; *nakhta* and *landay* (folksongs), 85; Persian poetry, 84. *See also* Literature

Political organizations: Afghan *Millat* (Afghan Social Democratic Party), 38; *Muassisah-e-Khayriyah-e-Zanan* (Women's Welfare Association, WWA), 184

Political organizations, Islamic, Shia: *Harakat-e-Islami* (Islamic Movement), 72, 74; *Hizb-e-Wahdat* (Unity Party), 38, 72, 74; Shura-e-Itifaq (Solidarity Council), 70

Political organizations, Islamic, Sunni:

Hizb-e-Islami (Islamic Party), 47–48, 72, 187; *Ikhwan al-Muslimin* (Islamic Brotherhood); *Jamiat-e-Islami* (Islamic Society), 67, 70, 72, 84

Political organizations, pro-Soviet. *See Hizb-e-Demokratik-e Khalq-e-Afghanistan* (Peoples Democratic Party of Afghanistan, PDPA), renamed *Hizb-e-Watan* (Homeland Party); *Sazman-e-Demokratik-e-Zanan-e-Afghanistan* (Women's Democratic Organization of Afghanistan, WDOA)

Political organizations, revolutionary. *See Jamiat-e-Enqilabi-e-Zanan-e-Afghanistan* (Revolutionary Association of Women of Afghanistan, RAWA); *Sazman-e-Azadi Bakhsh-e-Mardum-e-Afghanistan*, SAMA (People's Liberation Organization); *Sazman-e-Jawanan-e-Mutaraqi* (Progressive Youth Organization, PYO); *Shula-e-Jawid* (Eternal Flame)

Polygamy, 167–68. *See also* Marriage

Poppy cultivation, 17–18, 196. *See also* Agriculture

Progressive Youth Organization (PYO), 38, 43, 45, 67; women members, 185. *See also* Political organizations, revolutionary

Prophet Muhammad, 54–57

Prostitution, 180–81, 205–6

Purghu (shared oxen system). *See also* Agriculture

Pushtu language, 7, 93

Pushtu literature, 92–93

Pushtuns, 7–8, 34, 74; political power, 29–30; tribes split by Durand Line, 31

Al-Qaeda ("the base"), 49–50

Qalah (fortress) 120, 127. *See also* Architecture; Housing

Qirghiz, 10. *See also* Ethnic and religious groups

Qiyas (reasoning by analogy), 56. *See also Sharia* (system of Islamic law)

Qizilbash, 10. *See also* Ethnic and religious groups

Quran (Islamic holy book), 56; *Mawlawis,* 210–11; and Shia Muslims, 58; and Sunni Muslims, 57. *See also Sharia* (system of Islamic law)

Rabbani, Burhanuddin (interim president), 47, 72, 74

Radical Islam. *See* Islamic fundamentalism.

Radio, 105, 207–8. *See also* Media

Al-Rahman, Abd (king), 7, 9, 31, 211

RAWA, Revolutionary Association of Women of Afghanistan, 185–88. *See also* Political organizations, revolutionary

Rawalpindi Treaty, 31

Rebellions: Bala Hisar garrison (1979), 43; Chindawal ghetto (1979), 69; Ghilzai tribes (1930), 34–35; Khost (1924), 32; Kohistan (1930), 34; Nooristan and Dara-e-Paich (1979), 69; in rural areas, against Kabul regime (1978–1979), 70; Shinwari (1930), 33; anti-Soviet uprisings in various areas (1980), 71. *See also* Anti-state activities

Recreation. *See* Dancing; Festivals and feasts; Games, traditional; Music; Sports

Refugees, 73, 204–7; refugee camps, living conditions, 205–7; women refugees and prostitution, 205–6. *See also* Social class

Religion: ancient, 53–54; fundamentalism (*see* Islamic fundamentalism); and nationalism, 69, 70, 73–74; and politics, 69–70; in postindependence period, 65–66; under Soviet rule, 68–69, 70–73; under

the Taliban, 60, 62–63, 68. *See also names of religions*

Religious discrimination: against Isma'ilis, 60; against non-Muslims, 62; war on religion, 68–69

Republican order (1973–1978), 39, 40–42. *See also* Daoud, Mohammad

Revolutionary Association of Women of Afghanistan (RAWA), 185–88. *See also* Political organizations, revolutionary

Ruling class, 21–22, 64. *See also* Social class

Ruybar (liaison), 173. *See also* Engagement; Marriage

Sa'adi, Muslihaddin, 169

Sabbah, Hasan, 59–60. *See also* Isma'ilis

Samarqandi, Abu Hafs Hakim bin Ahwas Sughdi, 84

Sayyeds, 10. *See also* Ethnic and religious groups

Sazman-e-Azadi Bakhsh-e-Mardum-e-Afghanistan, SAMA (People's Liberation Organization), 38, 43, 45. *See also* Political organizations, revolutionary

Sazman-e-Demokratik-e-Zanan-e-Afghanistan (Women's Democratic Organization of Afghanistan, WDOA), 184–85. *See also* Political organizations, pro-Soviet

Sazman-e-Jawanan-e-Mutaraqi (Progressive Youth Organization, PYO), 67; split into factions, 38, 43, 45; women members, 185. *See also* Political organizations, revolutionary

Seminomads and nomads, 22–23; housing 128–32. *See also* Social class

Sewage and waste disposal, 124. *See also* Lifestyle, urban

Seyum-e-Aqrab (1965), 214. *See also* Anti-state activities

Shabnamah (night letters), 69. *See also*
  War of national liberation
Shafi'i School of Jurisprudence, 57.
  See also Sunni schools of jurispru-
  dence
Shafiq, Mohammad Musa (prime
  minister), 39, 63
Shahnamah (Book of Kings)
  (Firdawsi), 86
Shahr-e-Ghulghulah (City of Screams),
  28
Shah Rukh (Timurid ruler), 116
Sharia (system of Islamic law), 56, 66;
  and Taliban, 75
Shia Muslims, 57–58, 69–70, 72
Shia schools of jurisprudence, 58
Shuja (king), relations with Britain, 30
Shula-e-Jawid (Eternal Flame), 67. *See
  also* Political organizations, revolu-
  tionary
Shura-e-Itifaq (Solidarity Council), 70.
  See also Political organizations, Shia
Sikhs, 11; Sikh festivals, 155; Sikhism,
  62; traditional costume, 151. *See
  also* Ethnic and religious groups
Sina, Abu Ali (Avicenna), 87
Slavery, abolished by 1923 Constitution, 31
Social class, 21–26; dispossessed
  (lowest social class), 25–26; elites,
  21–22; entrepreneurs, 25; intelligentsia, 24; landowners 22; *Mullahs*
  (religious leaders), 23–24; nomads
  and seminomads, 22–23; peasantry,
  22; refugees, 25–26; workers, 25
Social interaction, at teahouses and
  bazaars, 135
Society of Islamic Scholars, 67, 75
Solar calendar, 154. *See also* Calendar,
  Muslim; Festivals and feasts; Holidays
Solidarity Council, 70. *See also* Political organizations, Shia
Soraya (queen), discards veil at 1928
  Loya Jirgah (Grand Assembly), 32

Soviet Union. *See* Union of Soviet
  Socialist Republics, USSR
Sports and games, 156–62; banned by
  Taliban, 162; *buzkashi,* 158–61
Student demonstrations, 214. *See also*
  Anti-state activities
Sufis, Sufism, 60–62. *See also* Ethnic
  and religious groups
Sunna (custom, tradition of Islam),
  56. *See also* Sharia (system of
  Islamic law)
Sunni Muslims, 56–57
Sunni schools of jurisprudence, 57
Superstition, 63; and choosing a
  child's name, 177

Tab khaneh (heating system), 128; *See
  also* Housing
Tajiks, 9, 74; political power, 33–34.
  See also Ethnic and religious groups
Takyakhana (shrine to Imam Hussein),
  75, 153. *See also* Muharram
Talaq (divorce), 179–80; and custody of children, 179. *See also*
  Marriage
Taliban, 48–50, 73–75; atrocities,
  75; controls on arts and media,
  101, 108, 208; controls on festivals
  and sports, 155, 162; exploitation
  of tribal and ethnic rivalries, 49
  (*see also* Civil war); interpretation
  of Islam, 216–17; oppression of
  women, 216–17; religious discrimination, 62; United States support,
  48. *See also* Cookery; Islamic fundamentalism; Omar, Mohammad,
  Mullah; al-Qaeda *tanoor* (oven)
Taqiyya (dissimulation in practice of
  faith), 60. *See also* Isma'ilis
Taraki, Noor Mohammad (president),
  44
Tariqah, 61–62. *See* Sufis
Tarzi, Mahmood, 91
Tatars, 10. *See also* Ethnic and religious groups

Tazi, Afghan hound, 5–6

Teahouses, 135. *See also* Lifestyle, urban

Television, 207. *See Also* media

Tents, 128–29. *See also* Housing

Timur (Tamerlane) (king), 28–29

Trade, 16, 23. *See also* Commerce

Transportation, 14, 77. *See also* Industries

Treaties and agreements: Anglo-Russian Treaty (1895), 31; Bonn Conference (2001), 50; Durand Line (1893), 31; Gandumak Treaty (1879), 30; Helmand Treaty (1973), 39; Rawalpindi Treaty (1919), 31

Tribalism; 29–30, tribal identity, 166–67. *See also* Families

Turbans, 147. *See also* Clothing

Turkmen, 9–10. *See also* Ethnic and religious groups

Ulama (religious leaders), 65, 66

Ummah (community of believers), 64

Union of Soviet Socialist Republics, USSR: and education, 214; reaction to occupation with anti-Soviet literature, 97–99; relations with Afghanistan, 30–32, 37, 41, 44; Soviet occupation of Afghanistan (1979–1989), 45–46, 204–6. *See also* Democratic Republic of Afghanistan (Kabul regime)

United States, intervention in civil war, 49–50; and Bonn Conference (2001), 50

Unity Party, 72, 74. *See also* Political organizations, Shia

Uzbeks, 9. *See also* Ethnic and religious groups

Veil, 148; political aspects; 149–50, 170. *See also* Clothing

Village settlement patterns, 125–27; *See also* Lifestyle, rural

Virginity, 176–77. *See also* Marriage; Women

War, civil. *See* Civil war

Warlords, 48–49, 188, 217–18

War of national liberation, 65–66, 69–70, 73–74, 214–15; expressed in literature, 95–98; use of *shabnamah* (night letters), 69

Water supply and distribution, 18–19, 125–26, 197

Weaving, 188–90. *See also* Handicrafts

Widows, 168. *See also* Marriage

Witchcraft, 63

Women: education, 181–82; health-care access, 178–79; laws governing marriage, 183; participation in politics, 183–88; role in family, 168–71, 198; symbolized in *National Geographic* magazine, 170–71; and Taliban, 217; virginity, 172, 176–77; women activists, 186–87; women's movement, 183, 185. *See also* Engagement; Families; Marriage; Prostitution

Women's Democratic Organization of Afghanistan, WDOA, 184–85. *See also* Political organizations, pro-Soviet

Women's Welfare Association, WWA. 184. *See also* Political organizations

Workers, 25. *See also* Social class

Yurts, 129–30. *See also* Housing

Yusuf, Mohammad (prime minister), 37–39

Zahir, Mohammad (king), 35–36, 40, 67; educational policies, 214

Zoroaster, Zoroastrianism, 26, 53–54; and *Naw Rooz*, 54

About the Author

HAFIZULLAH EMADI is a former academic who serves as a consultant to Focus Humanitarian Assistance and monitored the October 2004 elections in Afghanistan. He has written four books and numerous articles and essays on Afghanistan.

Recent Titles in
Culture and Customs of Asia

Culture and Customs of Taiwan
Gary Marvin Davison and Barbara E. Reed

Culture and Customs of Japan
Norika Kamachi

Culture and Customs of Korea
Donald N. Clark

Culture and Customs of Vietnam
Mark W. McLeod and Nguyen Thi Dieu

Culture and Customs of the Philippines
Paul Rodell

Culture and Customs of China
Richard Gunde

Culture and Customs of India
Carol E. Henderson

Culture and Customs of Thailand
Arne Kislenko